BROOKLYN DODGERS IN CUBA

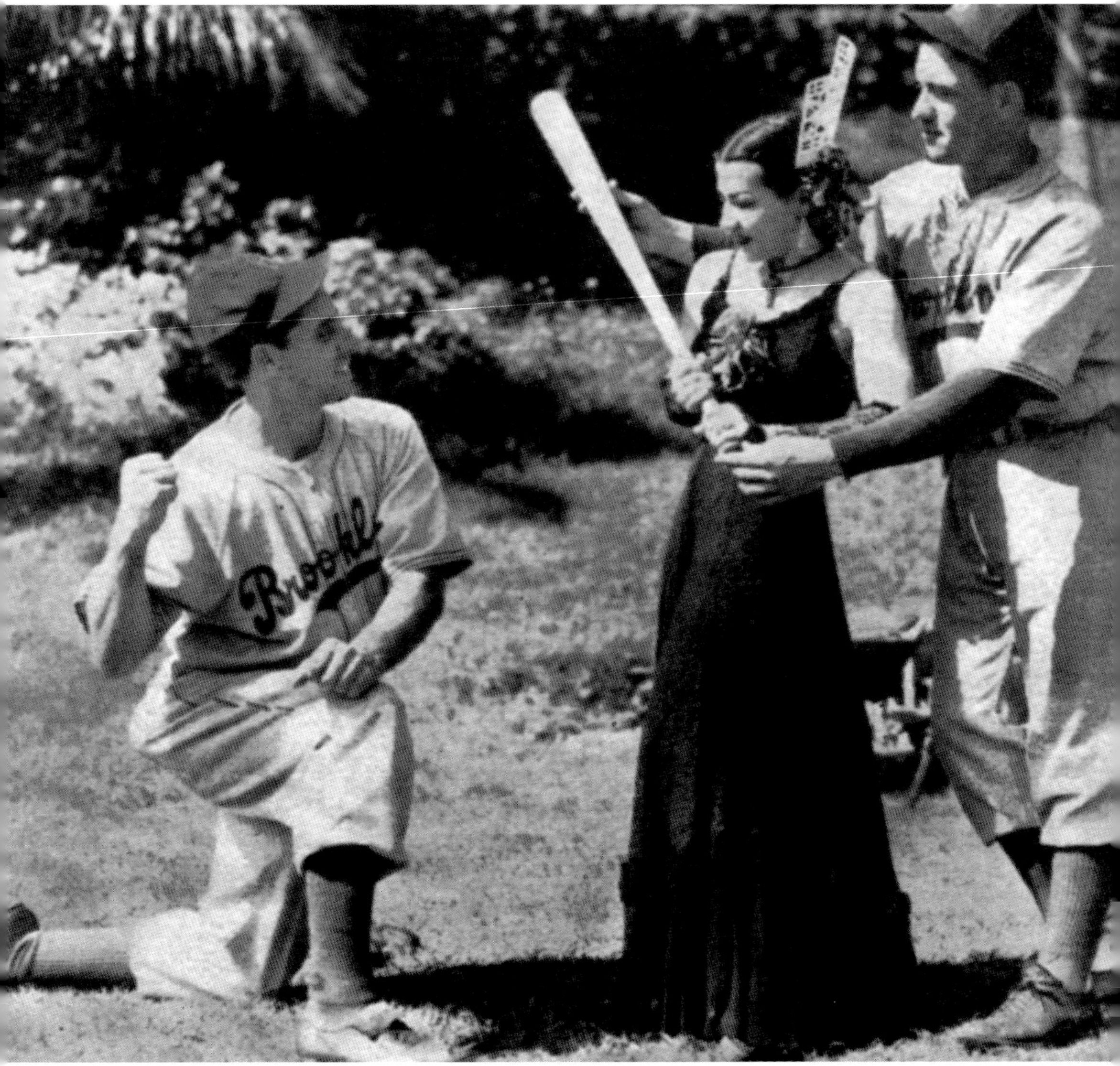

Brooklyn Dodgers Johnny Rizzo and Arky Vaughan traveled to Cuba in 1942 for the team's spring training trip. While there, they provided some batting tips to Señorita Isis of Havana.

FRONT COVER: Brooklyn's 1941 interpreter/utility third baseman, Monchy de Arcos (upper left) drills Charlie Gilbert, Johnny Hudson, and Pee Wee Reese on the proper ways to conjugate Spanish adjectives at Cuban umpires. (Courtesy Jim Allyn Archive.)

COVER BACKGROUND: Cerveza Tropical Stadium in Havana is pictured on opening day in 1930.

BACK COVER: Not wanting to offend his hosts, Hugh Casey did his best to honor the local customs in the spring of 1947.

BROOKLYN DODGERS IN CUBA

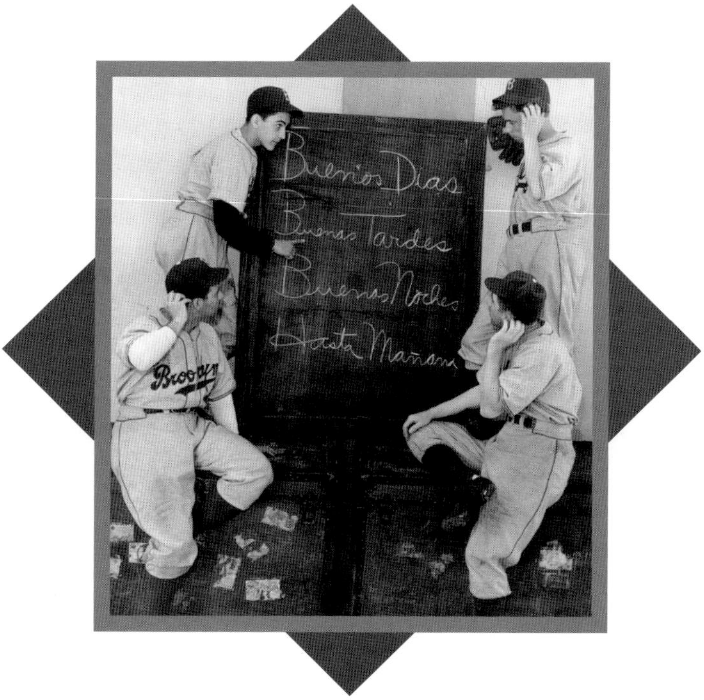

Jim Vitti

ARCADIA
PUBLISHING

ISBN 978-0-7385-7427-1

Published by Arcadia Publishing
Charleston, South Carolina

Printed in the United States of America

Library of Congress Control Number: 2010935095

For all general information, please contact Arcadia Publishing:
Telephone 843-853-2070
Fax 843-853-0044
E-mail sales@arcadiapublishing.com
For customer service and orders:
Toll-Free 1-888-313-2665

Visit us on the Internet at www.arcadiapublishing.com

This book is dedicated to the boys of spring—all those guys of the greatest generation that played baseball in Cuba during the preseason before bringing it back to Ebbets Field for the summertime.

CONTENTS

ACKNOWLEDGMENTS

Thanks to: Mark Langill and Gary Miereanu of the Dodgers; Judy Walsh and Susan Aprill of the Brooklyn Public Library; Brent Shyer of www.walteromalley.com; the New York Public Library; Jim Meier; Bill Swank; Bill Stetka of the Baltimore Orioles; Dagoberto Rodriguez, chief of Cuban Interests Section, Washington, D.C.; and Larry Register.

en Cuba: La Biblioteca Nacional de Jose Martí, Havana; Luis Fernández, Ministerio de Relaciones Exteriores, República de Cuba; Fidel Castro Ruz, president/council of the State of Cuba, República de Cuba; Lic Olga Lopez Rodriguez, Instituto Nacional de Deportes, Educación Fisica y Recreación, Havana; Danylo Sirio, vice president, Special Projects, ICRT (Cuban National Cable Network); Armando Jimenez, director, Cubavision Internacional; Lucia Newman of CNN Havana (and family); Luís Zayas, trainer, Cuban National Baseball League; Antonio Valdez; Pedro Alfonso; Ismael Sené; y Severo Nieto.

Also thank you to the ballplayers and their families: Rugger Ardizoia, Joe Astroth, Ed Bailey, Jack Banta, Rex Barney, Bobby Brown, Cy Buker, Ed Chandler, Johnny Van Cuyk, Cliff Dapper, Scat Davis, Solly Drake, Carl Erskine, Elroy Face, Boo Ferriss, Ed FitzGerald, Bob Friend, Tony Giuliani, Jesse Gonder, Dick Hall, Bill Harris, Gene Hermanski, Cal Hogue, Eddie Joost, Clyde King, Fred Kipp, Marty Kutyna, Bob Lennon, Lefty Locklin, Don Lund, Bob Mabe, Dick Manville, Conrado Marrero, Lefty Martin, Skip Mauch, Ralph Mauriello, Pat McGlothin, Lefty Minner, Bobby Morgan, Don Newcombe, Luis Olmo, Claude Osteen, Jack Paepke, Lynn Parrott, Don Pavletich, Eddie Pellagrini, Lee Pfund, Dave Philley, Billy Raimondi, Frank Robinson, Preacher Roe, Elmer Sexauer, Carl Scheib, Stretch Schultz, Vin Scully, Shotgun Shuba, Charlie Silvera, Duke Snider, Liz Stansky, Eddie Stevens, Pete Suder, Joe Tepsic, Preston Ward, Jim Waugh, Lou Welaj, Yaz, and Gus Zernial.

All photographs are from the Los Angeles Dodgers, the Brooklyn Public Library/*Brooklyn Eagle* Collection; the Walter O'Malley Foundation; Cesar Lopez, www.cubanball.com; TranscendentalGraphics, www.theruckerarchive.com; *Sporting News*; National Baseball Hall of Fame; Library of Congress; Vero Beach Chamber of Commerce; Baltimore Orioles; Bill Loughman Collection; and Lance Richbourg Jr., unless otherwise credited. Baseball cards are courtesy of Topps. Other memorabilia is courtesy of the Jim Allyn Collection—thanks to you and Rophe for always being there.

INTRODUCTION

When you think Brooklyn Dodgers, you think of Ebbets Field, with men in fedoras hollering through rolled-up scorecards and Jackie Robinson in heavy flannels, taunting the pitcher from third base.

You do not think sandy beaches, palm trees, grand casinos with natty waiters speaking in Spanish, or Fidel Castro in fatigues, surrounded by soldiers toting machine guns. Yet they came together on La Isla de Cuba. The Brooklyn Dodgers held spring training there, way back then, and the stories are the stuff of legend.

Dodger Van Lingle Mungo holed up in the fabled Hotel Nacional, with not one but two women. A husband pounded the door, cursing in two languages and wielding a machete.

Brooklyn ballplayers headed to Ernest Hemingway's bungalow to drink all night. They donned boxing gloves to pummel each other, taking lamps, fixtures, and furniture down with them.

Jackie Robinson landed a tryout to break baseball's color barrier. He stayed at a dirty hotel apart from the rest of the team, where a cockroach crawled out of the soup.

Leo Durocher, fabled manager, ran the club while honeymooning with his movie star wife, fighting with umpires who did not speak English, and feuding with the Yankees owner over who was buddies with gamblers (resulting in Leo's full-season suspension on trumped-up charges).

Dodger rookie Ed Chandler was arrested in mid-game against the Yankees and paraded across the field in flannels and handcuffs, much to the delight of thousands of jeering, bottle-hurling fans. Another Dodger, Sam Nahem, was a lawyer, but could not spring Chandler from a night in jail. "All he was able to get me was a sandwich," Chandler said.

Stu Locklin warmed up before a game against a Cuban team as Fidel Castro walked onto the field in full battle fatigues, looked right at him, patted his sidearm, and said, "Tonight, we win." They did.

Legendary Dodger broadcaster Vin Scully watched guerrillas enter the lobby at the Hotel Nacional carrying machine guns and drinking heavily.

A Brooklyn rookie was harshly reprimanded by Durocher for tearing up his hands on fishing line while chasing a great fish in a true-to-life Hemingway-esque adventure. Bumpy bus rides across dusty rutted roads took players to ballparks set amid jungles, and they stayed in a castle with bats flying through the pane-free windows. A Cuban left fielder, fed up with fan taunts, headed for the clubhouse and emerged with his pistol, heading toward the bleachers in search of his hecklers.

Brooklyn ballplayers on a quick flight back to the United States watched an engine burst into flames, then witnessed the other engine burst into flames, causing them to wonder if they would ever see Flatbush again.

Old timers such as roughnecks John McGraw, Ty Cobb, and even Babe Ruth paved the way, barnstorming across the island (and its saloons). Other American ball clubs set up spring drills in Havana, like the New York Giants (1937) and Pittsburgh Pirates (1953). Mel Ott, Carl Hubbell, and even Joe Garagiola played there.

Some all-time Dodger greats like rookie Duke Snider, Sandy Koufax (before he became the great ballplayer he is now remembered as), Don Drysdale, and Tommy Lasorda (a pitcher who was not afraid to brush anybody back) all played in Cuba. There were stops in the Dominican Republic, Venezuela, Puerto Rico, and other exotic ports of call, with various and sundry revolutions going on all over, seemingly all the time.

Machine guns, drunken nights, horse tracks, dice, tropical beauty, and señoritas galore were just a pleasant 90-mile steamship jaunt across the Gulf. Strap on your sidearm and head to the ballpark—it is the Brooklyn Dodgers in Cuba, and you are in for some steamy fun.

1

EARLY ON

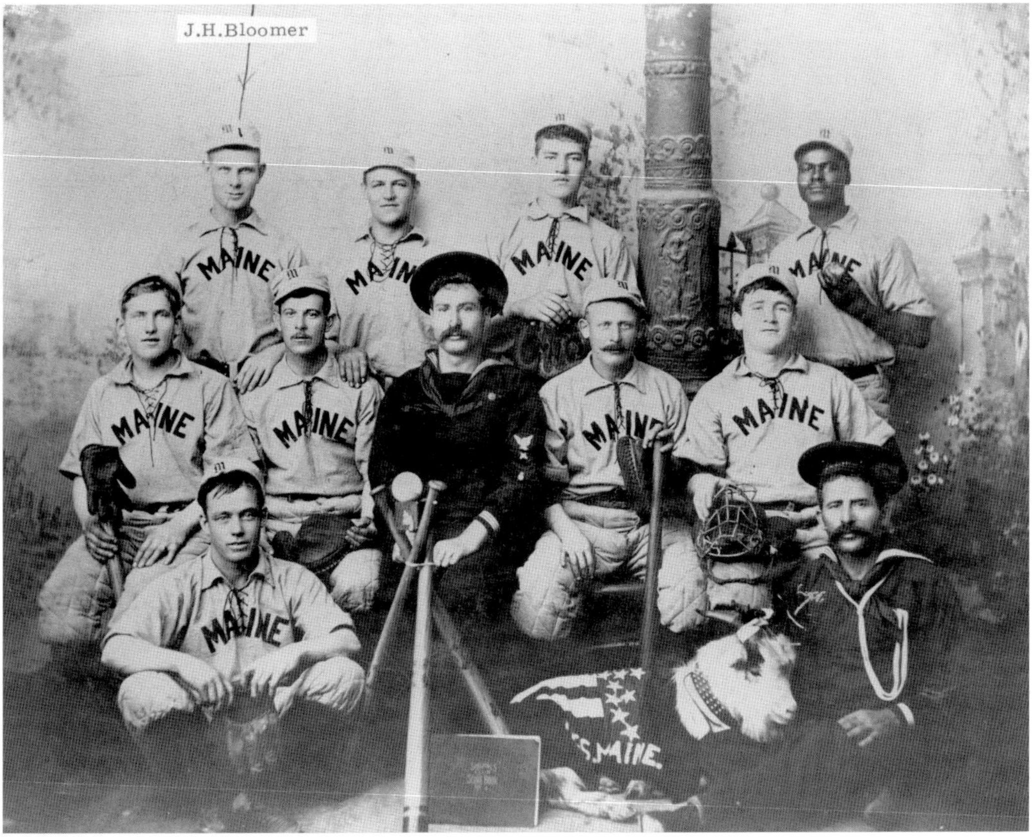

Americans and *cubanos* first played baseball on the island in the 1860s when U.S. Navy warships patrolled Havana Harbor, and the sailors introduced the game on shore leave. In 1891, the first U.S. All-Star team came through. Over the years, more than a dozen big league teams (and legends like Babe Ruth) played in Cuba. The Brooklyn Dodgers maintained the strongest ties, starting in 1900. The USS *Maine* team arrived in 1898. When an explosion sank the ship, 284 sailors died. Of the 89 survivors, only one ballplayer made it—J. H. Bloomer.

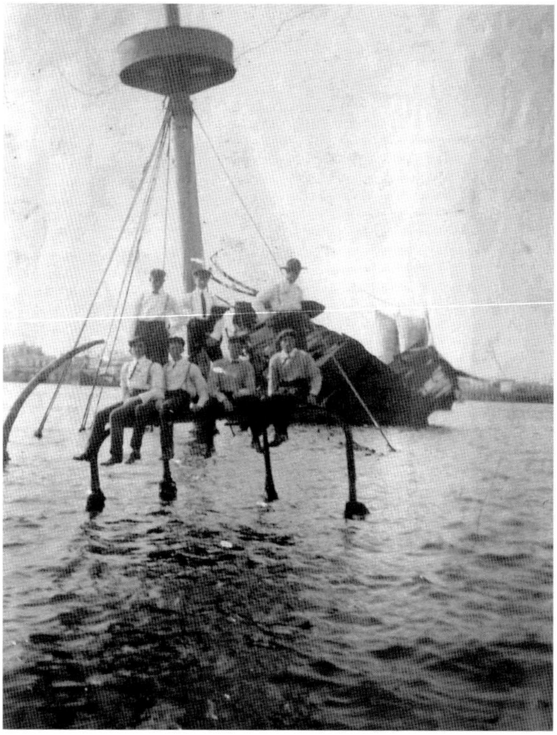

When Tampa's team traveled to Havana in 1904, ballplayer Jim McGuicken brought his camera. Cuba won the series 4-2, and the guys went sightseeing. Six years after the *Maine* incident, the wreckage was still in its half-sunken spot. At left, several Tampa ballplayers pose aboard the former ship. It has long since been removed, but a large monument at the site (on land) includes a pair of cannon from the sunken ship.

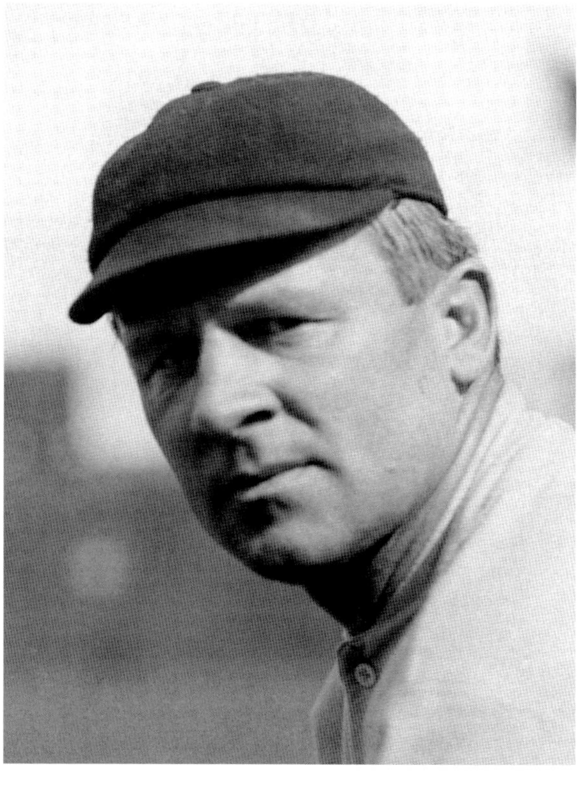

Hall of Fame manager John McGraw helped pioneer the American-Cuban baseball link. He played with the first U.S. All-Stars there in 1891 and kept coming back for decades. "The barnstorming buccaneer of baseball," the *Los Angeles Times* noted in 1932, "has cruised the Spanish Main demonstrating baseball to those sitting in darkness, playing cricket and ukuleles. He has invaded the Hawaiian Islands, the Philippines, Ceylon, the British Isles and Brooklyn with baseball teams."

Christy Mathewson was already a superstar when McGraw-managed teams began visiting the isle. The year this Cuban baseball guide was published in 1908, Matty won 37 ball games. Three years later, Mathewson recorded a trio of victories during the Giants visit, pacing his squad to a 9-3 mark against local teams.

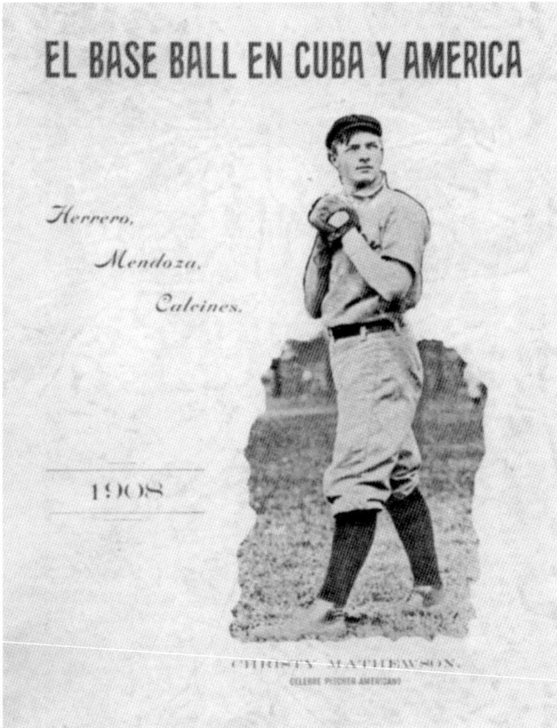

In 1909, the defending league champs, the Detroit Tigers, played a dozen preseason games in Cuba. They finished 4-8, getting a no-hitter in one, but were without Ty Cobb. The next spring, Cobb showed for the last five contests. Detroit managed a 7-5 mark, 4-1 with Cobb and 3-4 without him. He hit .368 during the series.

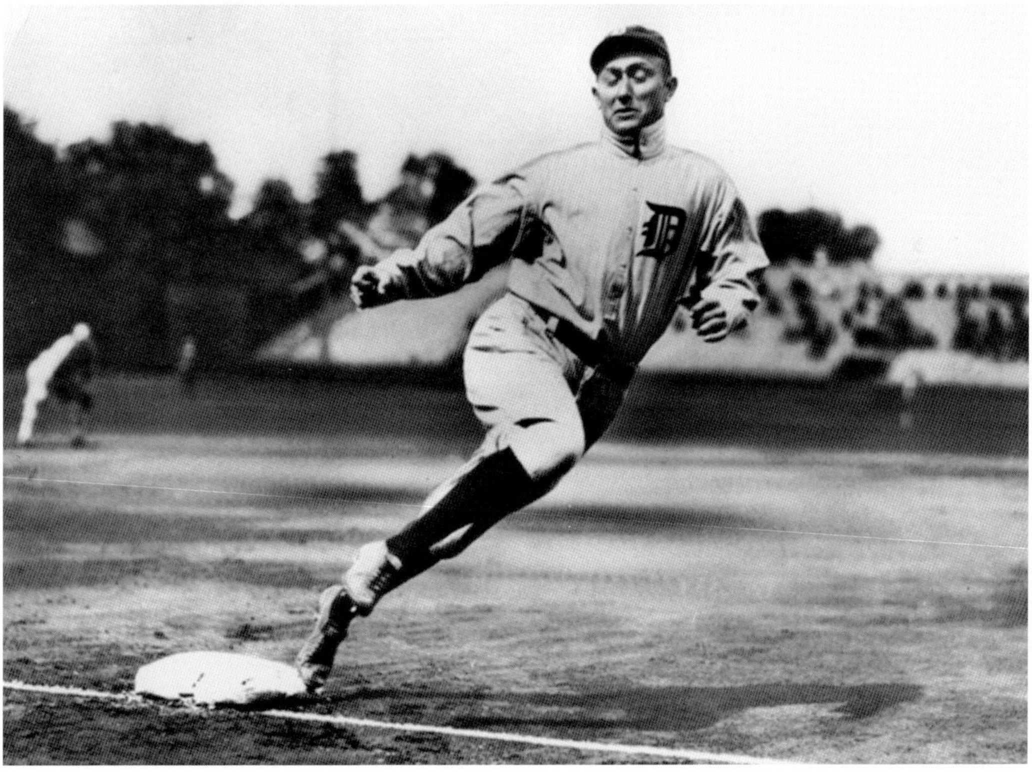

In 1920, Babe Ruth showed up late during the 10th game of 12 to play for McGraw's Giants, on loan from the rival Yankees. He smacked several homers, including the longest one in Almendares Park history. According to legend, he then headed off to inspect the local breweries and distilleries.

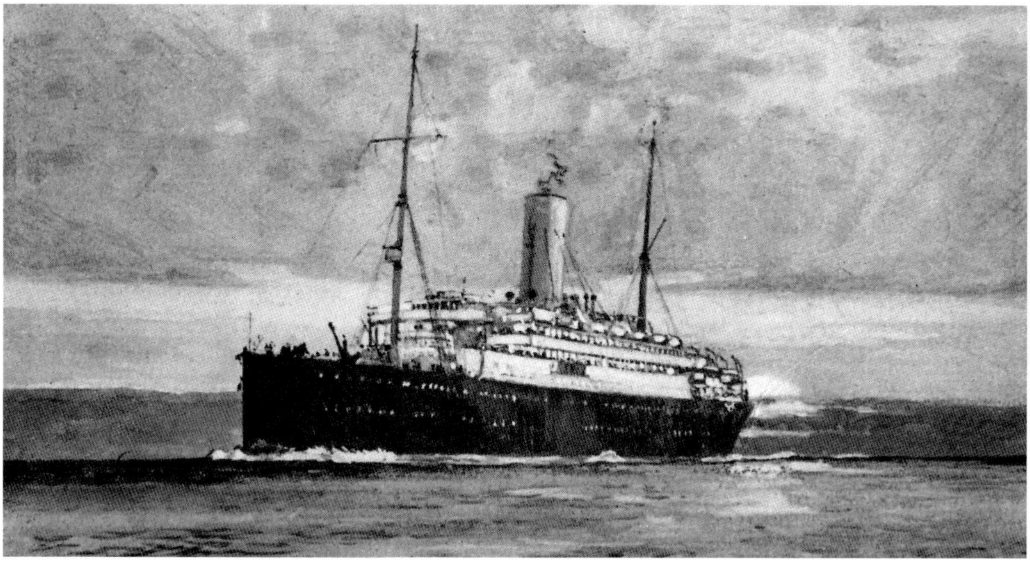

Before they became the mighty Yankees, the New York Highlanders tried spring training in Bermuda in 1913. They sailed aboard the Royal Mail steamer *Arcadian* with team president Frank Ferrell on hand "to tell the ball players to not lean too far over the rail of the ship," according to the *New York Times*. But, "the players experienced a rough trip, and several suffered from seasickness." When they arrived, most "spent the day sightseeing and getting rid of their sea legs."

THE OLEANDERS

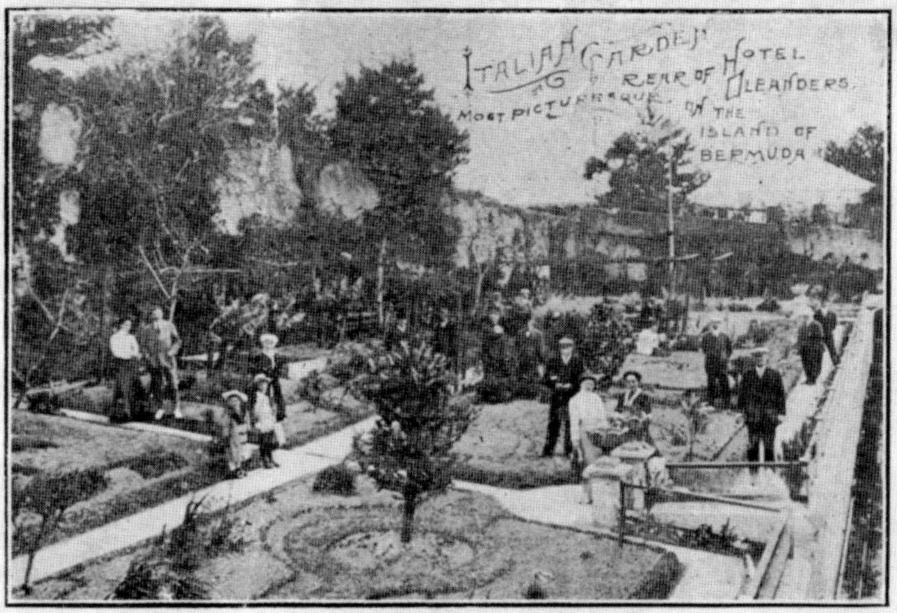

The pre-Yanks stayed at the Oleander Hotel. "The hotel is only four minutes' walk from the Hamilton Cricket Grounds, where the team will play," observed the *Times*. "Manager Chance will preside over a regular training table, which will be an innovation in baseball," the paper reported, laying out a diet similar to that of Atkins today. "The club will ship from this city all meats, including roast beef, lamb, ham, and bacon; also, butter and water. Pastry, hot bread, and seasoned dishes will be tabooed."

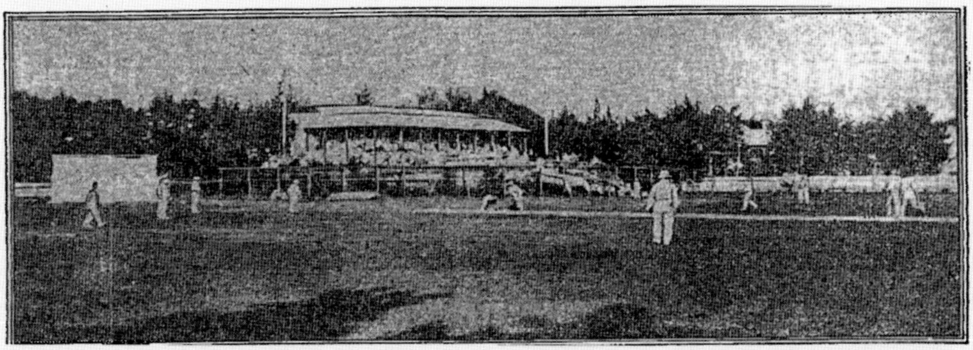

THE YANKEE'S PLAYING FIELD AT BERMUDA

The Hamilton Cricket Grounds became two baseball fields. The Highlanders brought the Jersey City Skeeters along and took the series 6-3. "The conditions in Bermuda could not be better," said the club's owner. "The players, completely trained, are almost ready to travel at their fastest gait." But the Highlanders went 57-94, and the entire team managed only eight home runs (Babe Ruth was still in school then). They did not return.

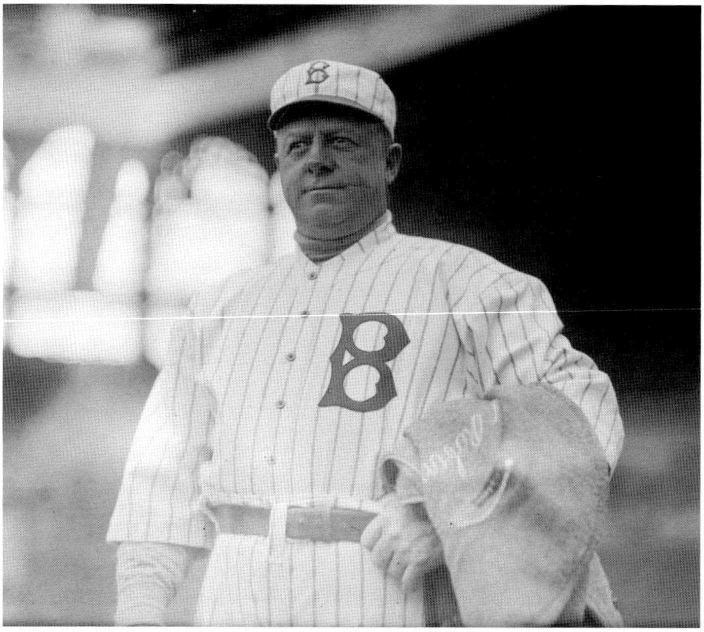

The Dodgers (known as the "Superbas" then) first visited Cuba in 1900, going 4-0 against locals. In 1913, they went 4-3, and in 1921, they posted a 10-5 mark under manager Wilbert Robinson. The team took his name, the Brooklyn Robins. Robinson, or "Robbie," led their first formal Cuban training camp in 1931. Hall of Famer Robinson first played there in 1886, and he coached for McGraw's Giants during the 1911 trip.

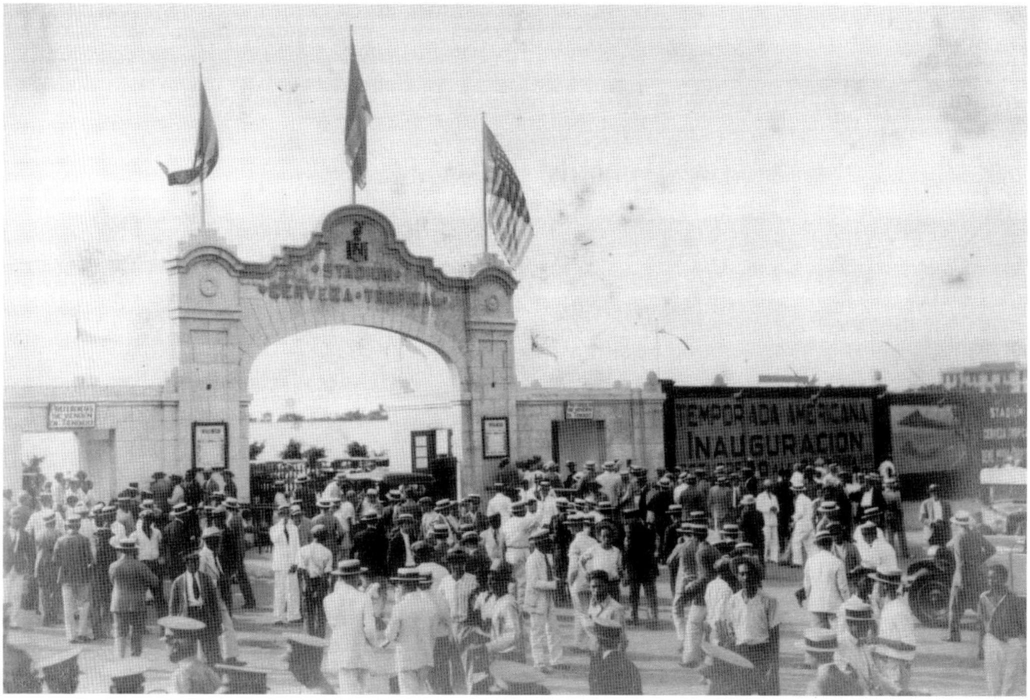

The 1931 Brooklyn Robins practiced at the brand-new cavernous Cerveza Tropical Stadium, seen here on its opening day in the fall of 1930. The name means "tropical beer," appropriate because it was adjacent to the Tropical brewery, owned by the same businessman who owned the stadium. This photograph was given to Boston Brave Lance Richbourg, who toured Cuba with an American All-Star team to inaugurate the field.

The Robins employed three future Hall of Famers on their roster: Dazzy Vance, Ernie Lombardi, and Al Lopez. Lopez was a local favorite because of his Cuban heritage; he had played there the previous fall as part of the All-Star series. Lopez, best known for his post-playing exploits, led the 1954 Cleveland Indians and 1959 Chicago White Sox to the World Series.

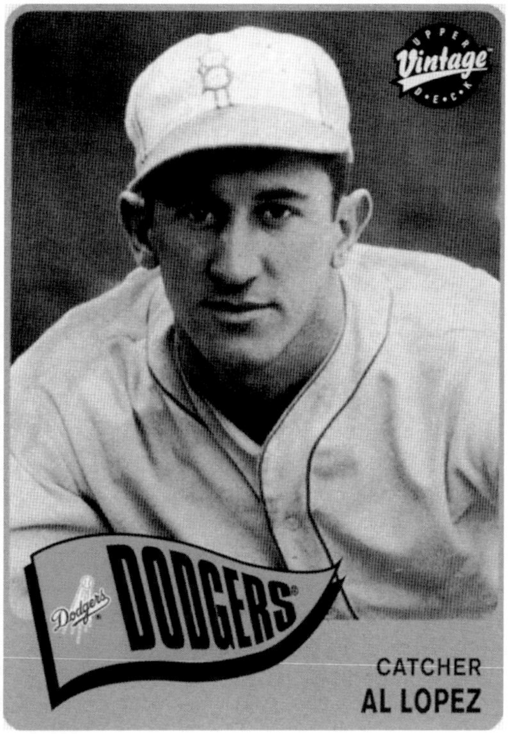

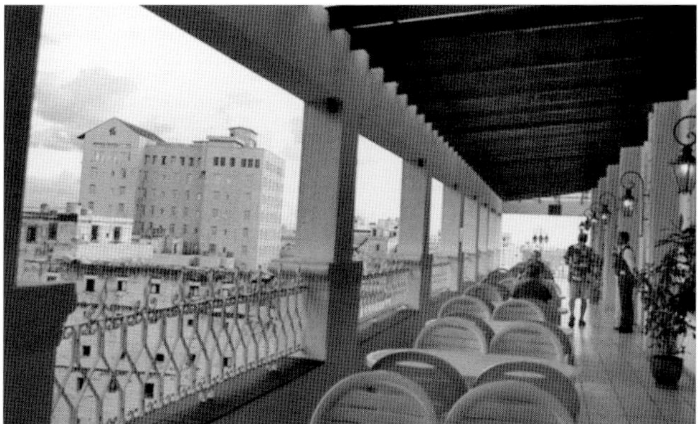

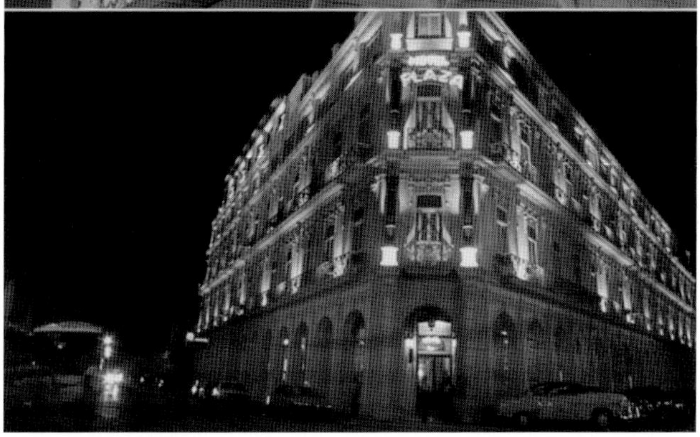

The ballplayers found themselves hosted at the ritzy Plaza Hotel, as noted in the *Brooklyn Eagle*. " 'I've heard about the life of Reilly ever since I was a little boy,' sighed Rube Bressler, stretching out in a wicker chair in the lobby of the Plaza, 'and at last I've found out where Reilly lived.' "

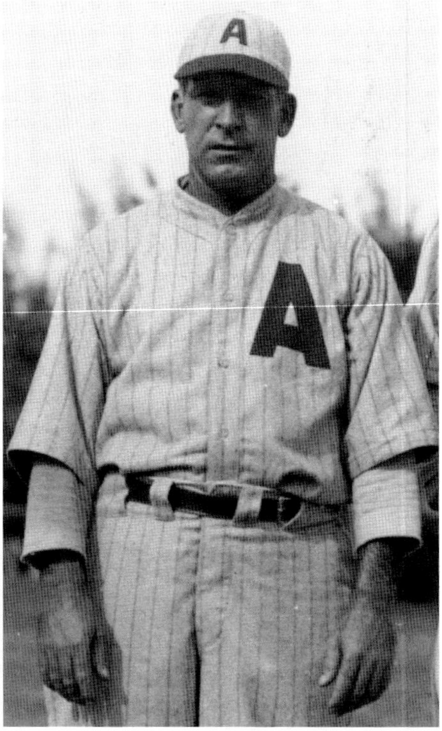

Local talent got into the act. Brooklyn's Cuban-born Dolf Luque recommended Cheo Ramos for a tryout at the Cerveza Tropical Stadium. Ramos got a contract and made the trip back to Florida with the squad. The *Times* reported he "played right field for the Dodgers and drew cheers from his compatriots for several fast fielding plays." He did not last long in the states but enjoyed a stellar career in Cuba, coaching for Luque's 1946–1947 champion Almendares team.

The wirephoto caption explains the Robinsons are examining his hunting canteen. Robbie once ran a saloon with McGraw, but in 1931, the U.S. Prohibition had not reached Cuba. "Some of the boys, following an old American custom, attempted to completely exhaust Cuba's beer supply, and did make an alarming dent in the cerveza on hand," said the *Brooklyn Eagle*. "The Hotel Plaza," said the *New York Post*, was next to Sloppy Joe's saloon, "which made it convenient. Robbie always knew where he could round up enough players when it came time for an exhibition game."

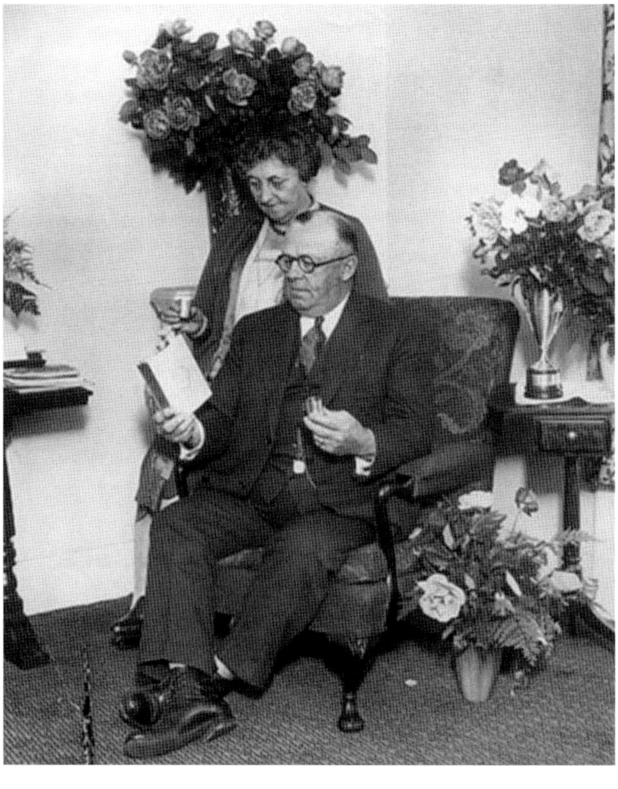

Even after McGraw's departure, the Giants maintained their Cuba ties under Hall of Famer Bill Terry. The team set up their spring training camp there in 1937 and finished 2-4-1 in exhibition games at the Tropical. Most of the games were against local squads, but they also split a series against "Dizzy" Dean's St. Louis Cardinals. The Cards had migrated over in 1936 to go 2-2 against locals; Leo Durocher played shortstop for the Redbirds, foreshadowing his return as Dodger skipper.

The New York club was loaded with Hall of Fame talent, like Mel Ott, who hit 511 homers. Ott arranged to sail from New Orleans with his family, apparently unconcerned about the ongoing political turmoil in Cuba. "There were revolutions or social uprisings or what not every so often in Cuba," the *Times* warned, "and possibly Owner Stoneham was taking a grave risk in putting valuable property like Hubbell and Ott where there was danger of damage from random shooting."

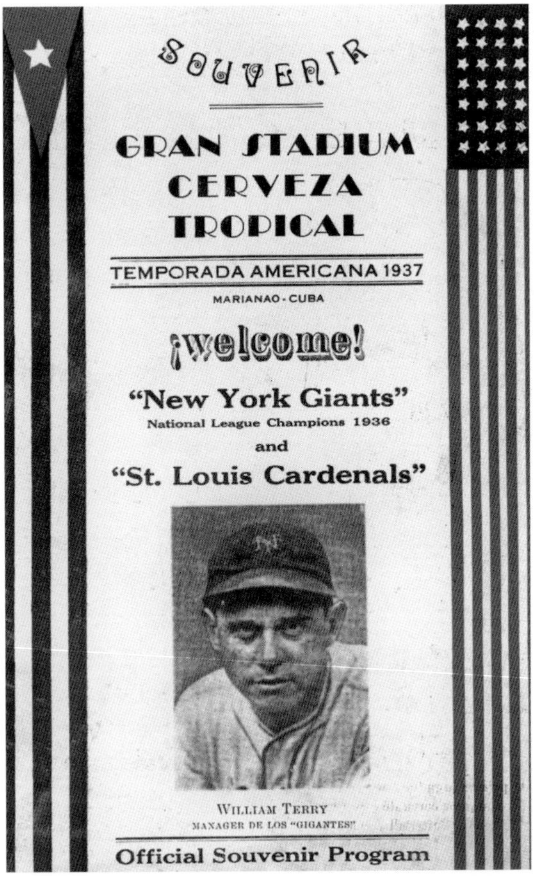

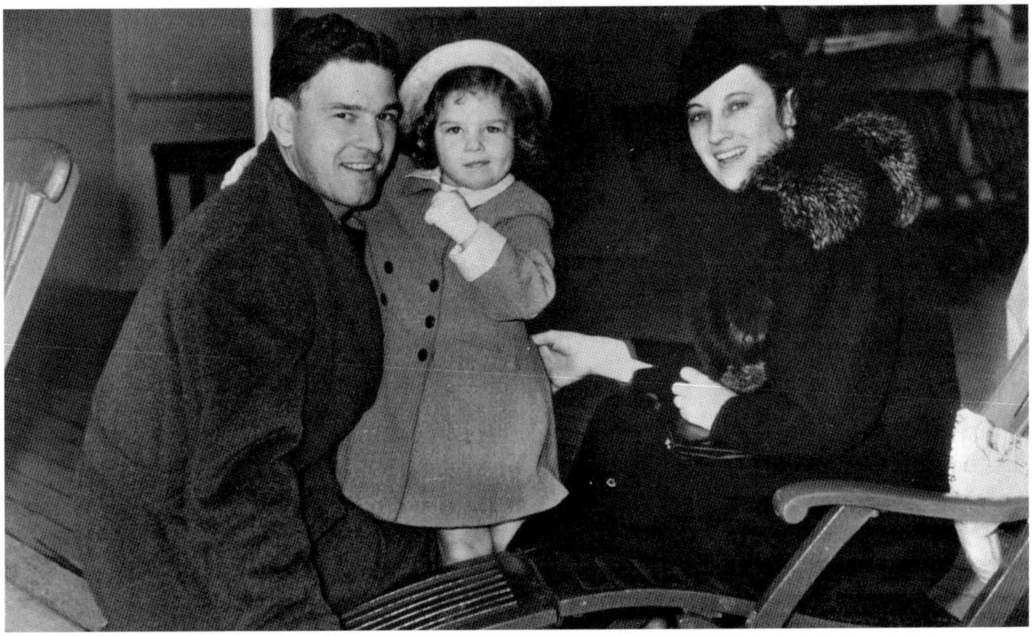

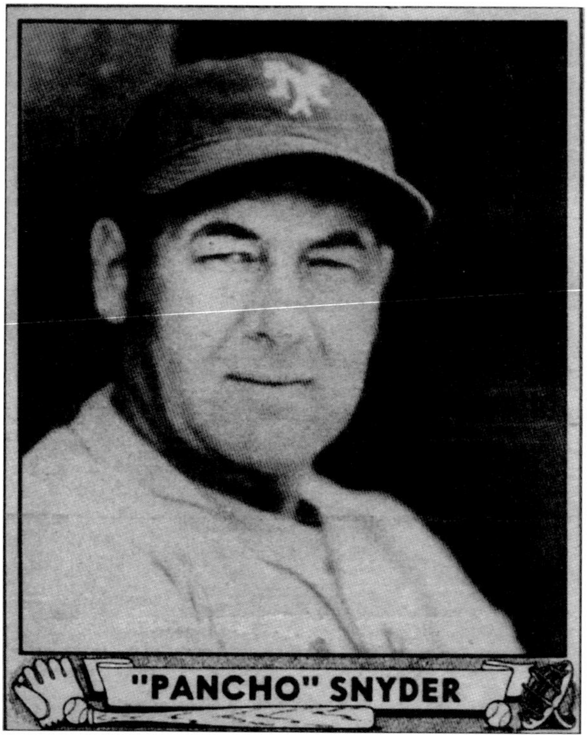

Coach Frank Snyder got nicknamed "Pancho" in Mexico. Snyder led the Giants to Cuba before manager Bill Terry arrived. "If Señor Snyder doesn't mind, they'd like to sit on level ground until the sidewalk stops coming up to meet them," said the *Post*. "The boys were not themselves as they tottered off the boat like a crowd emerging from a 52nd Street spot at 4 o'clock in the morning."

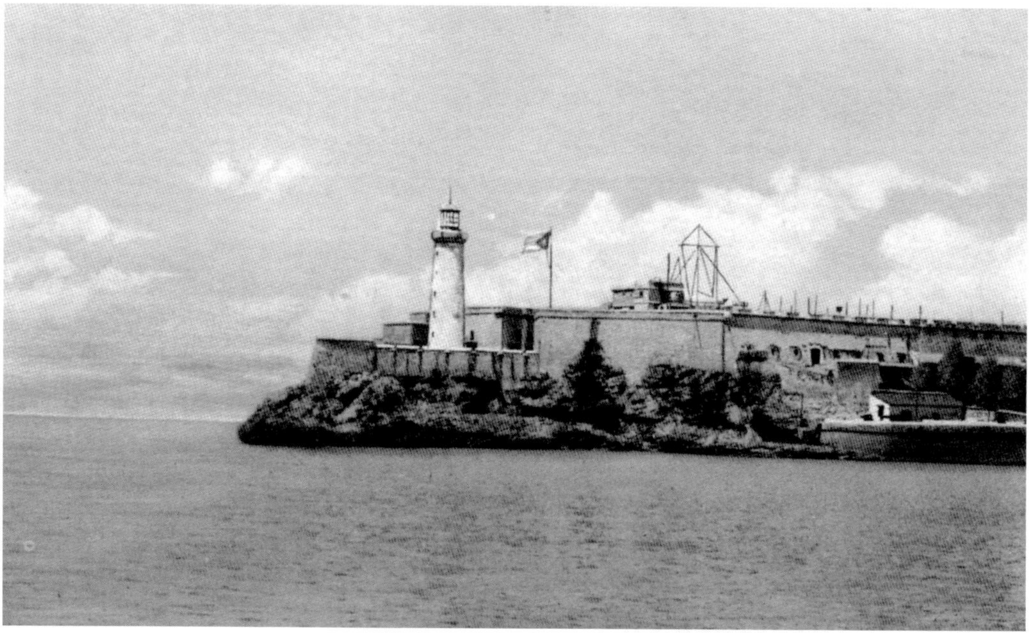

When sailing into Havana Harbor, ships pass the landmark Morro Castle, which has stood sentry since 1589. The *Post* story continued, quoting Giant executive Eddie Brannick, " 'Wonderful city. Went through Morro Castle yesterday and saw how these Spaniards used to defend themselves against those gangs from Pittsburgh.' "

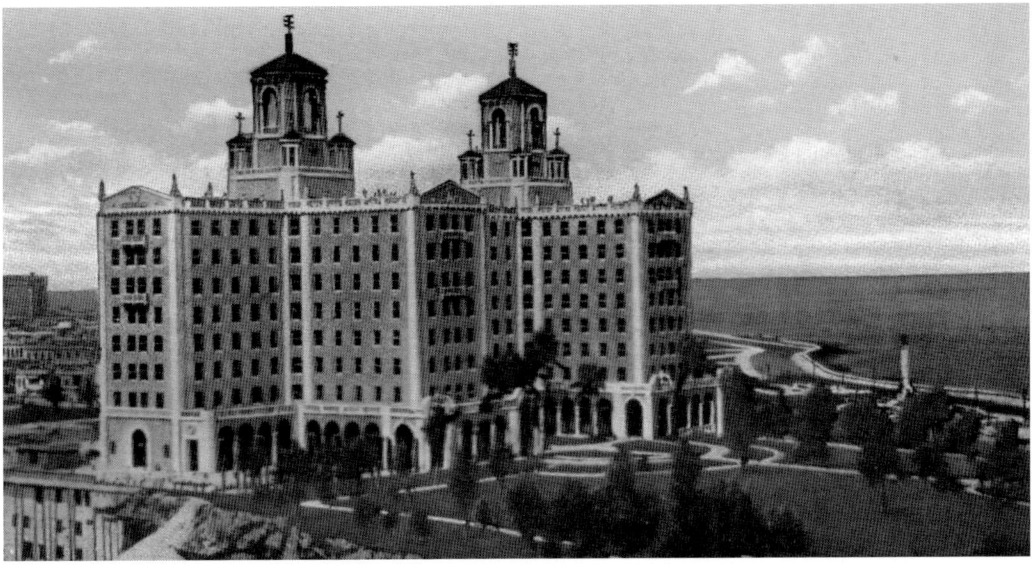

Four years earlier, in 1933, the team hotel, the Hotel Nacional, was sieged during a coup. "For a moment yesterday," the *Post* reported, "the Giants thought another uprising was on the way, there would be another shelling of the Nacional, a new tenant was on the way into the President's palace and maybe it would be best to forget about breakfast and head for the storm cellars. But the soldiers and sailors marching past and the gunboats in the harbor were merely celebrating 'Grito de Baire,' Cuba's 4th of July."

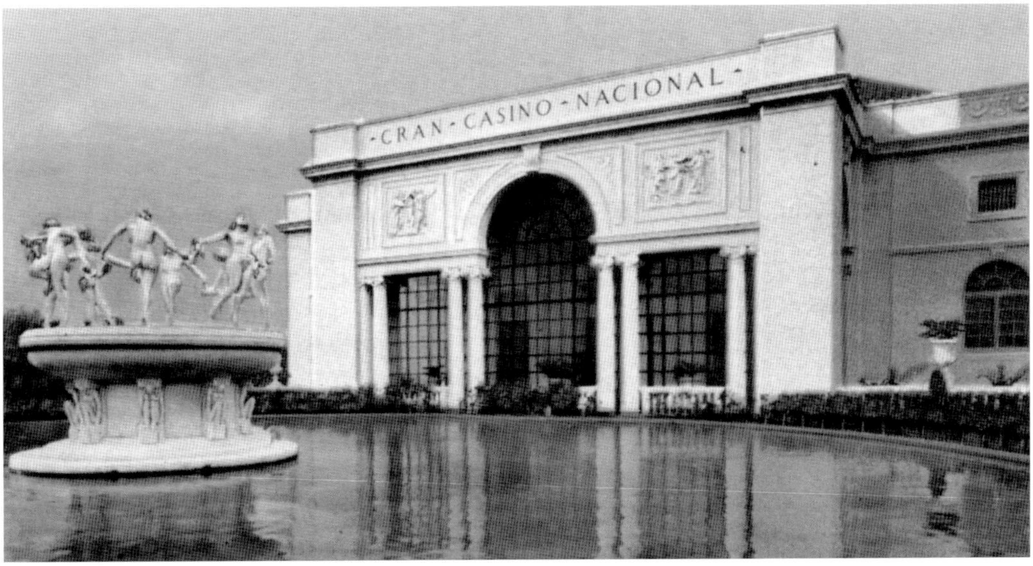

"The costly and beautifully-equipped National Casino, once the property of Charles Stoneham and John McGraw, has tables for baccarat and other games," wrote the *Post*. "They get mainly a play that doesn't exceed $5 at a time and observation indicates average winnings and losings seldom exceed $100. The dice tables are always crowded, though." Yet the waiters "hate all customers and will not serve meals the same day they're ordered."

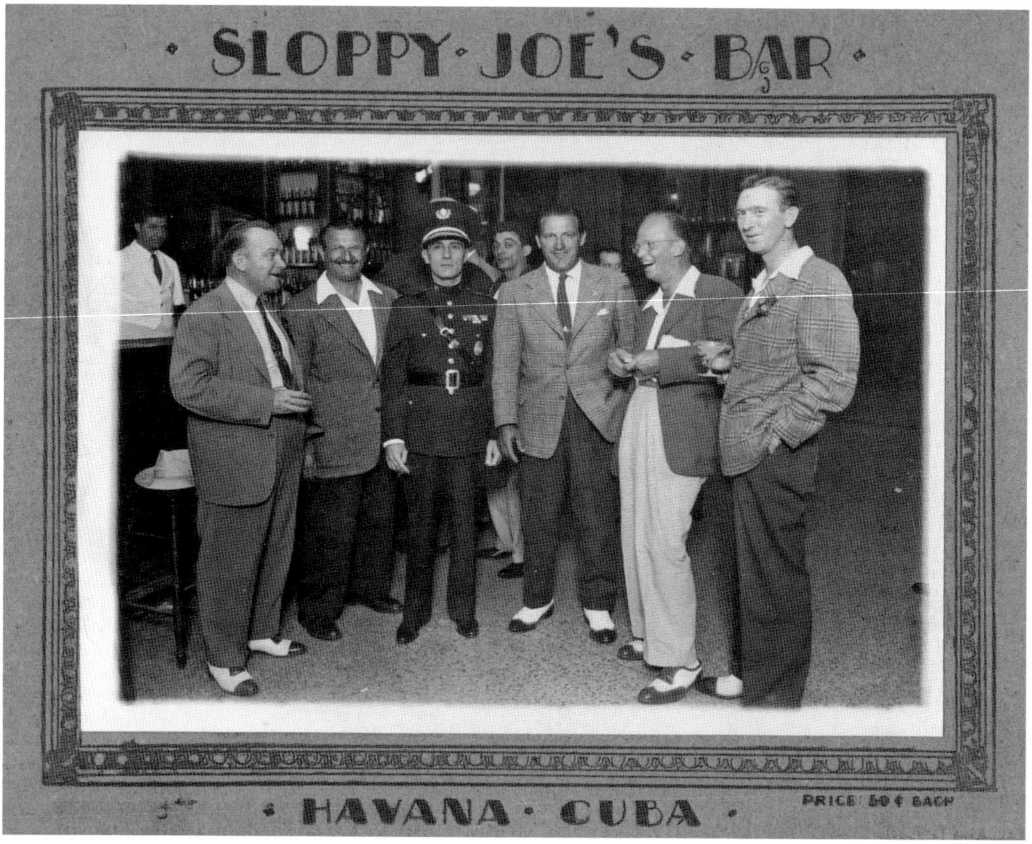

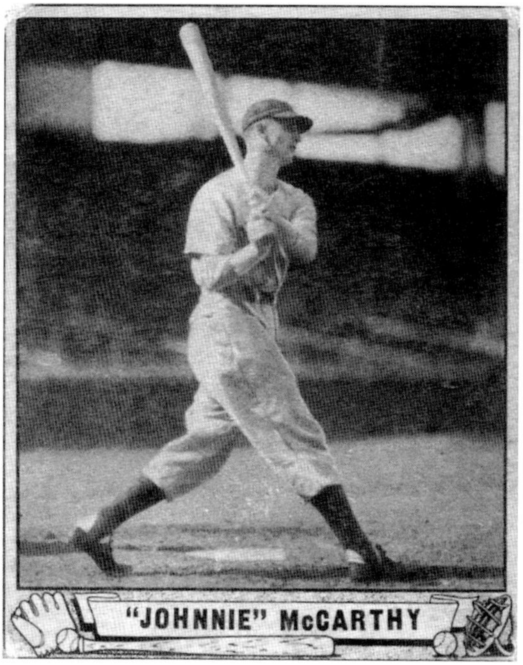

Ducky Medwick (third from right), Ewell Blackwell (right), and sportswriters pose at Sloppy Joe's. The *Post* said, "Ballclubs have come before, but never a club as well behaved as these Giants. The proprietors, who remember the Dodgers, can't understand. It was hard to tell where they did most of their training—the ballpark or Sloppy Joe's. 'What does *el jefe* Terry do?' they ask, 'lock los Gigantes in their rooms?' "

Johnny McCarthy and a few of his Giant mates found themselves lost one afternoon. As the *Post* recounted, "They stopped in an open-faced bar and grocery store at the corner. McCarthy tried first. He pointed to his feet, groaned, made motions to indicate a telephone call and an automobile ride. The proprietor smiled and took a box of corn cure off the shelf."

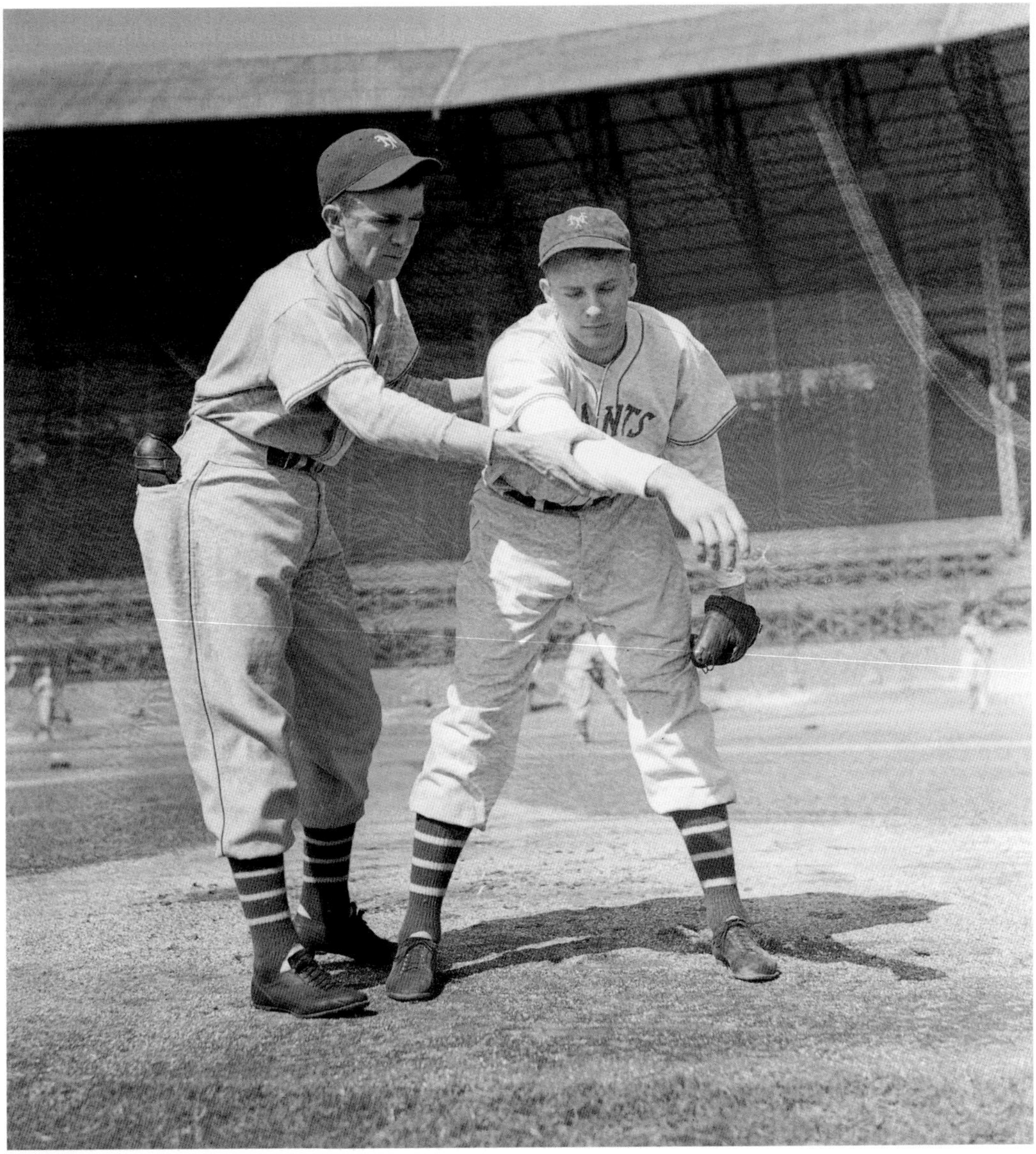

Hall of Famer Carl Hubbell's kid brother John got a Cuba tryout with the Giants that spring, and it helped the lost team. The *Post*'s coverage continued: "Things didn't get any better when a policeman, sword and revolver hanging from his belt and a rifle over his shoulder, appeared. He only shrugged when the Giants tried to make him understand and sat down and had a beer. 'We Giants,' McCarthy was yelling to the lottery ticket salesman who had just dropped in. 'Giants! Ott, Mancuso, Hubbell.' It was as though a bomb had exploded. 'Ooooobil?' asked a dozen Cubanos. 'Ooooobil? Carlos Ooooobil? Gigantes pitch, yes?' 'Yes,' yelled McCarthy. 'Him Ooooobil,' and pointed to Hooka's kid brother Johnny. Young Ooooobil had a lame back today from all the slaps they gave him, a sore hand from signing autographs and the idea of just how well known his big brother is in this world. So have the Giants. They were brought home in so many cars it looked like a parade."

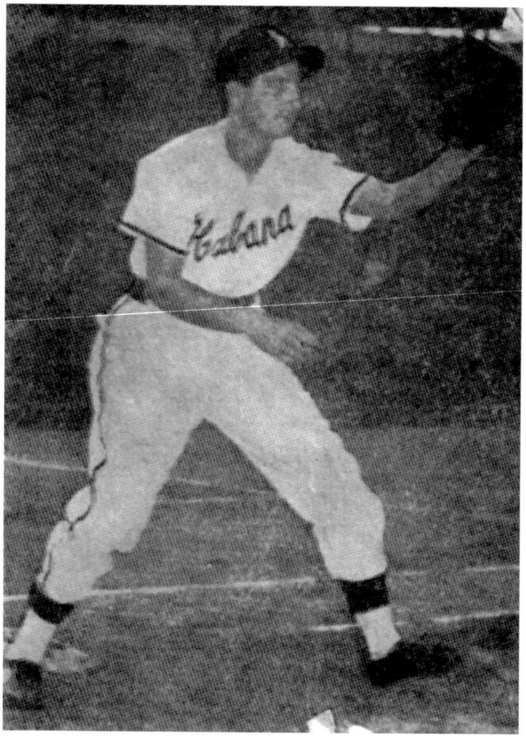

Cuban Regino Otero landed a Giants tryout. He finally made the big leagues eight years later, appearing in 14 games for the 1945 pennant-winning Cubs. Reggie's lifetime batting average at the American baseball show was .391. He also starred with the Angels in the old Pacific Coast League and returned to Cuba as a Cincinnati Reds coach in 1959, when the team played an exhibition series against the Los Angeles Dodgers.

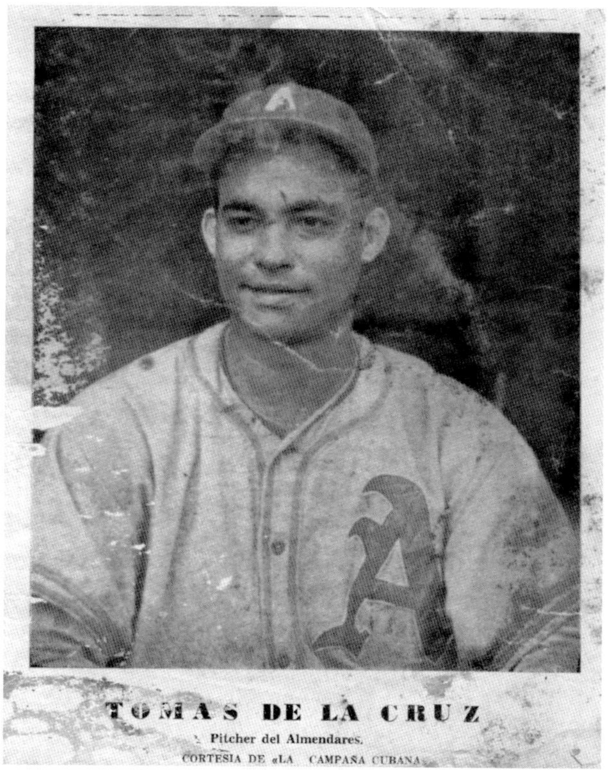

Local Tomas de la Cruz was also allowed to tryout for the Giants. Like Otero, he had toiled for years on Cuban diamonds and eventually got a cup of coffee at the show. Tommy pitched for the Reds in 1944, winning nine with an impressive 3.25 ERA.

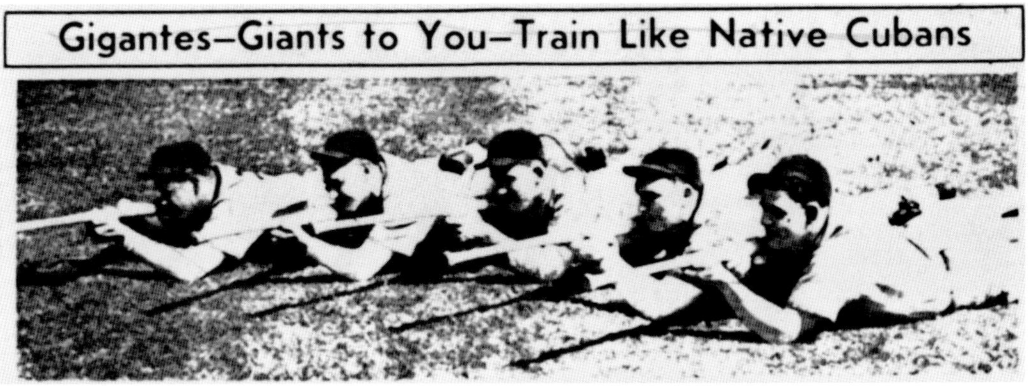

Hank Leiber, George Davis, Joe Moore, Jimmy Ripple, and Mel Ott "train their sights on the left-field fence," the caption said. The *Times* quoted Giant executive Eddie Brannick: " 'Colonel Batista is on our side—I hope! We play against his team.' Ah, Colonel Batista had a ballteam? 'Sí, The Cuban Armed Forces,' " said Señor Secretario. If the Giants had any diplomacy, the score would have been Cuban Armed Forces, 139, Giants, 0.

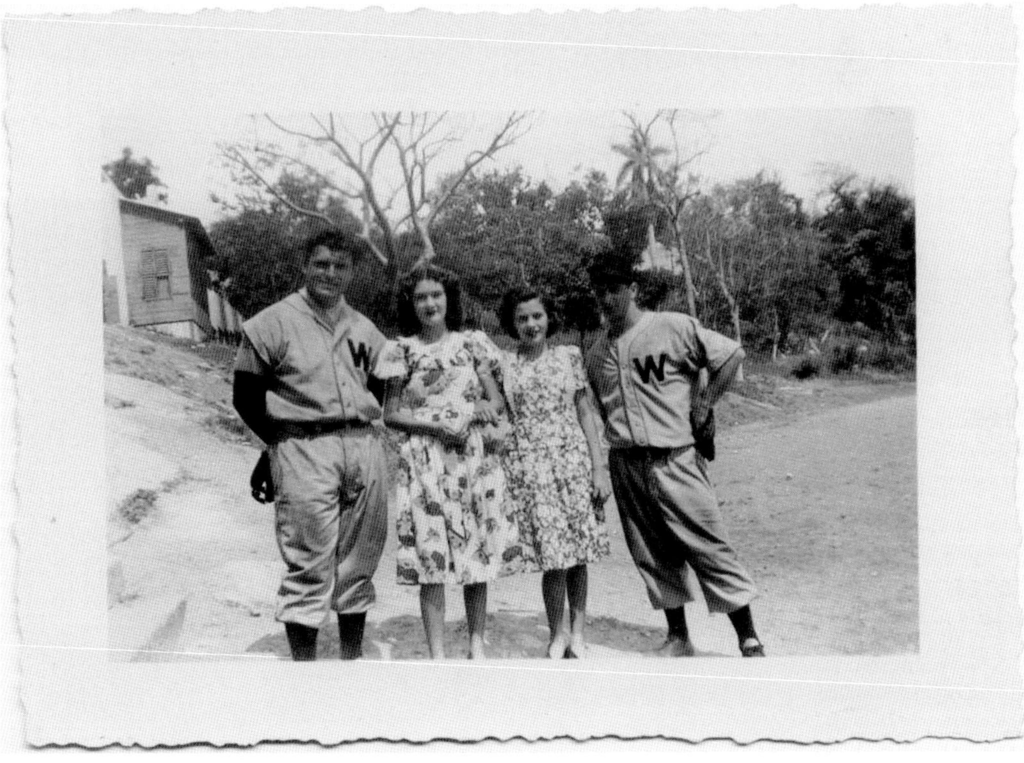

The Washington Senators toured Cuba in 1946; they won all five games against local teams and split two with the Red Sox. While there, owner Clark Griffith received a medal from the Cuban government for signing so many locals. His players practiced diplomatic relations for their country too, befriending numerous nationals on the *isla*. Here Bert Shepard and Marino Pieretti pose with two unidentified Cuban women.

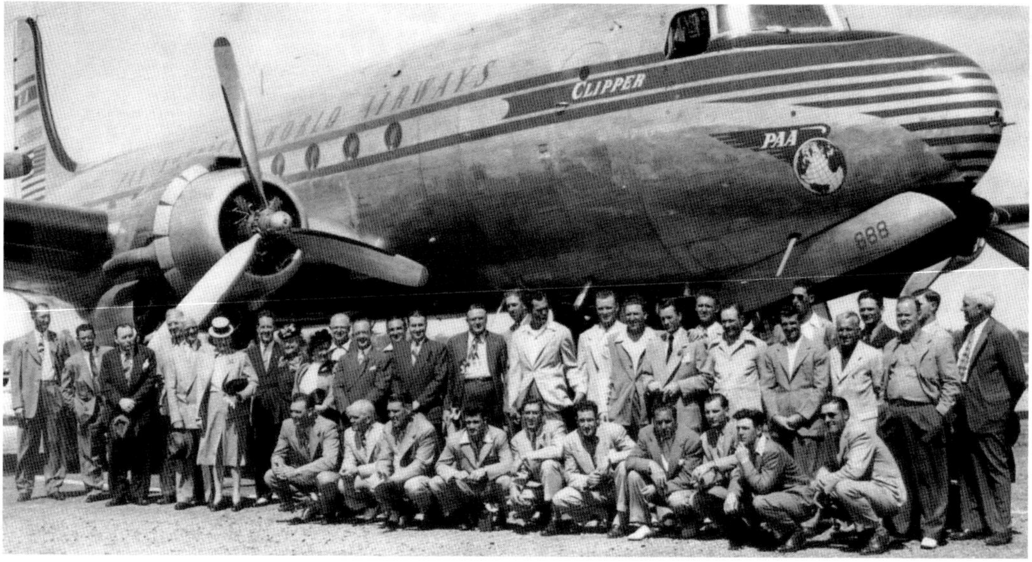

The Red Sox traveled to Havana in 1941 (without Ted Williams), went 1-2 against Cincinnati, and lost to a local team. In 1946, they flew back for more. "We took a plane over, which wasn't too common back then," recalls Dave "Boo" Ferriss. Ted Williams made the ride this time; he is towards the right in the above photograph, wearing shades. In the win against the Senators, Williams smacked a triple and two singles. That year, Williams went on to take MVP honors and Ferriss won 25 games on the way to the American League pennant.

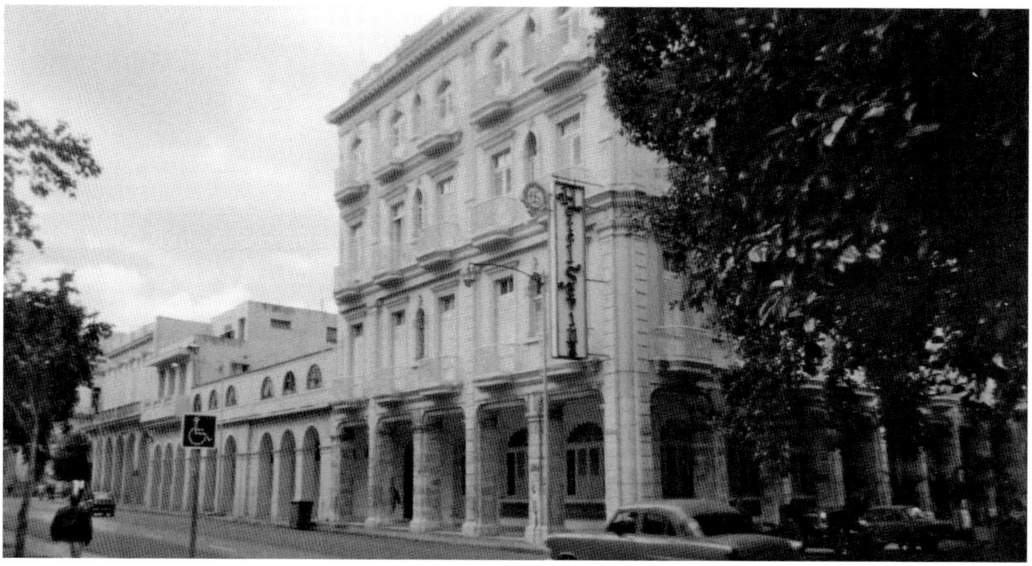

The Hotel Sevilla is still open. Ferriss remembers, "Bobby Doerr and I roomed together. One night at 2:00 a.m. there was a loud noise. We peeped out the door. Several Cuban police officers were in the hall, a few doors down. We shut the door quick and went back to bed. The next morning, we heard someone had been murdered there! That was scary, but otherwise the trip was good."

2

1941

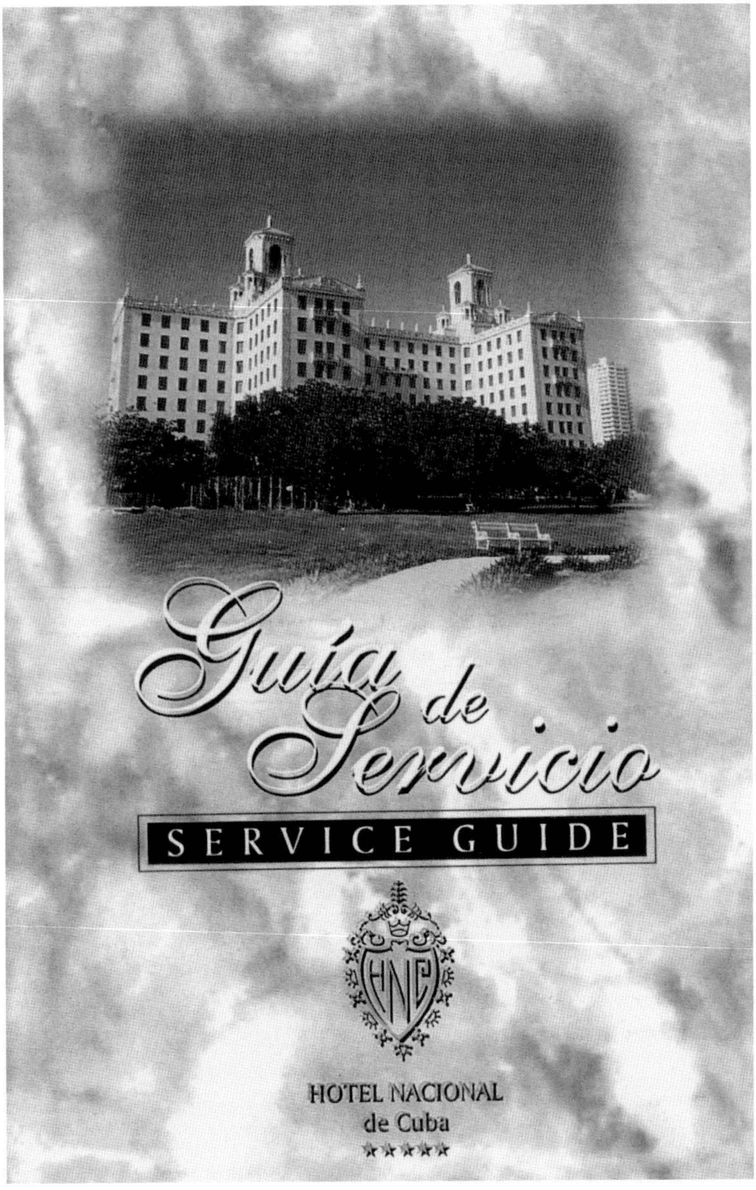

The Dodgers, also lovingly referred to as the "Bums," would win the pennant in 1941. MVP Dolph Camilli led the league in homers, while Pete Reiser had the best batting average. Pitchers Kirby Higbe and Whitlow Wyatt each won 22. For spring camp, some players sailed over to Cuba from Miami, but most flew, which was a rather novel innovation for that era. The AP reported an "enthusiastic welcome," with "officials, a band, a parade, and police escorts to the palace before bunking down at the Hotel Nacional."

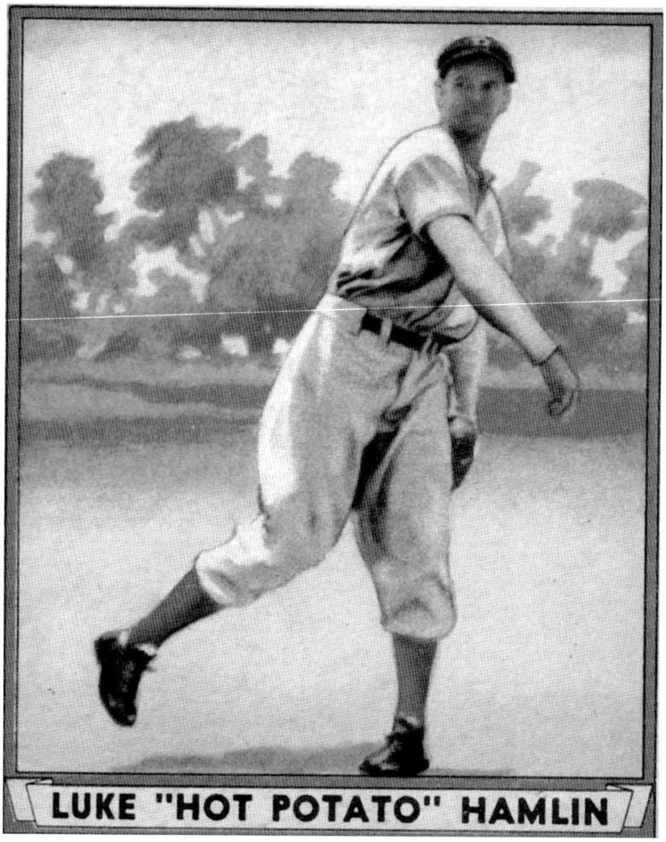

Here is a baseball card of Luke "Hot Potato" Hamlin. The 1941 Dodgers may be the all-time nickname team, with players such as "Ducky" Medwick, "Pee Wee" Reese, and "Cookie" Lavagetto. They also had guys whose real names were imaginative, like Van Lingle Mungo, Kirby Higbe, and Vitautis "Vito" Casimirus Tamulis. Their talent was world class, as one of every five guys on the roster ended up in the Hall of Fame (Billy Herman, Reese, Medwick, Leo Durocher, and Paul Waner).

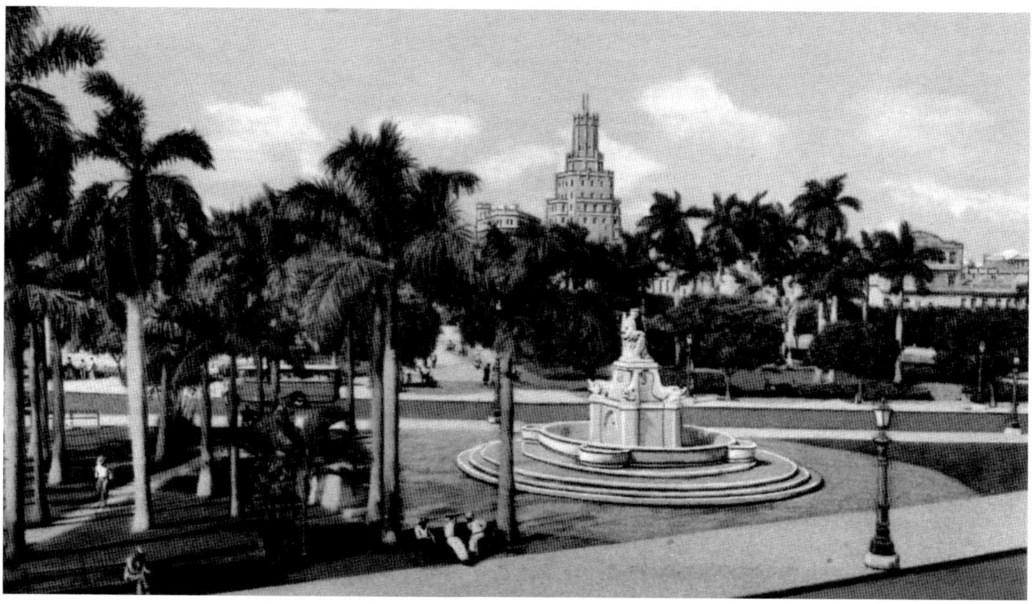

The tropics in February were a stark contrast to a lot of hometowns. "I went to Cuba from the land of ice and snow," says catcher and Minnesotan Tony Giuliani.

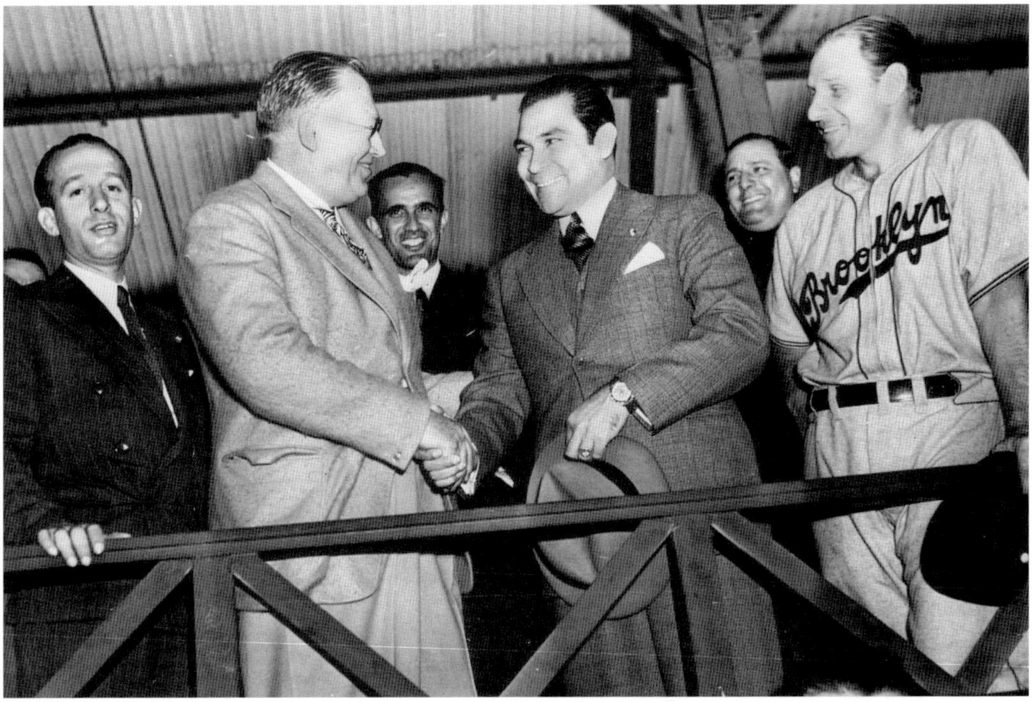

"The Dodgers," the *New York Herald-Tribune* revealed, "have been welcomed by everybody from President Batista to the local Boy Scouts." Batista personally greeted Leo Durocher and the other Brooklyn brass in 1941. He was still in power years later until he was overthrown by Fidel Castro's revolution in 1959. Like Castro, he was a big baseball fan. He also knew the benefits of American clubs coming down, so he offered the team financial incentives to train there.

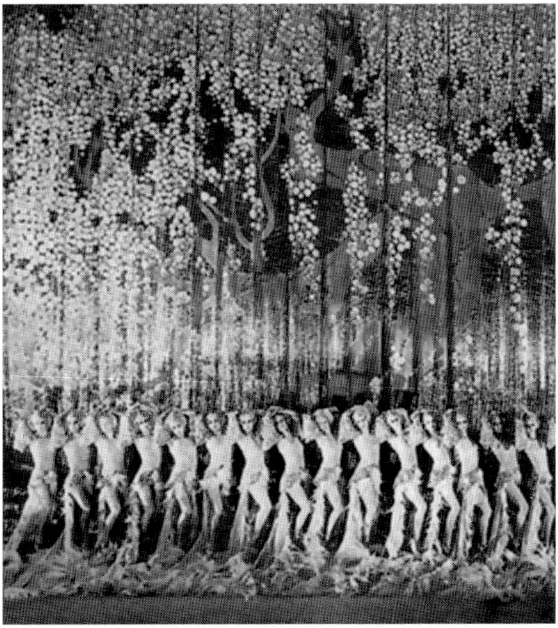

Manager Leo Durocher took charge right away. "The Dodgers may not yet dispossess the Reds from the top of the league but they've already ousted—the brutes!—a bevy of girlies from the Hotel Nacional in Havana," said the *Brooklyn Eagle*. "Yes, they've all been evicted! This may not be exactly Emily Post, but it's Durocher's way of getting distractions off the scene. He had the dancing troupe moved to another nearby hotel."

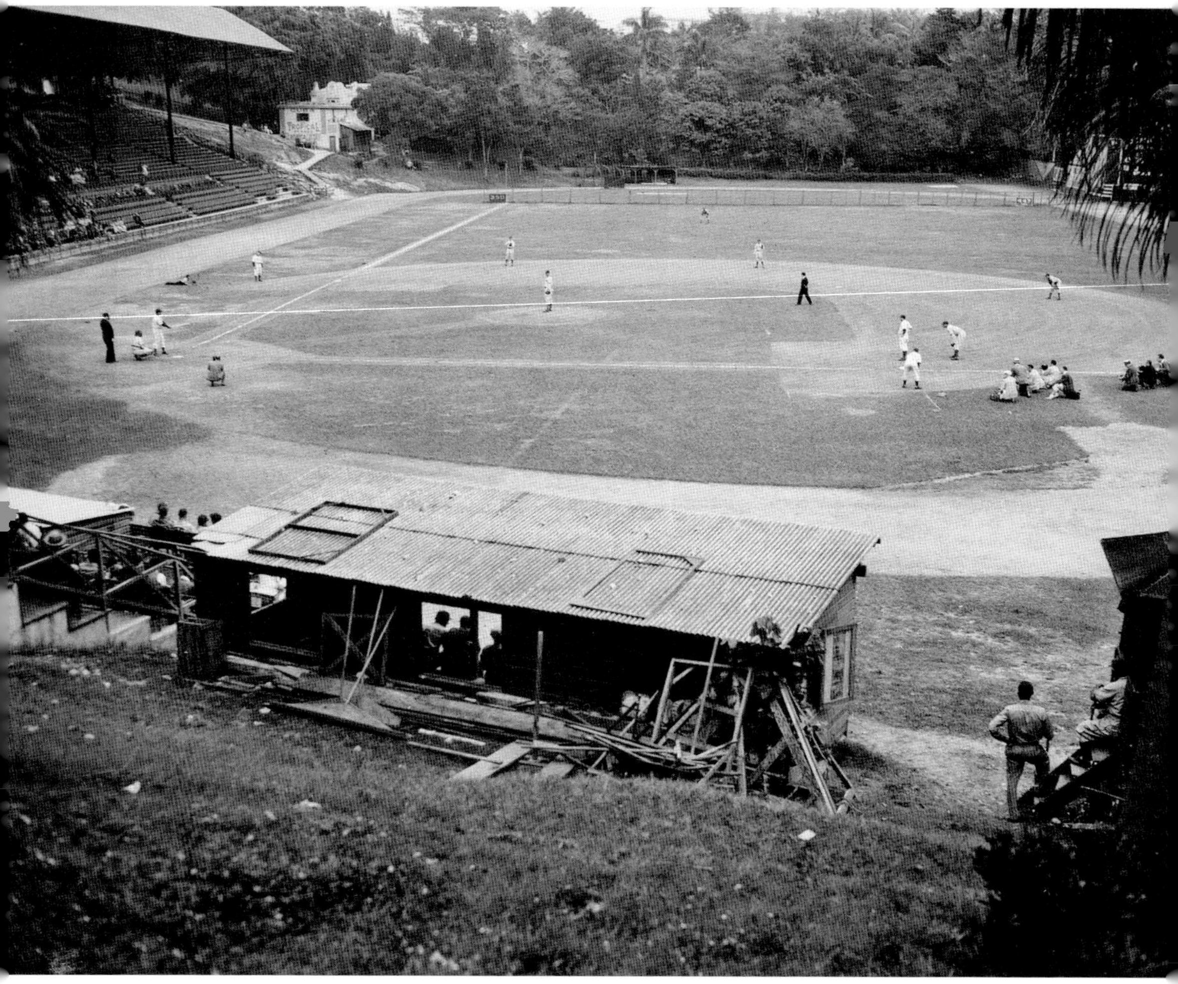

Cerveza Tropical Stadium, site of the 1931 sessions, was again their home for both workouts and exhibition games. "Tropical Stadium is so spacious," reported the *Herald-Tribune*, "that plans are under way to move the outfield fences in several feet so home runs over the wall will be possible. The centerfield barrier is 505 feet from the plate."

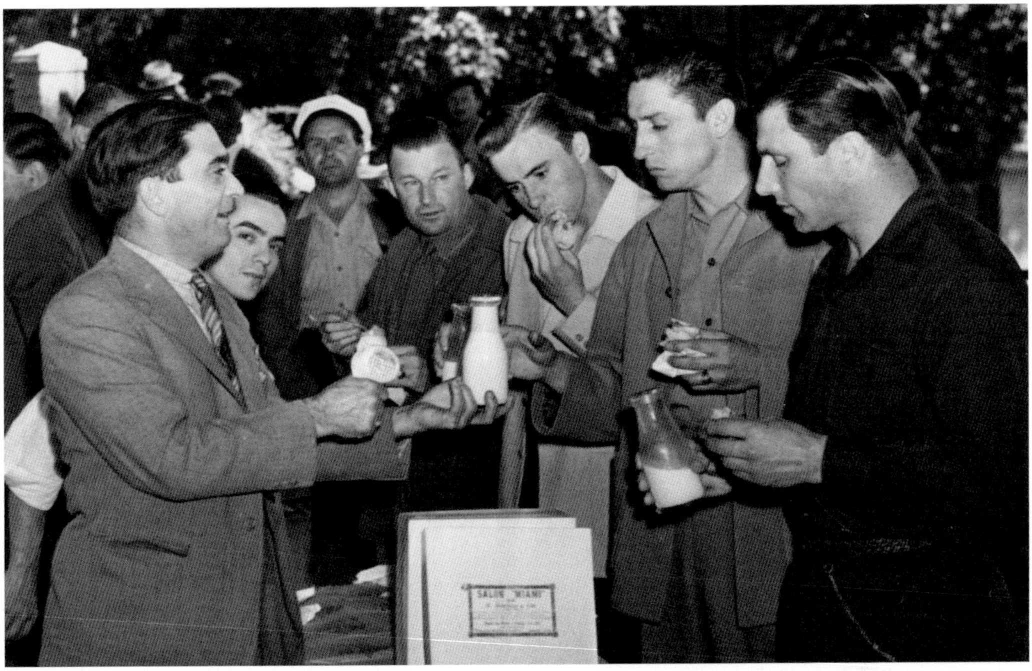

"Durocher put the players on a milk diet," the *Herald-Tribune* said, "strange, [as they were] close to the Tropical Brewery. In their hands were glasses of milk, but on their minds were foaming tankards of malt brew." The *Times* commented, "Leave it to Branch the Non-Alcoholic Rickey. Branch ordered Vitamin B-1. His pitchers lacked something; might have been B-1. On the other hand, it might have been a good curve ball."

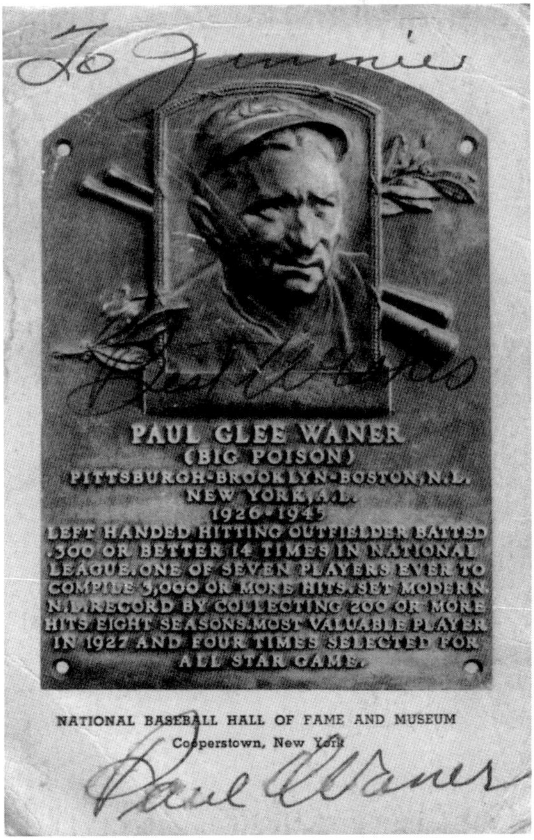

Durocher's discipline extended Paul Waner's career. "Old friends he'd meet on chandeliers and under tables in his delirious days and nights as a Pirate," said the *Post*, "wouldn't know the Waner of today. He's surrounded by temptation. But so far he hasn't had anything stronger than a malted milk." His seriousness paid off because two seasons later, Waner, at age 40, hit .311.

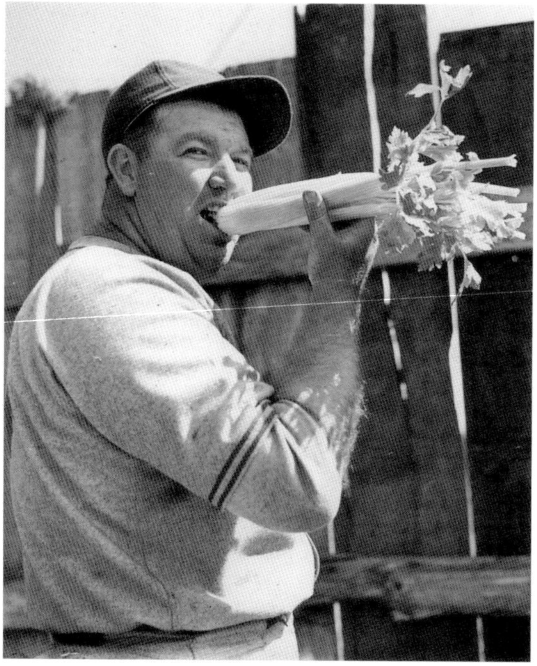

Joe Gallagher's nickname was "Muscles," but somehow, during the wintertime, he experienced a little settling. To help with his diet, the 1941 coaching staff directed him to the vegetable garden. Here Joe seems to enjoy a large stalk of celery.

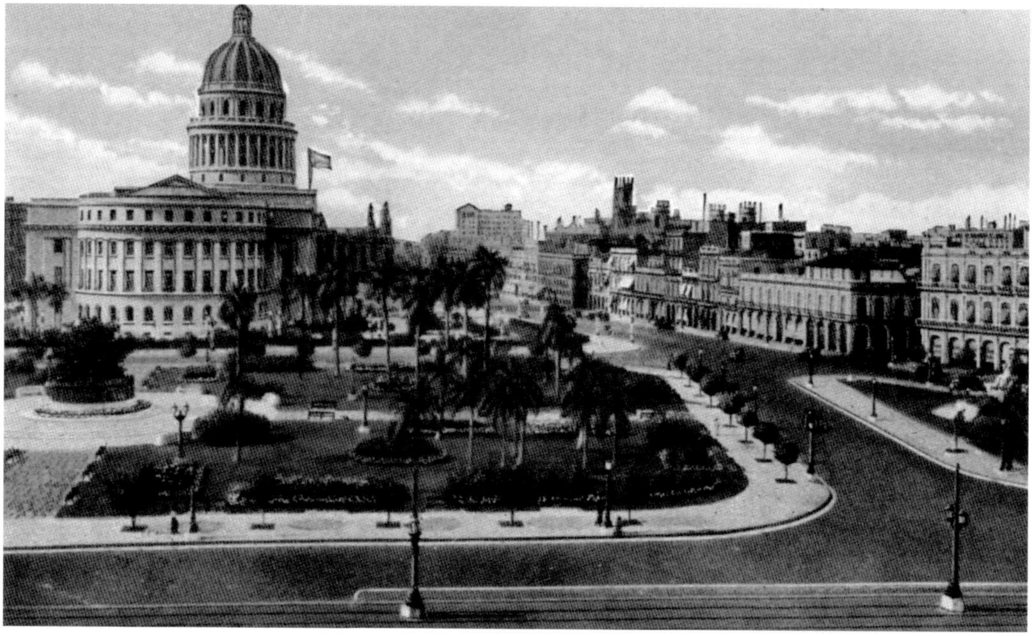

Transportation in Havana was not always smooth. "When the athletes filed down this morning, there was no bus," noted the *Times*. " 'Where's the bus?' barked Durocher. '*Muy a menudo llega tarde*,' wailed the bus manager. 'I'll say he's tardy,' yelled Durocher. '*Busqueme* half a dozen taxis; pronto!' They were obtained amid a cacophony of Spanish punctuated by the raucous remarks of Lippy Leo about the Cuban bus companies. Even the bus manager doesn't know where his driver went with the bus."

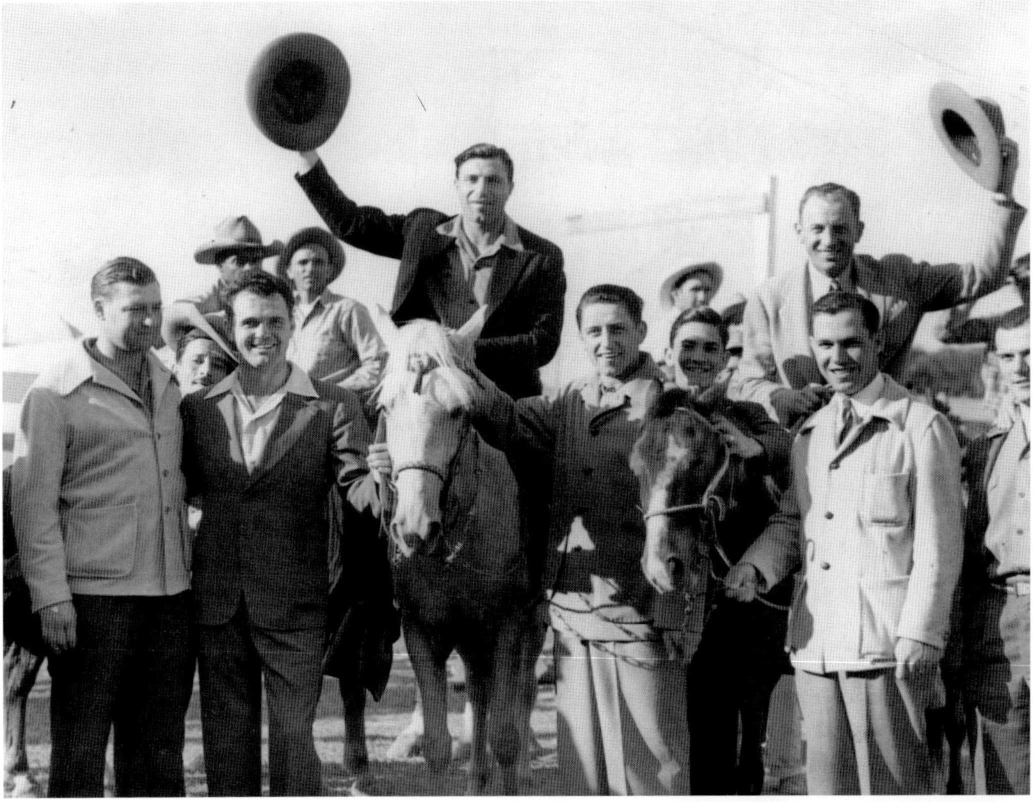

Not long after the non-bus incident, All-Star Dolph Camilli began riding Havana horses as an alternate mode of transport. "No speedballer, storm, or airship ever scared me," he told the *Daily News*, "and I never thought a mere bus would, but the buses here do. They race through the streets like mad, and I doubt whether all four wheels are ever on the ground. They never stop to let passengers on or off—you've got to hop 'em, like hoboes grab freight trains."

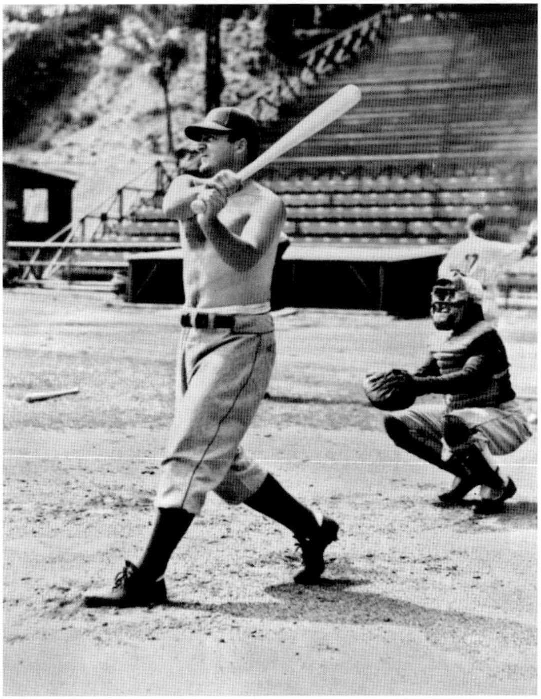

Finally, the boys made it to practice. New England boy Ducky Medwick found Cuban Februaries to be just too doggone hot for a heavy flannel jersey, so he took his off to work out. Ducky spent 17 seasons at the show as a 10-time All-Star en route to cooler Cooperstown.

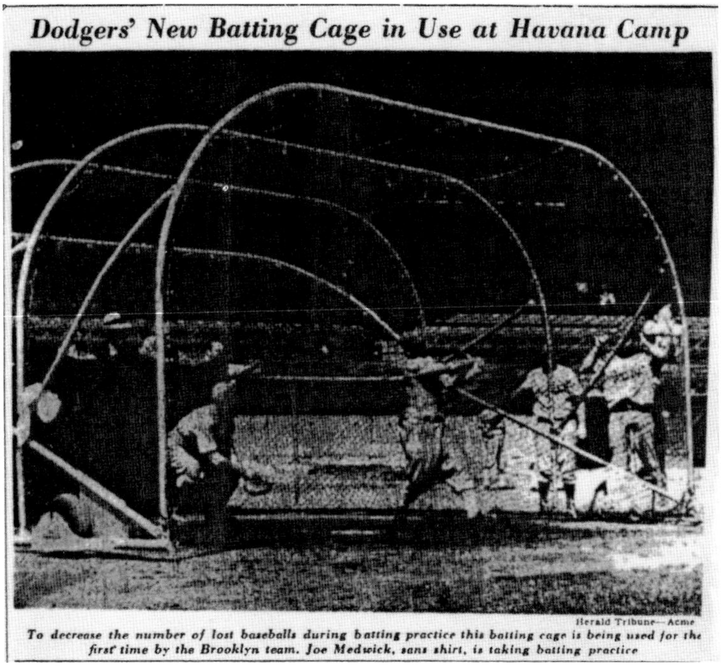

Dodgers' New Batting Cage in Use at Havana Camp

Herald Tribune—Acme

To decrease the number of lost baseballs during batting practice this batting cage is being used for the first time by the Brooklyn team. Joe Medwick, sans shirt, is taking batting practice

Larry MacPhail, Dodger president in 1941, was always innovating. He tried primitive batting helmets (plastic discs in zippered ball cap pockets), and his Bums were among the first to use batting cages. "There was a time fans suggested the Dodgers be confined in a cage," observed the *Daily News*, "but those days are gone. The new idea will save the club no end of expense in foul balls."

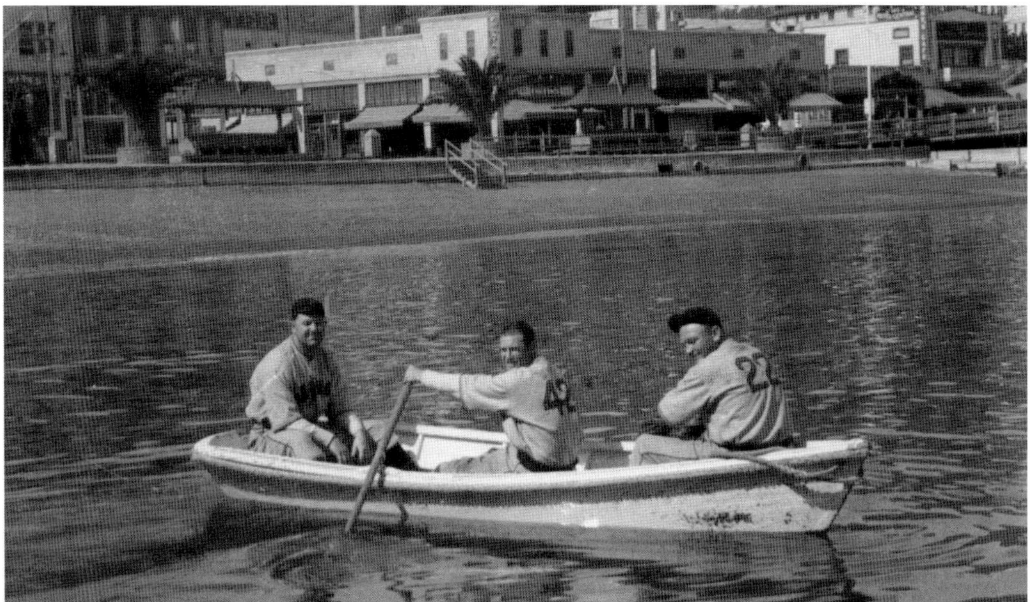

Latecomers always managed to disrupt things. "Blimp" Phelps, afraid of heights, missed the plane. "The big buzz of the Dodger camp is the strange case of Ernest Phelps," said the *Brooklyn Eagle*, "otherwise known as the Blimp that does not fly." Phelps finally managed to cross the bay but lost his starting job and was shipped to Pittsburgh. Earlier with the Cubs, Blimp managed to make the spring training trip to another island, Catalina. He is seen here on the left with skiffmates Bud Tinning (center) and Dutch Seebold (right).

Mickey Owen was late too. "Owen's mother has written to MacPhail," said the *Post*, "asking him to bring the young catcher into line." He arrived, "tired from the long trip but he will not feel much better after he emerges from the salary conferences tomorrow with Dodger officials." He ended up the number one catcher but became infamous for a World Series passed ball that led to a Dodger defeat.

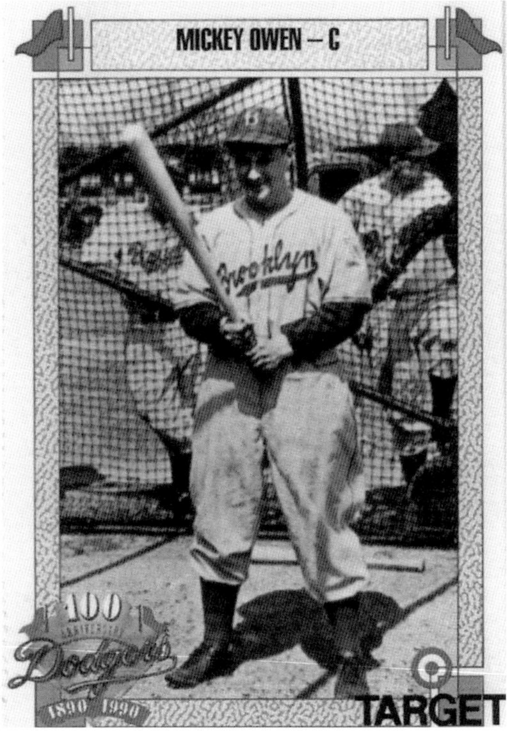

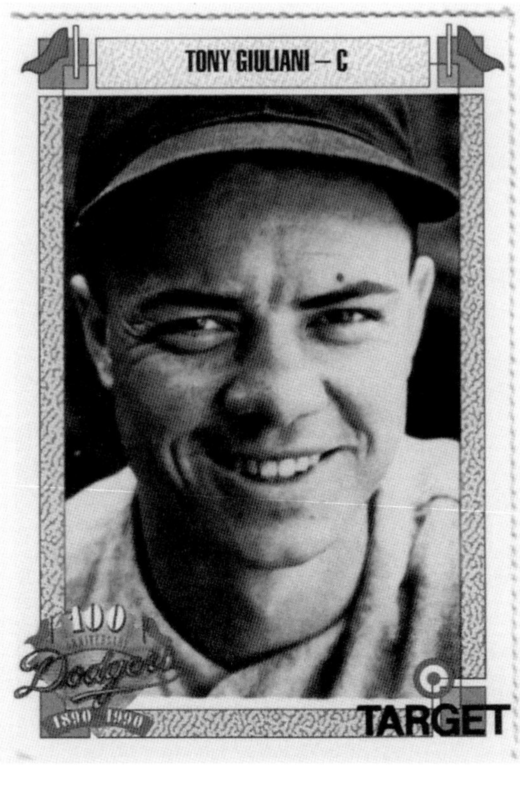

Tony Giuliani sent his contract back unsigned and was barred from Cuba. The *Post* reported he was considering a new profession in his native Minnesota as a wine taster at a vineyard, adding, "This is unique among Brooklyn ballplayers, because many Dodgers of the past have carried on the two businesses at the same time." The two sides worked it out, and Giuliani joined his mates, but he only appeared in three games that season.

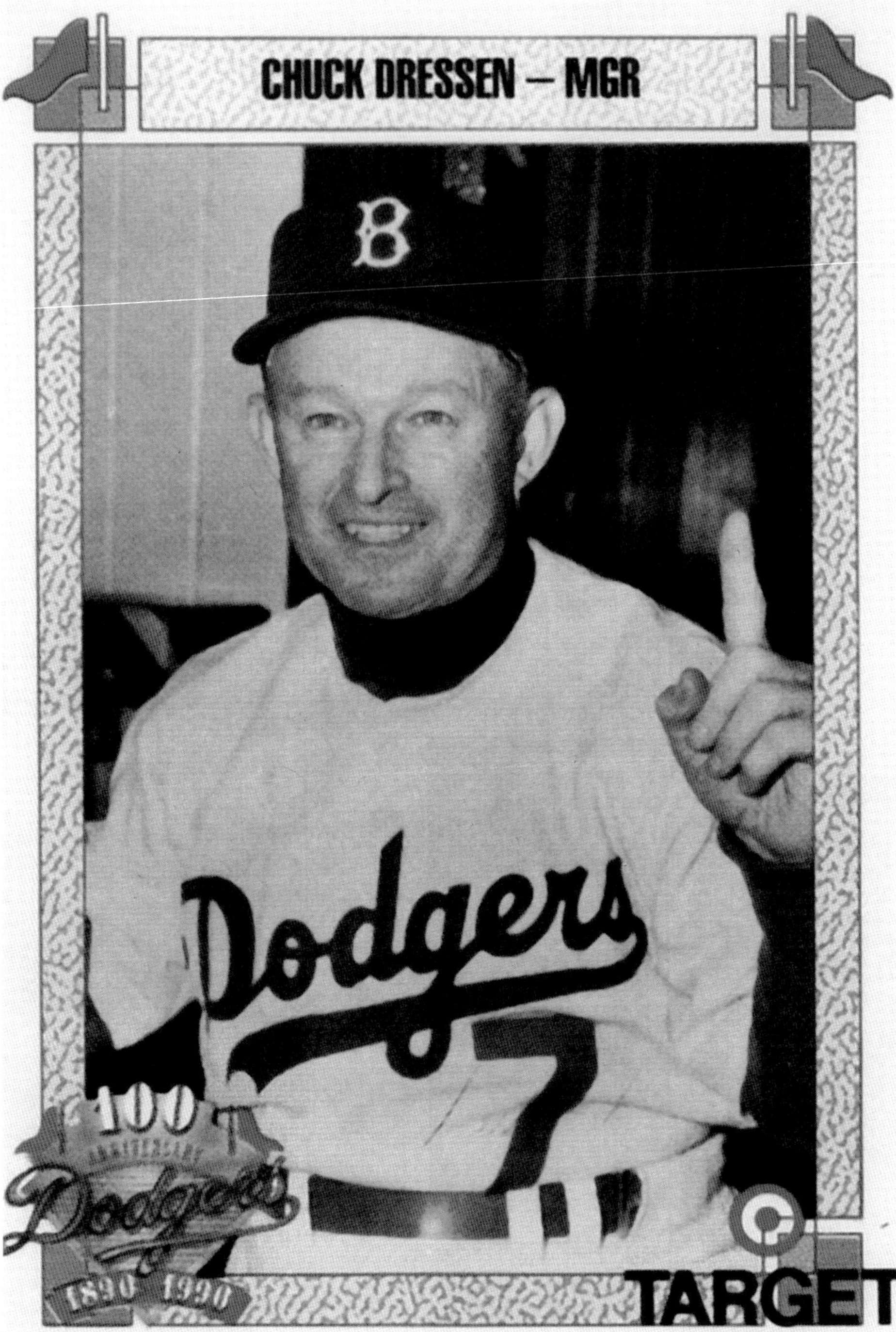

The Dodgers split the team for intrasquad games before the other opponents arrived and named the two halves after the coaches, the Estrellas Corriden and the Estrellas Dressen. "*Estrellas* in Spanish means stars, but in this case was strictly hyperbole," smirked the *Herald-Tribune*. "Neither side has progressed sufficiently to merit any sort of adjectives. The Dressens won, 8-4."

Gambling ran rampant in Cuba before the *revolución*. "Cubans, watching the Dodger games, have thought up almost every conceivable bet to make on baseball," AP said. "All during the game, bookmakers run up and down the aisles quoting prices, not only on who's going to win, but also on the color of Larry MacPhail's sports jacket creations." It is interesting to note that this national lottery ticket includes an image of a baseball player.

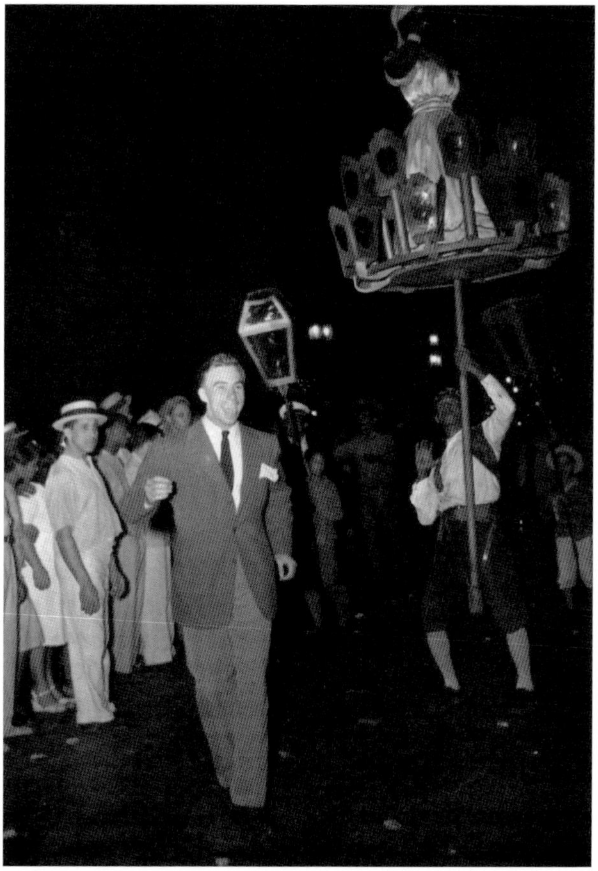

"Some of the guys went out, *en la compania de la mujer*—as the companion of a woman," Giuliani recalls. "So be careful! But we couldn't dwell on that, on what wasn't on the field. We had curfews. Some of the fellows went out and had fun. I suppose they had some libations. That's part of the night foolery. But they had to get back to the hotel before midnight. Durocher would send the coaches out around 11:00 p.m. to look for 'em." Here Pee Wee Reese engages in a Mardi Gras–like celebration that certainly took place before 11:00 p.m.

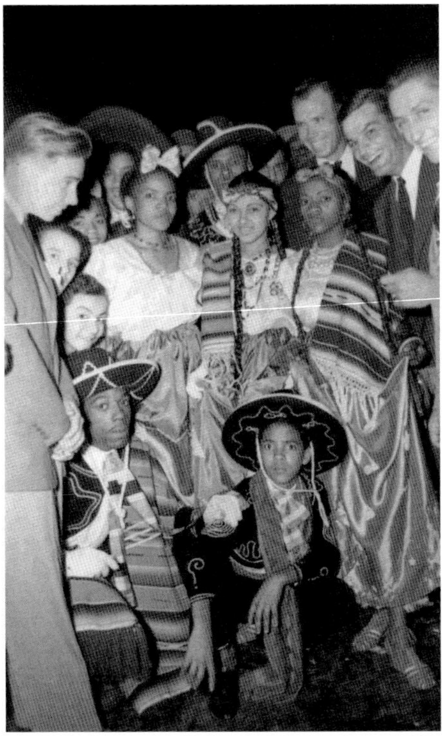

Reese and his Dodger pals immersed themselves in the Spanish culture, although the language barrier occasionally got in the way. "A guy can't enjoy a movie around here," Reese complained to a sportswriter. "There are about 200 picture houses in Havana showing American talkies, but they all flash Spanish titles on the screen. The Cubans don't understand English and they drown out the dialogue by reading and discussing the Spanish titles—and not in drawing room whispers, either."

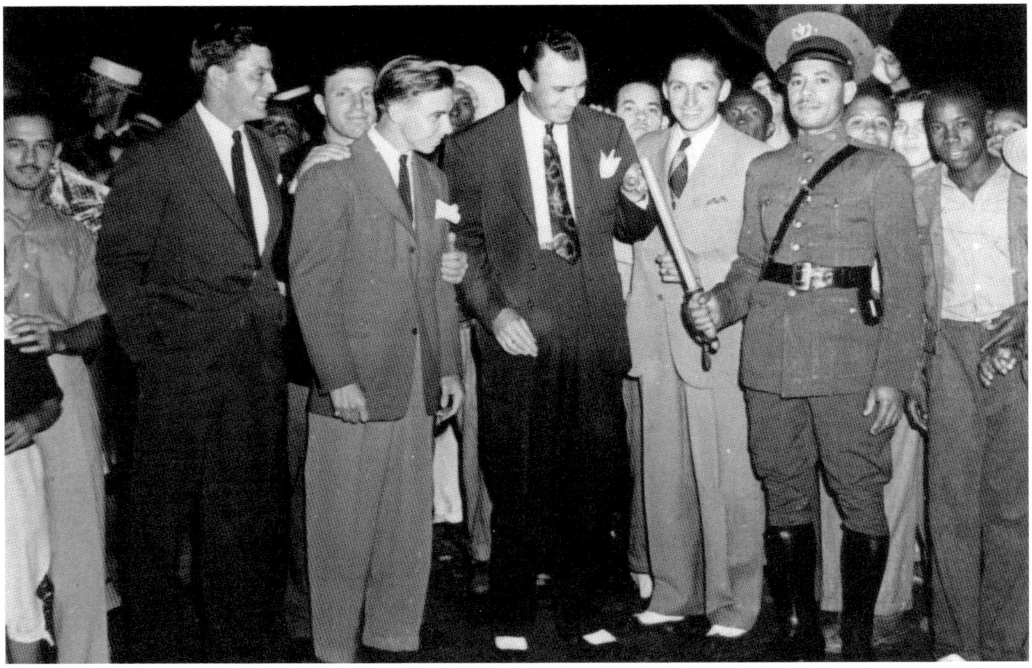

"You'd think the war had reached Cuba, to see all the soldiers here," wrote the *Post*. "They're all heavily coated with medals, too. Probably even got 'em for penmanship." Above, Dolph Camilli, Reese, Tex Carleton, and Pete Coscarart take a look.

All things baseball become topsy-turvy in Cuba. For instance, Hall of Fame Cleveland pitcher Bob Lemon played for the Indians in Cuba as an infielder in the spring of 1941, on the way up to the majors.

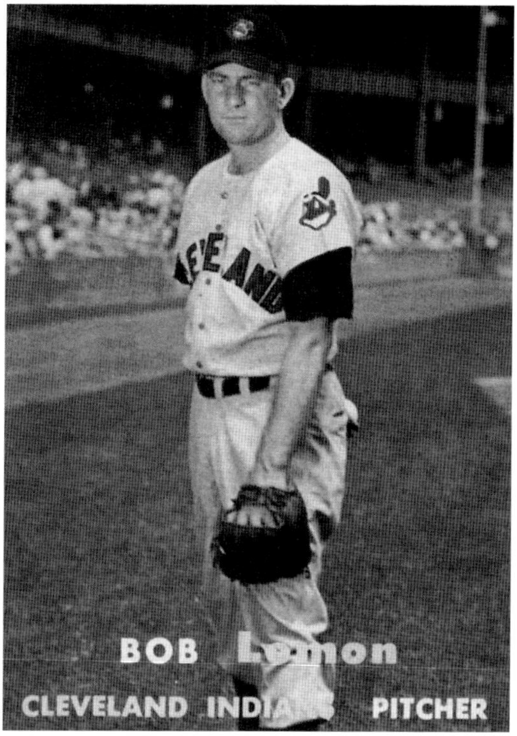

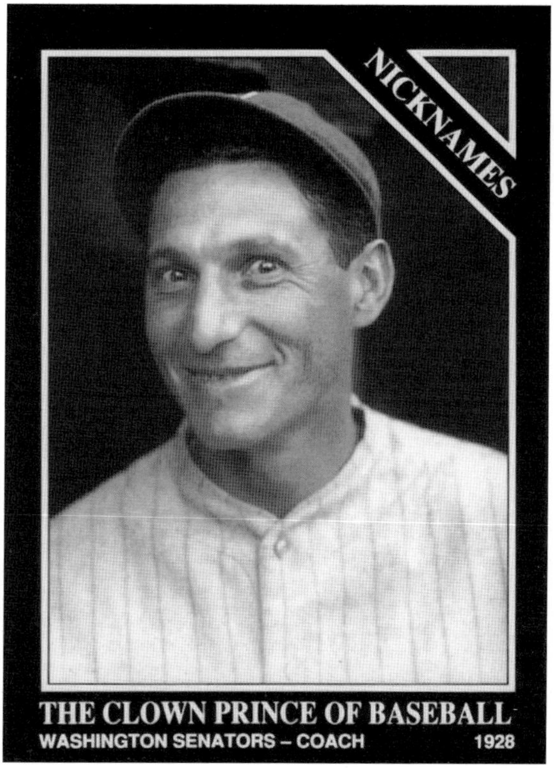

Al Schacht pitched for Washington 20 years earlier, but in 1941 he was a comic. When he arrived, he "had trouble passing customs," the *Post* reported. "He made the mistake of identifying himself as an author in his questionnaire. When an interpreter told him officials wouldn't go for that, Mr. Schacht wrote 'comedian.' They believed him, but there's some doubt about that, too. He'd better be funny this weekend."

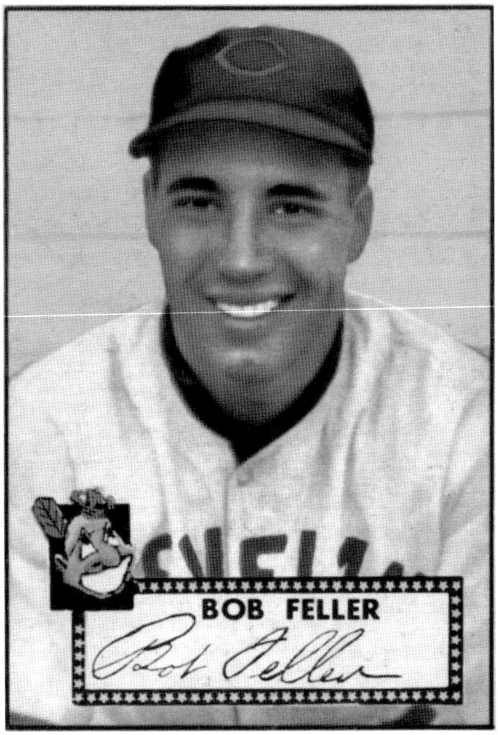

Cleveland Hall of Famer Bob Feller beat the Dodgers 8-4, but the bigger headline was what happened off the field. He was supposed to match up against Dodger hurler Van Lingle Mungo, but Mungo ran into some trouble at the hotel a few hours before game time, as further explained in chapter three.

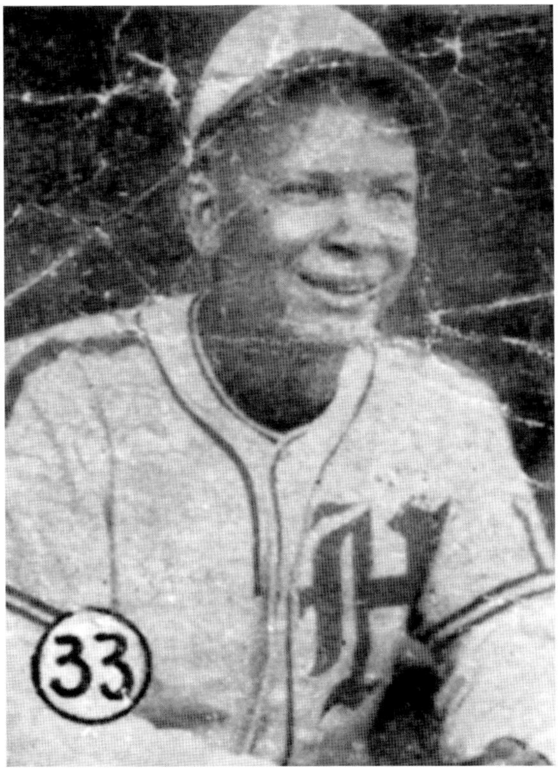

The next day, the Brooks fought back and "almost ran the Cubans off the field," said the *Eagle*, winning 11-4. Still, the best performance was a local one. "For the Cubans, the most amazing player was Julio Rojo, a catcher who is 52 years old and spry beyond his years."

In the final game, the Cubans were leading 7-2 behind the pitching of Gil Torres. Late in the game, a fan had a heart attack and an ambulance carted him to the hospital. The fan was Gil Torres's father, Ricardo, who had been quite a ballplayer himself in Cuba.

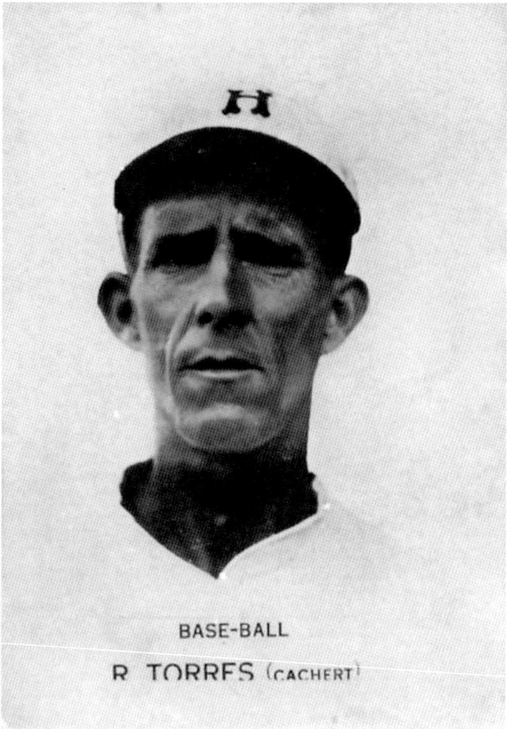

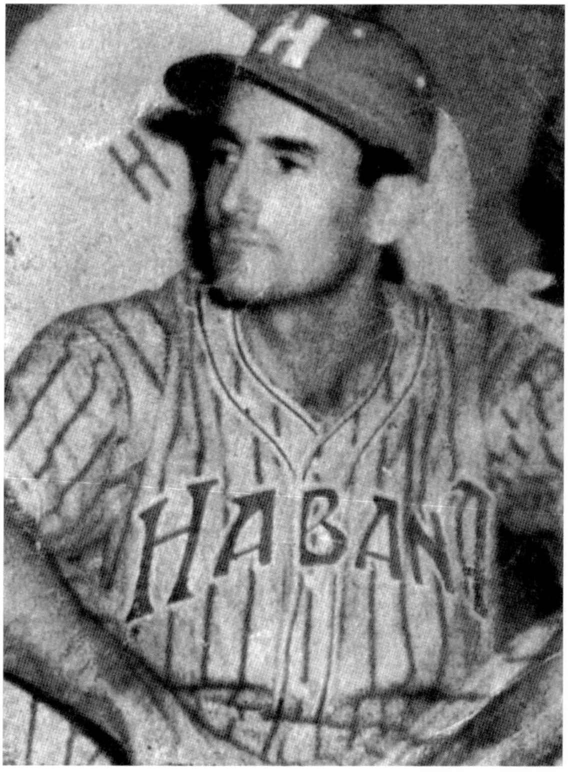

For some reason, Gil Torres stayed in the game. Understandably, he unraveled and gave up five runs in the next two frames. But the Dodgers had to catch their ride, so the game ended as a 7-7 tie after nine innings. Fortunately, Papa Torres recovered and lived to see nearly 20 more seasons.

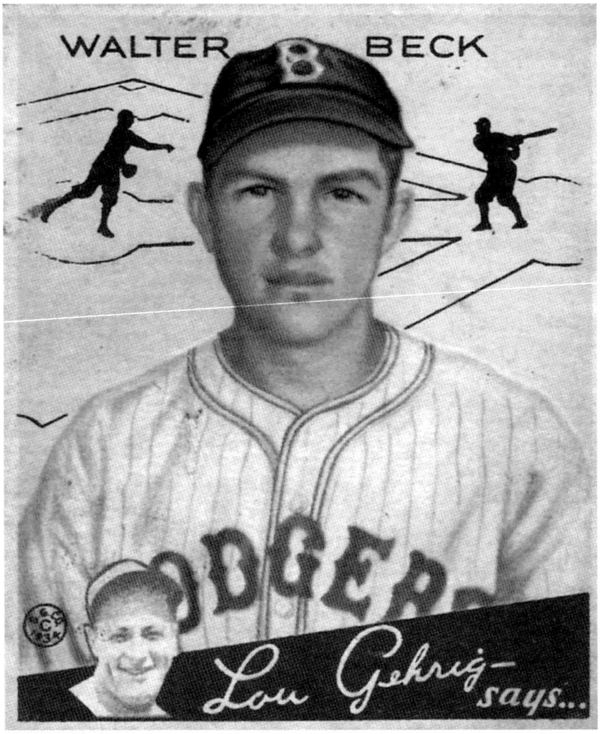

"The Dodgers made the trip across the Gulf without losing as much as a ballplayer or a trunk," said the *Herald-Tribune*. "Safe on the mainland, the Dodgers went to work at the Phillies' base. This was taking a chance, because of the danger of acquiring the Phils' habits." Philly always finished last, and that year, their ace, Walter Beck, went 1-9. His nickname, "Boom-Boom," tells the tale—there is no worse possible nickname for a pitcher!

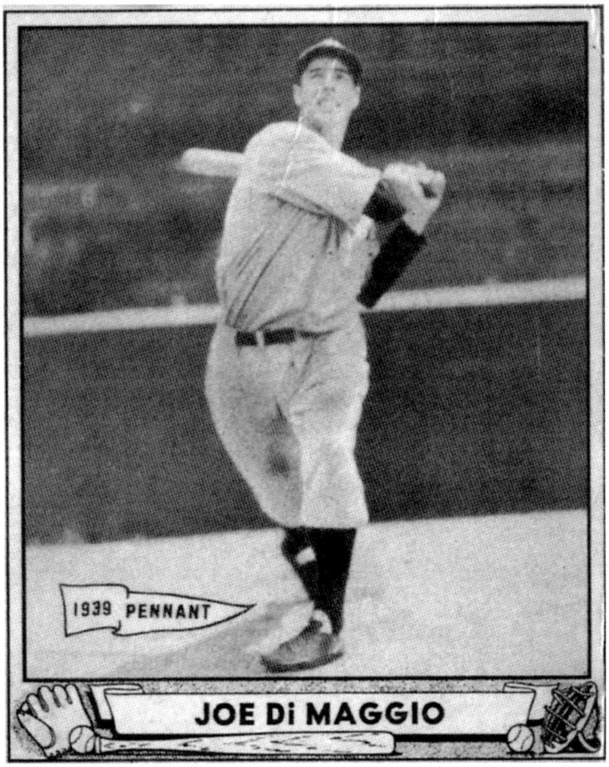

A few weeks later, far from Havana at chilly Ebbets Field, the Dodgers played their final exhibition game, a World Series preview against the Yankees. "Before a half-frozen crowd of 18,834, one of whom actually built a fire in a box back of the visiting dugout during the eighth inning," the *Times* reported, "the Yankees won when Jolting Joe DiMaggio doubled in the ninth frame."

3

"PAPA" HEMINGWAY, VAN LINGLE MUNGO, AND OTHER DIVERSIONS

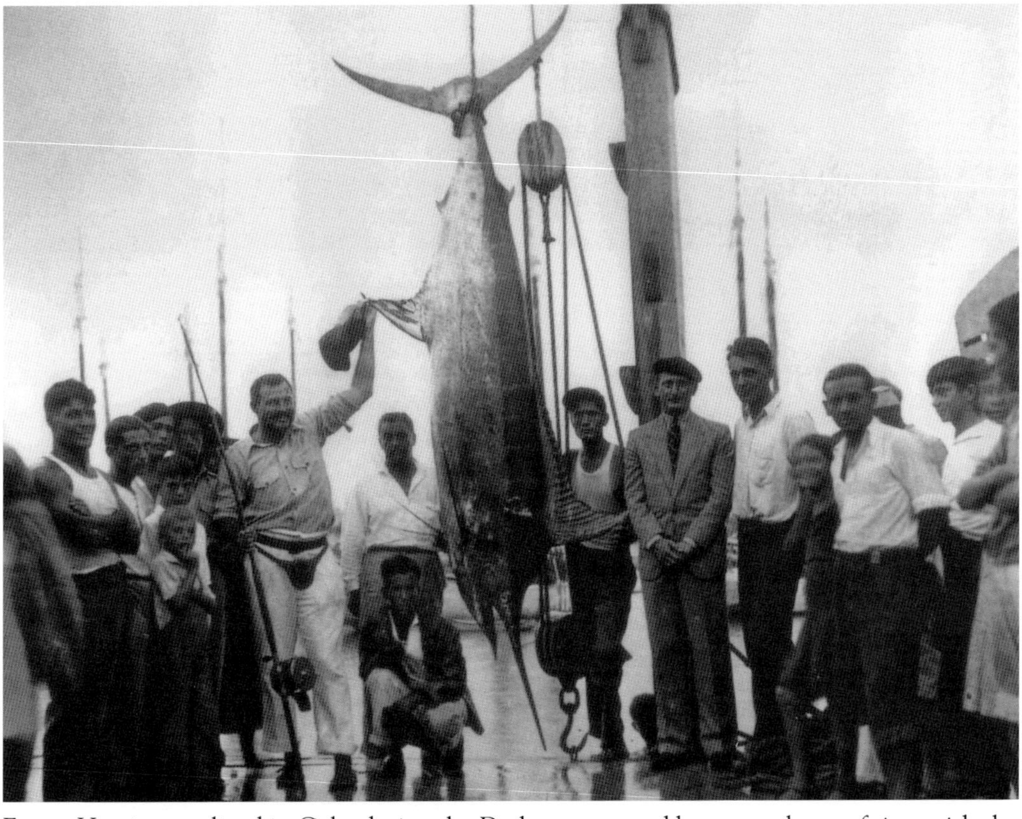

Ernest Hemingway lived in Cuba during the Dodger years, and he spent plenty of time with the ballplayers. They did not engage in good clean fun but in entertainment involving guns, cards, money on the table, lots more liquor on the table, fish tales, and fistfights. Other Dodgers found trouble without "Papa" Hemingway's help: Van Lingle Mungo brought scandal to the 1941 camp with two women, one angry husband, and his massive knife; several lawsuits; the Cuban army; and a slick early-morning getaway. For good measure, a few Dodgers found themselves in jail as well.

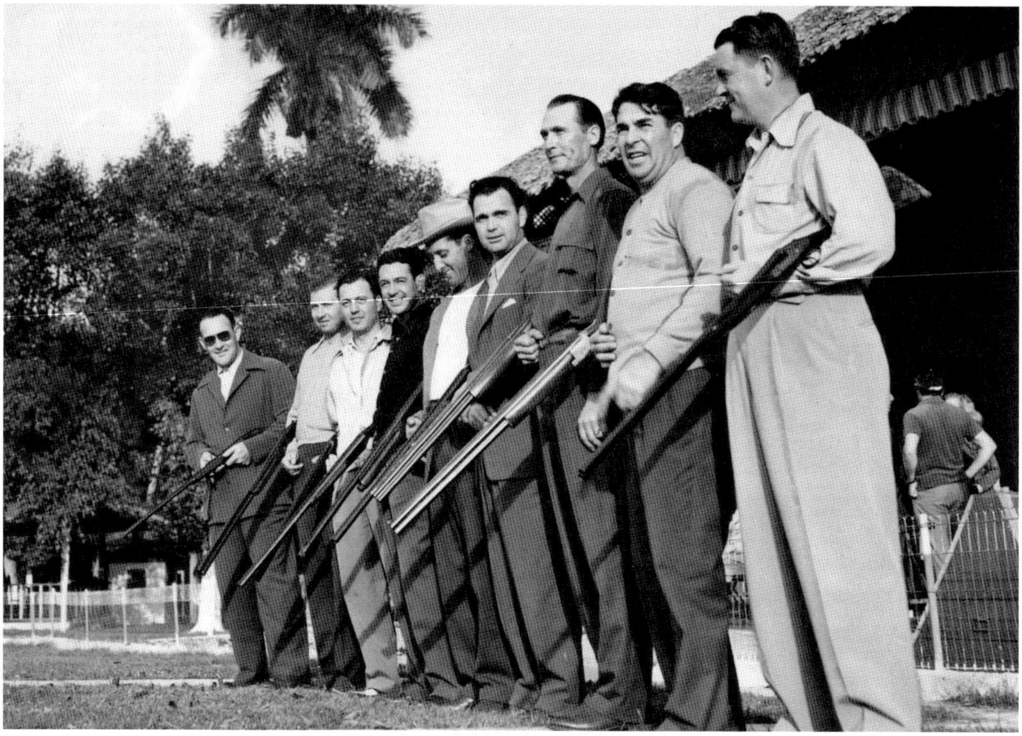

From left to right, Johnny Allen, Hugh Casey, Billy Herman, Augie Galan, Johnny Rizzo, Lew Riggs, Curt Davis, Fat Freddie Fitzsimmons, and Larry French prepare to seek pigeons at the Club Cassadores de Cerro. "You can't ask for better shoots than when the Dodgers are training," Hemingway told A. E. Hotchner, "and we have match-ups with Hugh Casey, Billy Herman, Augie Galan, Curt Davis and some of the others who are all crack shots."

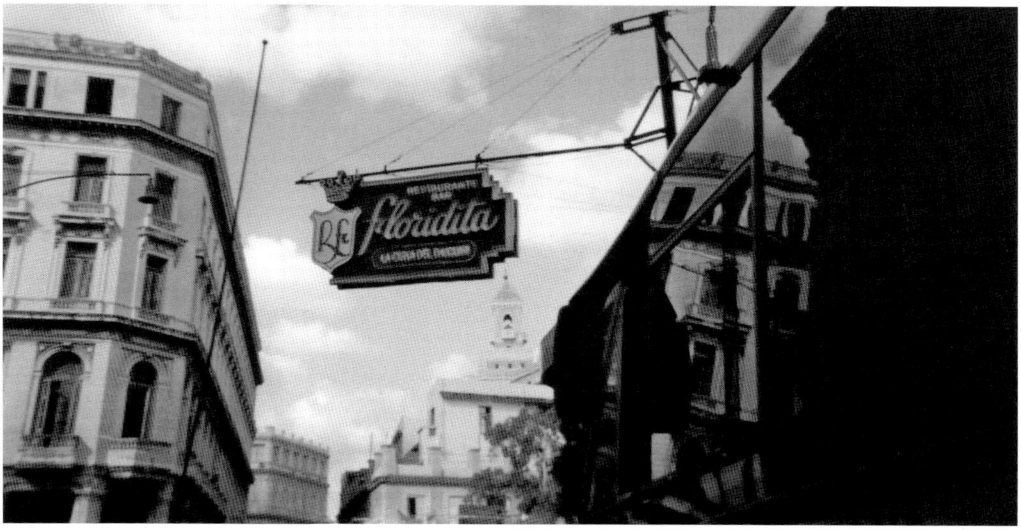

Legend has it that the Daiquiri was invented at La Floridata for Hemingway; doubtful, but one might argue it was perfected for Papa here. It is still open for business in downtown Havana.

Kirby Higbe and Hugh Casey would go to Ernie's after practice. One evening, Higbe recalled later, at "about 3:00 a.m., Ernest said to Case, 'Let's go to my house and put the gloves on a spell.' They put the gloves on and stood there toe to toe in the living room, belting each other. They wrecked two fine chairs and a beautiful sofa. About 4:00 a.m., Ernest's wife couldn't stand it any more and she broke it up."

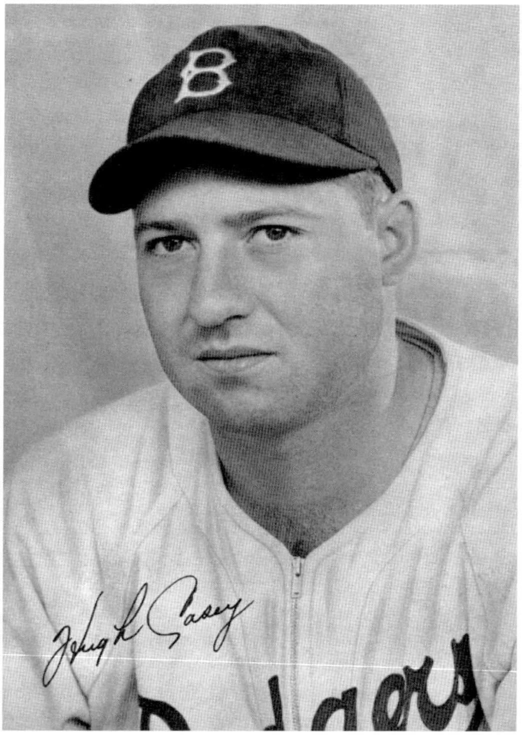

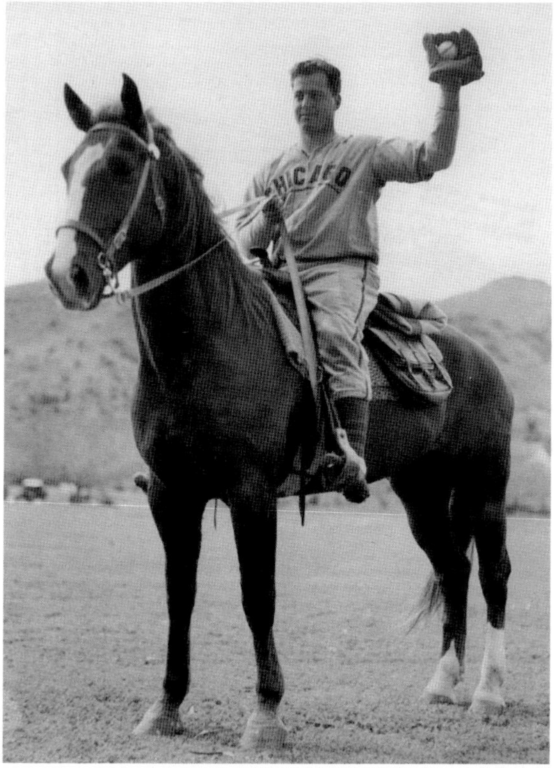

"Casey knocked him into the bookcase," Billy Herman said, "with a large crash on the terrazzo, like an explosion. It woke up his wife; she came downstairs. He told her, 'Oh, we're just playing. Go to bed, honey.' We were getting uneasy and wanted to get out of there. He said, 'We're drunk now, but tomorrow we'll be sober, and we can fight again. We can have a duel. Knives. Guns. Swords. Any weapons you want.' Well, we got out after that. He was the nicest guy in the world sober, but when he was drunk, he was like an animal."

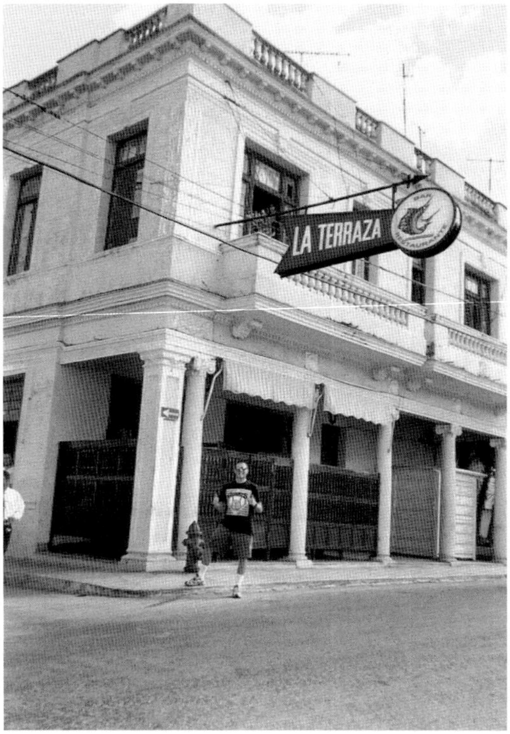

John McGraw brought some rough times to Havana years earlier, as Hemingway noted in *The Old Man and the Sea*: "He used to come to the Terrace sometimes too in the older days. But he was rough and harsh-spoken and difficult when he was drinking. His mind was on horses as well as baseball. At least he carried lists of horses at all times in his pocket and frequently spoke the names of horses on the telephone." The now quieter Terrace still serves patrons in Cojímar, just east of Havana.

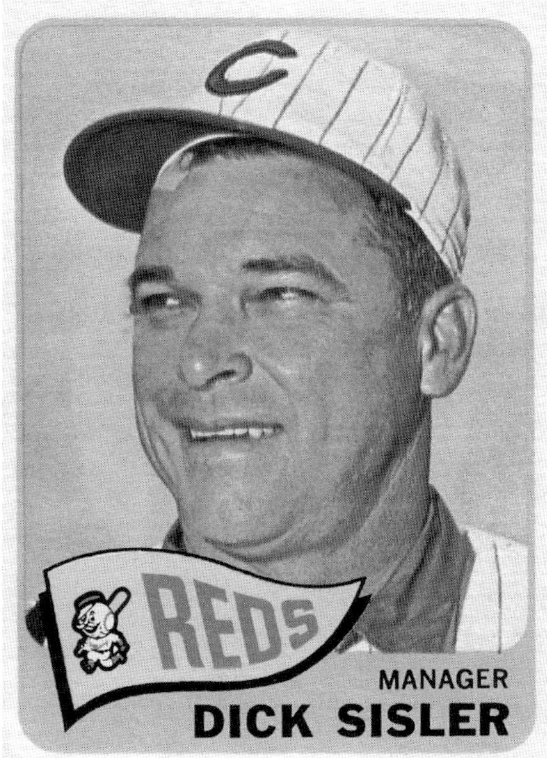

Hemingway wrote of several ballplayers in *The Old Man and the Sea*. " 'I think of Dick Sisler and those great drives in the old park,' the old man told the boy. 'There was nothing ever like them,' the boy replied. 'He hits the longest ball I have ever seen.' " Sisler clouted five homers in his first two Cuban games and blasted a 450-footer out of Tropical Stadium into the brewery across the street.

All dangerous things must come to an end. "The last night in Cuba," Higbe wrote, "Ernest and Case had a few rounds with the gloves. Then we sat sipping a few. Case started telling how he pitched different ballplayers, how he'd knock them down and dare them to get up. We left around 1:00 a.m. Case and I went back to our hotel and up the fire escape to our room."

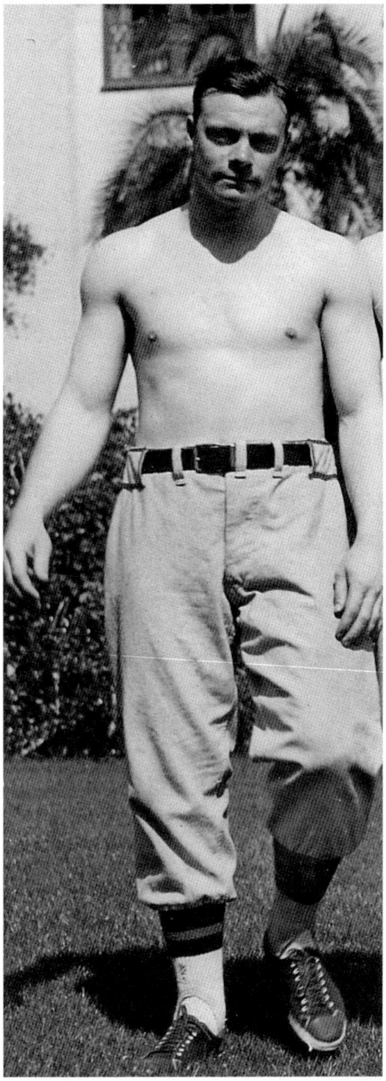

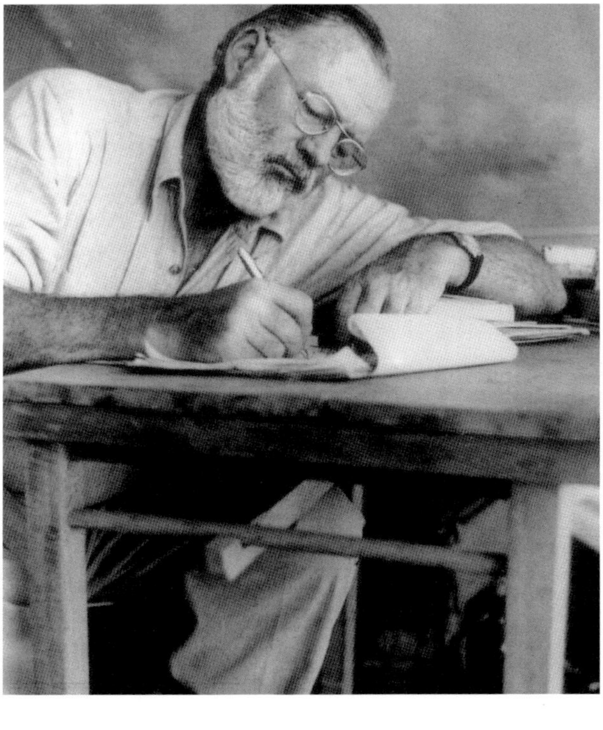

Once Higbe and Casey left, Hemingway was not quite ready to get back to work. "Have a terrific hangover," he wrote to editor and friend Max Perkins, "and can't write this morning (won't write rather as I don't want to turn out any hungover pages so write to you instead). Make allowances for that in reading. Had been working steady and went on big drunk with some of the boys down here night before last."

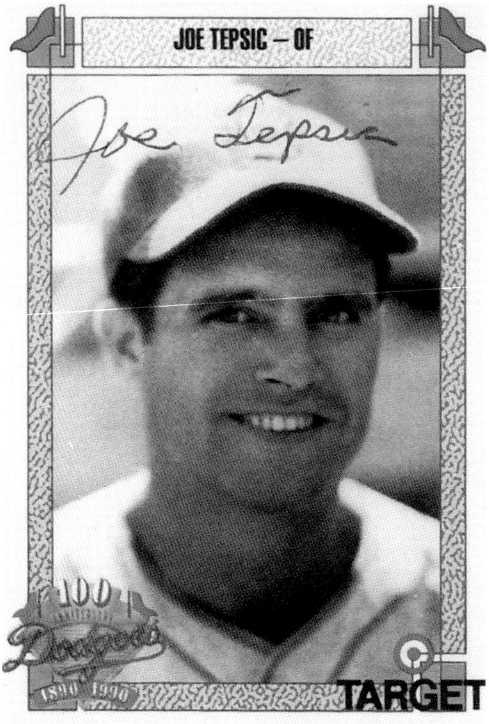

Dodger rookie Joe Tepsic did not realize it at the time, but one spring day in Cuba he lived out the climax of Hemingway's tale. "I went fishin'," Tepsic recalls. "I caught this big dad-gummed thing, and fighting it, my hands got all cut so I couldn't play. Durocher was real mad and fined me to teach me a lesson." Worse still, "I didn't get the fish—a shark got half! I had it, tryin' to reel it in, and he got the rest. So we just threw the other half in. I never did know what kind of fish I had. I didn't know anything about fish."

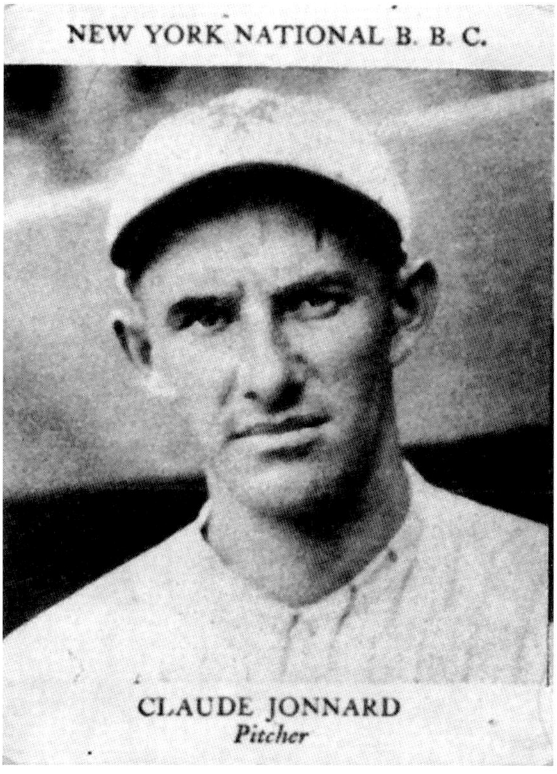

"Bubber Jonnard got into a fight with a local player," the *Brooklyn Eagle* reported one spring. "Both of 'em were arrested and carried away to jail where they spent the night. All you have to do is just thumb a guy out of the ball game and the police do the rest."

Van Lingle Mungo's pitching career pales in light of his 1941 off-the-field Cuban exploits. He arrived to practice drunk one day, threatening to hit manager Leo Durocher. Leo suspended Mungo; later Durocher saw him through a window. He recalls, "On one arm he had Lady Vine, the star attraction at the hotel. On the other, the woman half of the dance team Gonzales and Gonzales. I thought, 'Both of them?' "

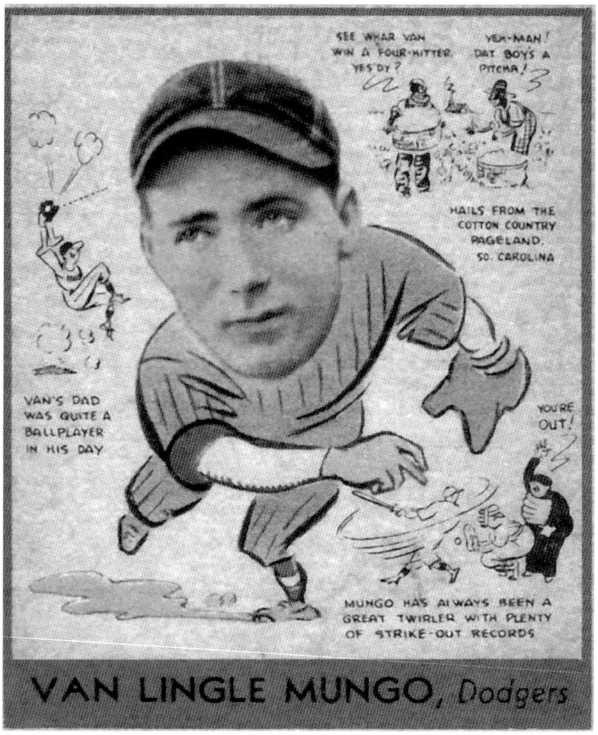

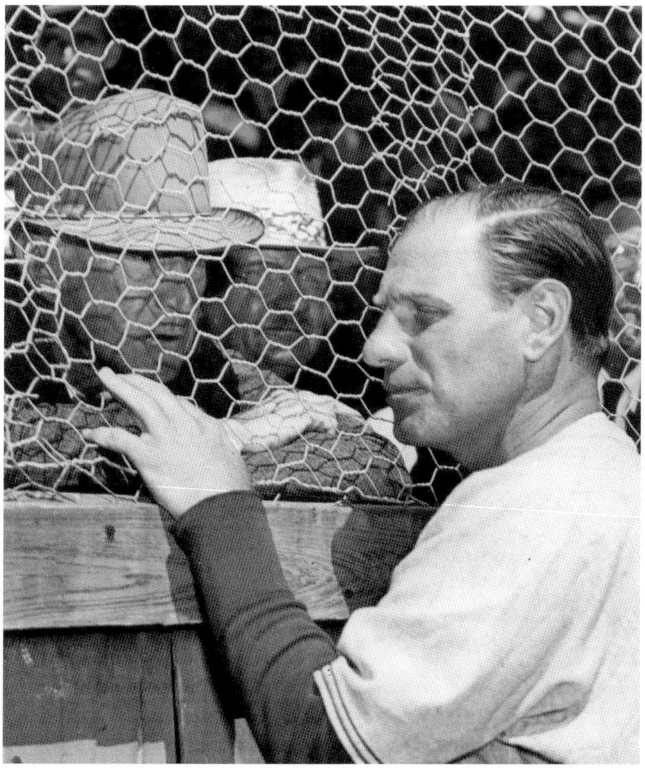

"At six in the morning," Durocher recounted, "I got a call. Will I come down to Mungo's room? I ran down, and there are two policemen and a couple of soldiers there. Plus Gonzales, the male member of the team. He's got a butcher knife in his hand this long. His wife hadn't come home all night. He found her in bed with Mungo and Lady Vine. The three of them. Mungo knocked him into the hall and bolted the door. And he's back there now with the butcher's knife to kill him."

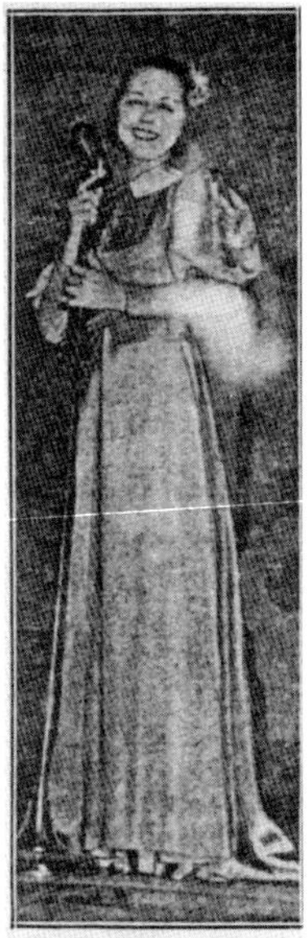

Ex-Hostess
Lady Ruth Vine (Lady is her first name) was official hostess at the Hotel Nacional until the Mungo incident. She's looking for a job now, too.

Señor Gonzales awoke to find his wife had never come home. "Panic-stricken," *PM* reported, "he called Lady's room, 273, and was told Lady had left orders not to be disturbed. He put on his bathrobe and went out and knocked on the door at 273 until the man in 274 asked him to stop. He went back and told the operator it was life and death, and she rang 273. Lady answered, said Cristina was there, at her request, since she was lonely, and did not want to be disturbed."

"Gonzalo's Latin temperament was thoroughly aroused," *PM* continued. "He pounded more at 273 and eventually was admitted by Lady, in pajamas and robe. Breathing fire, Gonzalo headed straight for one of the twin beds which was shrouded in a mosquito net. He yanked the net aside and there was Cristina, attired in a blue negligee. At the moment his eyes fell on Cristina, Gonzalo asserted, he was made the victim of an attack by a large, naked man, afterward identified as Mungo, pitcher estrella del Brooklyn." Locked out, "he returned momentarily, machete in hand, to extract revenge."

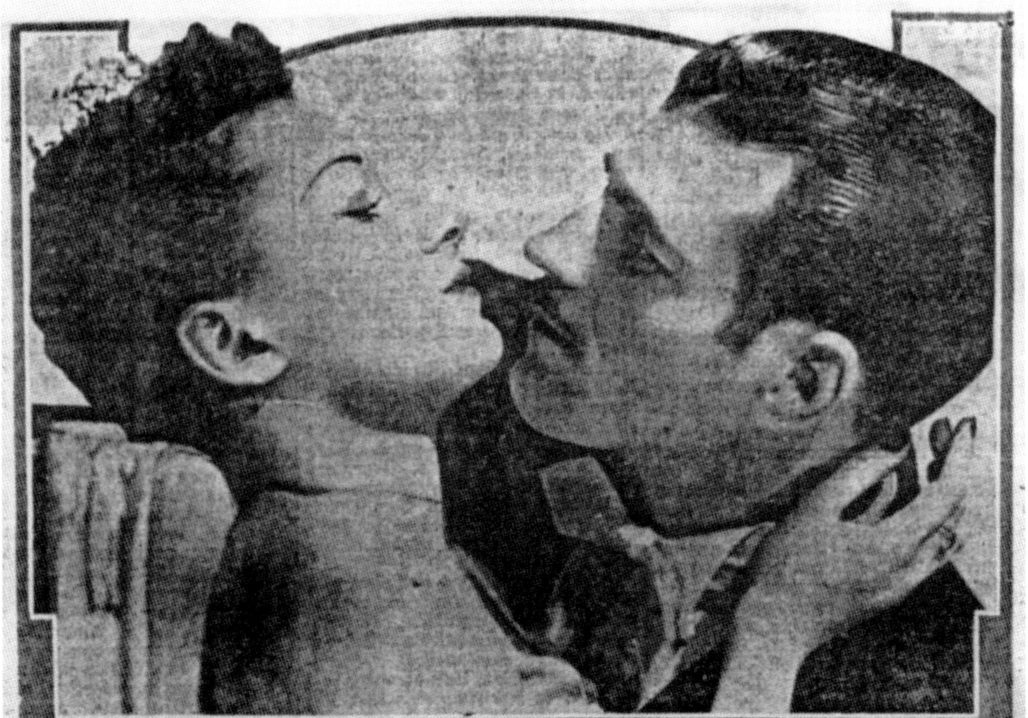

A Senor From Spain; a Senorita From Wilkes-Barre
Gonzalo (Francisco Collada Carreno) here looks soulfully into the teeth of Cristina (Miriam Morgan) in publicity shot of their dance team that shone at Hotel Nacional de Cuba, Havana, until Van Lingle Mungo happened on the scene.

"The bedlam issuing from 273 aroused the rest of the hotel," said *PM*. "The corridor and the room were full of waiters, managers, guests, Dodgers, and Van trying to get his pants on." Durocher added, "We finally got everybody to leave, the soldiers dragging Gonzales away. We smuggled Mungo out and hid him in the vegetable bin in the cellar. The police came back with warrants for Mungo, and they were searching for him. Gonzales is prowling the hotel with his black eye and butcher's knife. We're setting up the seaplane to fly him out. Somehow, we were able to smuggle him out. The police came running down the wharf behind him, blowing whistles, somebody threw a rope out of the plane, Mungo grabbed it, they pulled him aboard and he got out of Cuba."

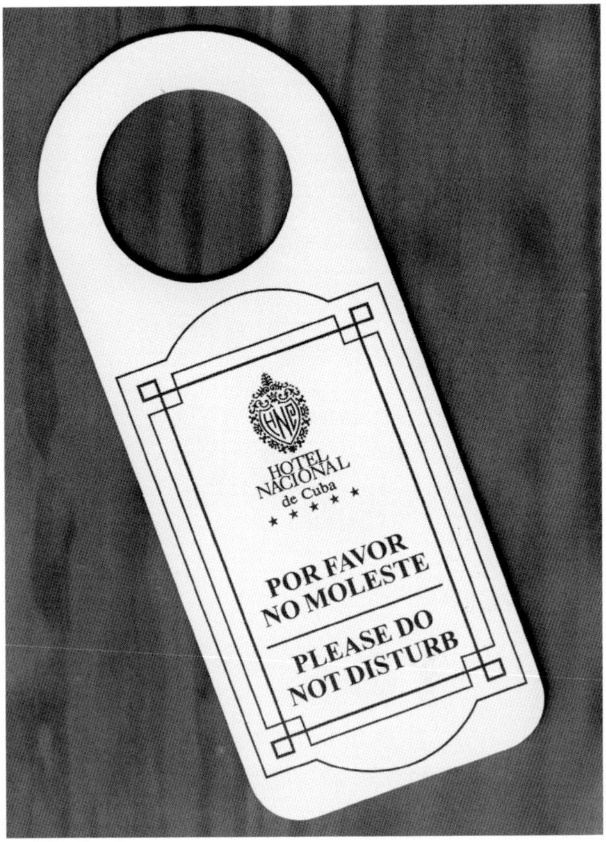

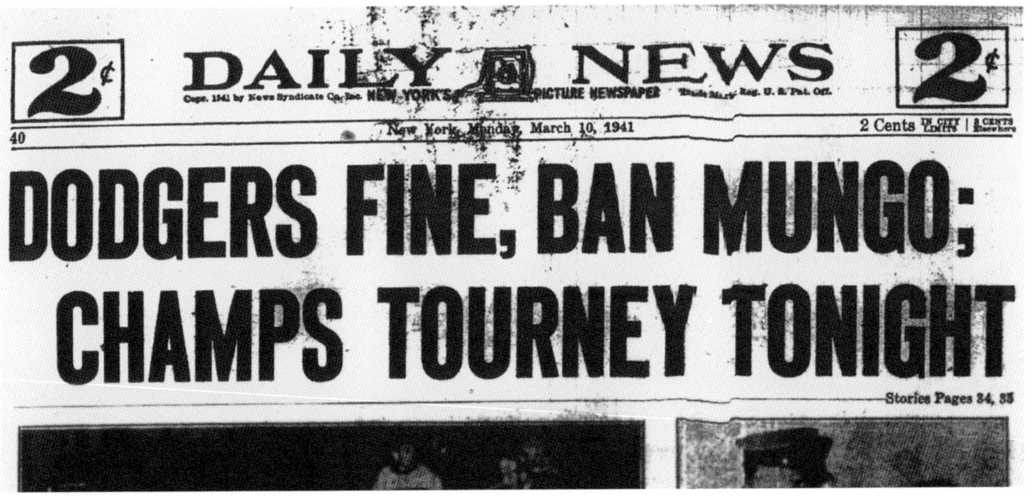

2¢ DAILY NEWS 2¢

NEW YORK'S PICTURE NEWSPAPER

40 — New York, Monday, March 10, 1941 — 2 Cents

DODGERS FINE, BAN MUNGO; CHAMPS TOURNEY TONIGHT

Stories Pages 34, 35

The *Post* concluded, "The bartenders missed Van today. So did a small army of soldiers, sailors, marines, and national police who reached the airport a few minutes after his Miami-bound plane had taken off." The story is doubly remarkable in the fact that it received so much coverage, as sportswriters back then looked the other way from numerous player indiscretions. Apparently Mungo's tale was simply too good (and too loud) to cover up.

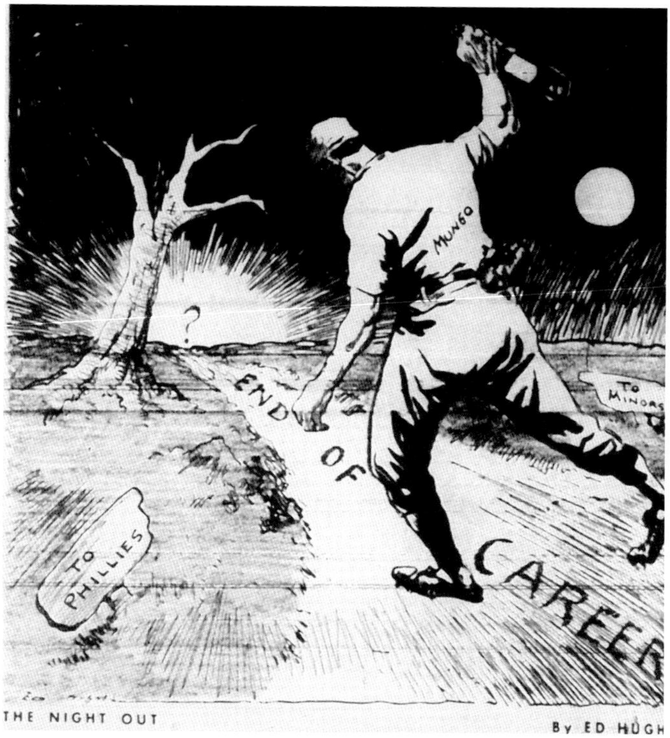

PM concluded, "Gonzalo was out of work. The hotel was taking no chances that Gonzalo, in twirling Cristina around that evening, might fling her into shark-infested waters. Cristina and Lady, out of work too, said they had been doing a Samaritan act, seeking to sober Van up. This work at last proved so tiring that they dumped him into one of Lady's beds and themselves fell into the other, knowing nothing more until the beforementioned dawn. Gonzalo is slapping suits on the hotel and another action will be taken against Mungo, something pretty terrible, you may be sure."

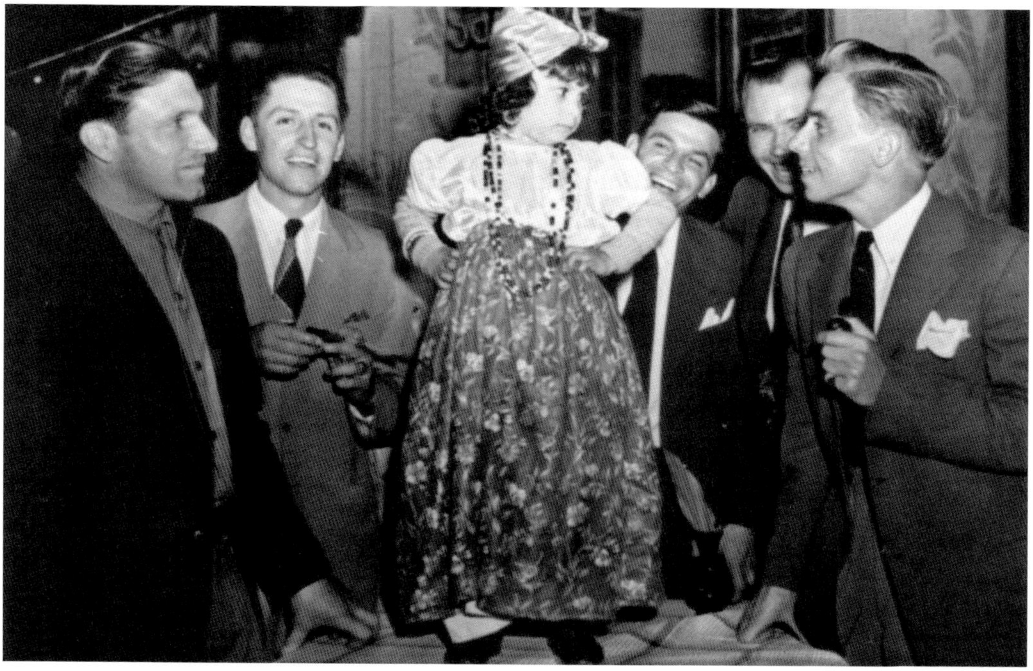

Without Mungo around, Dolph Camilli, Pete Coscarart, Tex Carleton, Curt Davis, and Pee Wee Reese (pictured from left to right above) wonder what kind of trouble they are about to encounter on a sultry Havana night.

Eddie "Lefty" Chandler was busted one hot Caribbean night—but not in a seedy bar. The Dodger rookie was merely sitting in the dugout during a game against the Yankees. His contract did not allow him to pitch yet, but the local promoter (who was buddies with the local law) took exception when he found out; he wanted every American to get into his event. The *policia* cuffed Lefty and paraded him across the field during the game. The fans howled and threw bottles.

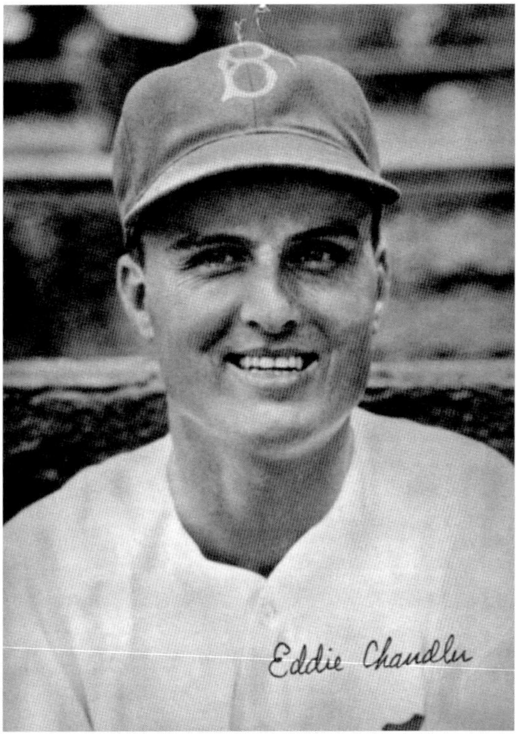

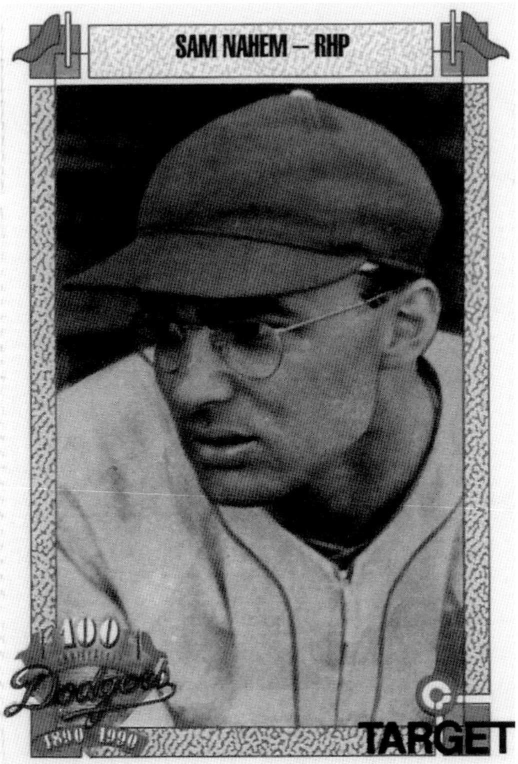

Dodger teammate Sam Nahem got the call—but not to pitch. Seems Sam possessed a law degree, so he was literally assigned Chandler's case that night! Yet despite his knowledge of American jurisprudence, Naham went 0-1 in the halls of Caribbean injustice that evening. "All he could get me was a sandwich," Chandler lamented. Lefty spent the night in jail before things could get cleared up the next morning.

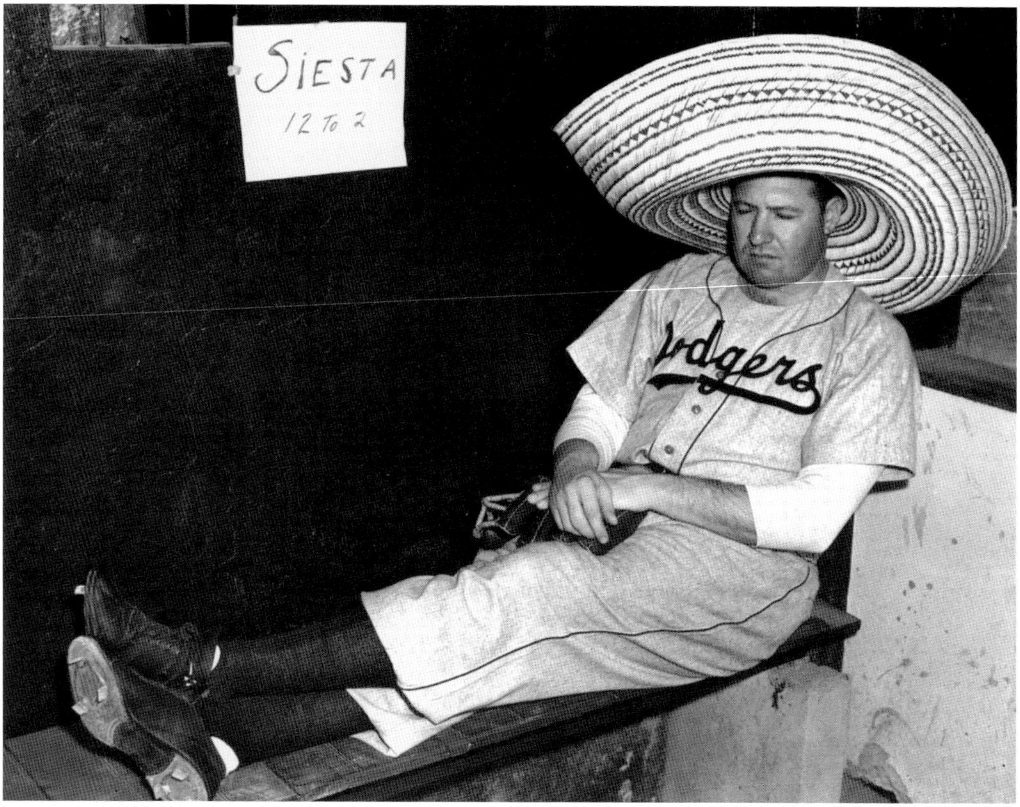

Hugh Casey needed a siesta after a stressful incident at the *aeropuerto*. Some of the Dodgers were playing cards while waiting for the plane. A man walked up, Kirby Higbe recalled, and "pulled a big pistol and stuck it right in Case's belly. He was going to take us all to jail for playing poker in the airport." But "somebody called Batista's office, and he sent a big shot down to call off the law. We just did make the airplane."

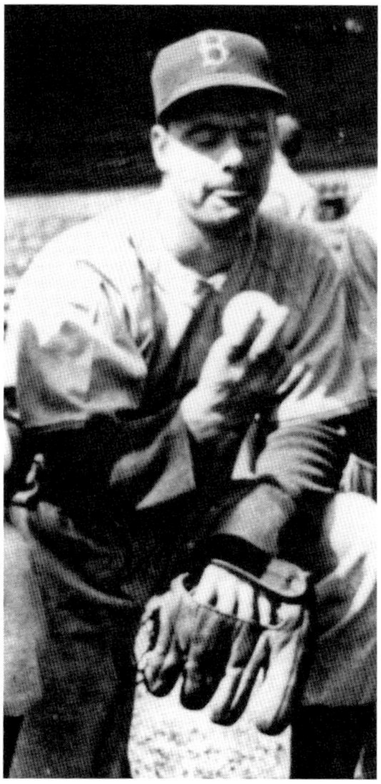

Kirby Higbe usually managed to be in the thick of incidents like these. "I wondered whether they would ever let us out of Cuba that day," Leo Durocher mused later. "They could be very stubborn about such things."

4

1942

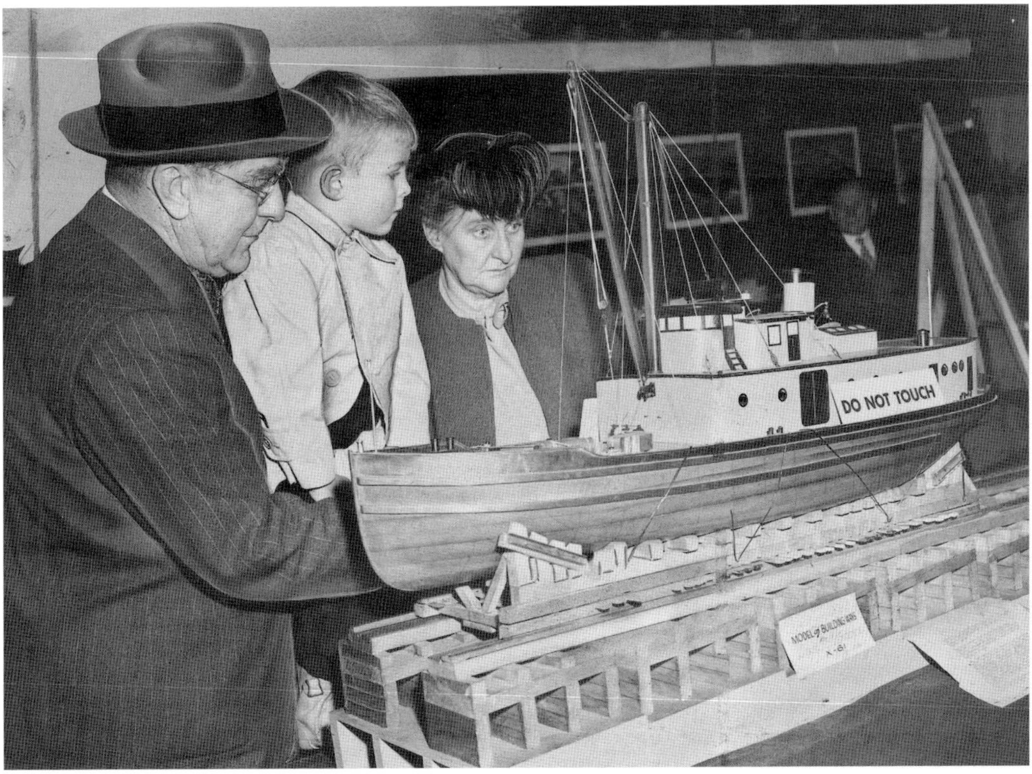

Fresh from their 1941 pennant, Brooklyn was delighted to return to Cuba. Unfortunately, it was just two months after Pearl Harbor. Wartime restrictions meant no sailing, so the team flew to Havana once again. Here Branch Rickey teases his wife that this is the ride to Cuba, with their four-year-old grandson Rickey Eckler looking on. The Dodgers fell to second and could not return in 1943; travel restrictions forced the Bums to train at nearby, frigid Bear Mountain, New York.

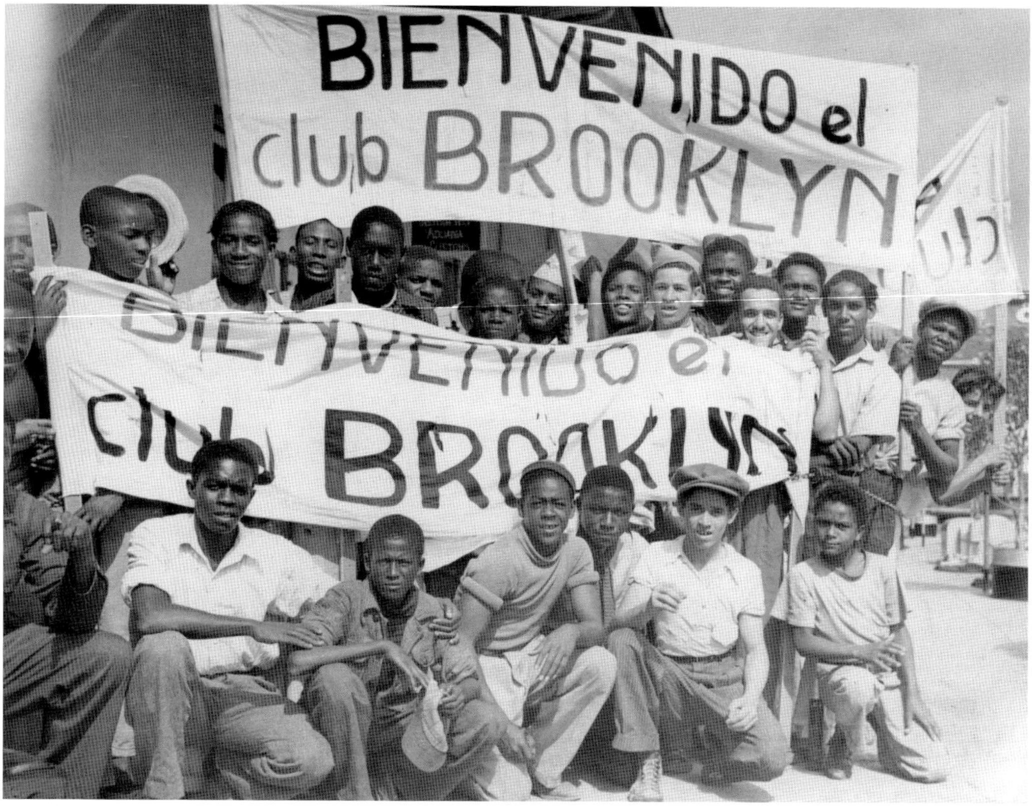

The locals have always been enormous fans, following the World Series in the papers and on the radio, just as their own season was kicking off. They showed up in large, vocal crowds to greet the American ballplayers.

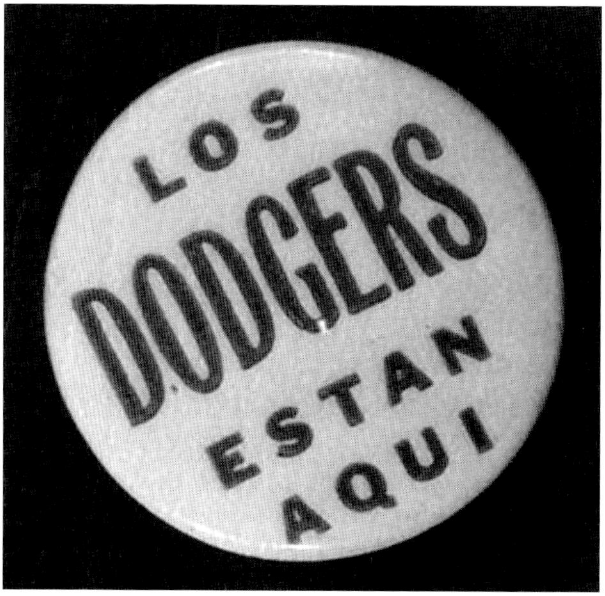

The team made buttons in Brooklyn to distribute on the island. "*Los Dodgers estan aqui*," the *Herald-Tribune* reported, quoting the buttons. "The foregoing phrase, roughly translated by no less a linguistic authority than Kirby Higbe means, 'We made it, bub.' Having added the above words to their Spanish vocabularies, the Brooklyn Dodgers disembarked at Havana this evening after a two-hour flight from Miami. The athletes sidestepped the whirl of Cuban life around them and registered at the Hotel Nacional, their spring training barracks."

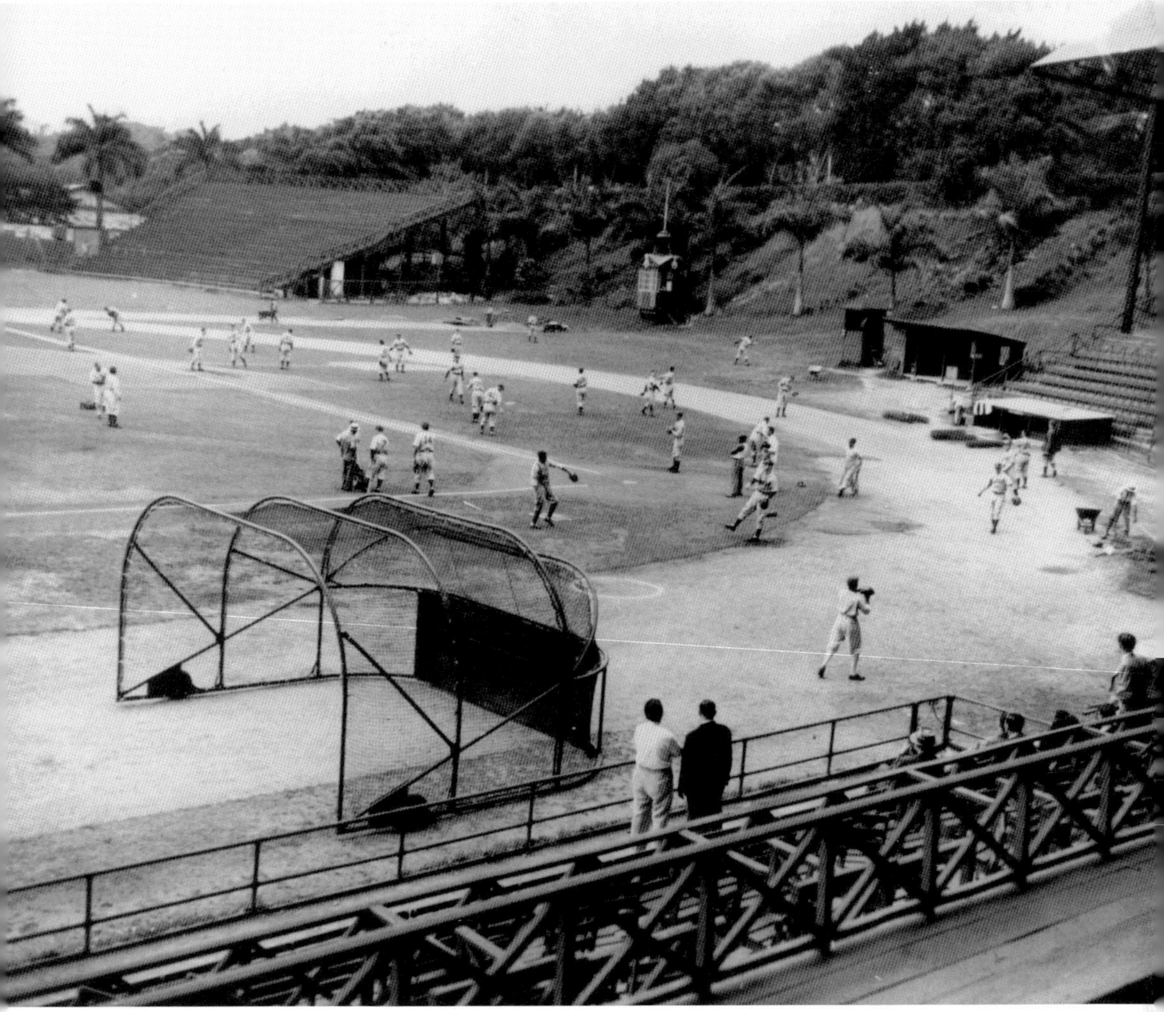

Once again, the enormous Tropical Stadium would serve as both the training grounds and the ballpark for exhibition games. The schedule called for a repeat series against the New York Giants, but the wartime travel issues put those games into question. When the owners got their heads together, they agreed the financial benefits were worth the risk, so the games went on as planned.

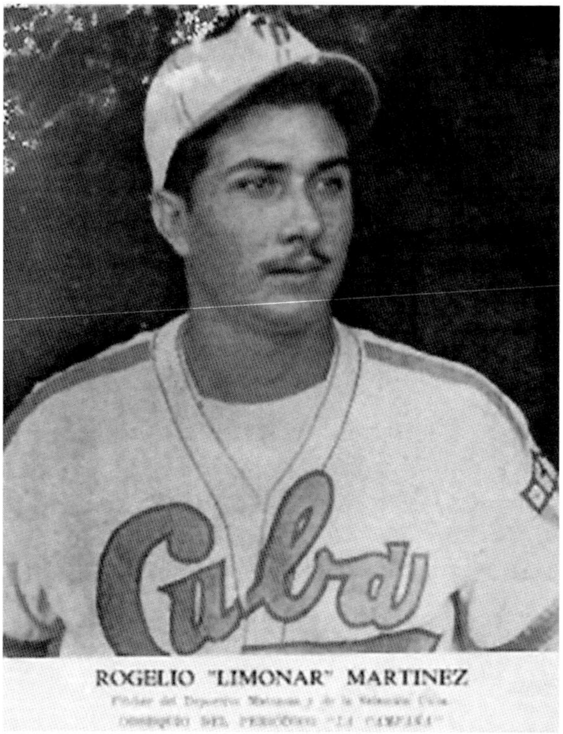

Rogelio "Limonar" Martinez, a Cuban local, scored a Brooklyn tryout. He did not make the squad, but the Senators signed him in 1947. He appeared in two major-league games in 1950 and had a solid career in the minors, winning 20 games for Tampa one season.

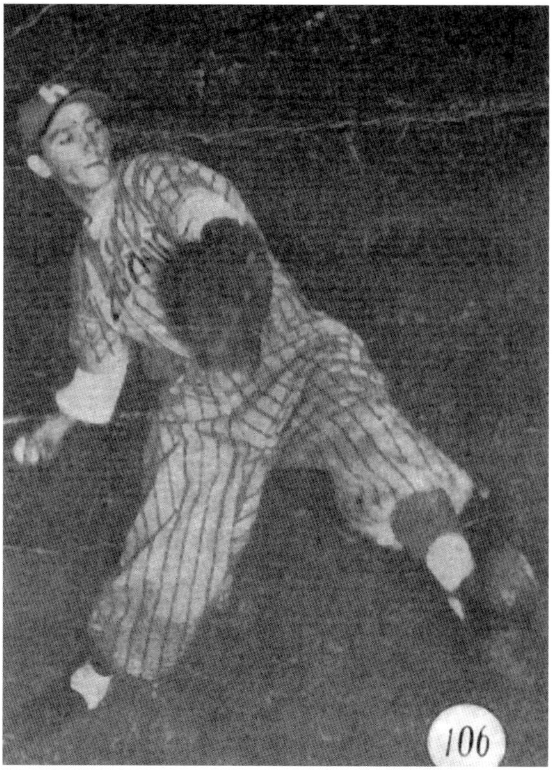

Cuban native Julio Moreno was also considered. Like his amigo, he did not make the Dodgers but landed a Senators contract in 1947. Moreno fared a little better, pitching four seasons at the show and 15 in professional baseball, on top of his successful Cuban career.

Kirby Higbe did not report to camp because the travel restrictions meant his wife could not come along, not to mention the fact he hated to fly. "Hig" made it as far as Miami and practiced with a high school team. When Durocher began fining him $100 a day, Higbe decided he could survive camp without his wife in tow. "If I'm going to win 30 games," he modestly told the waiting press in Havana, "I thought I'd better get over here." He ended up going 16-11.

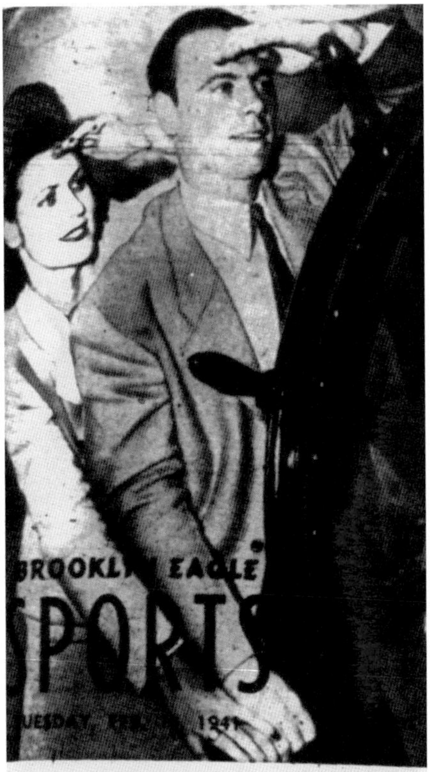

WE ARE—AND OFF TO WORK WE GO—The Dodger
d Havana for the first part of their Spring training s
f a safe arrival and decided to steer the S. S. Florida into

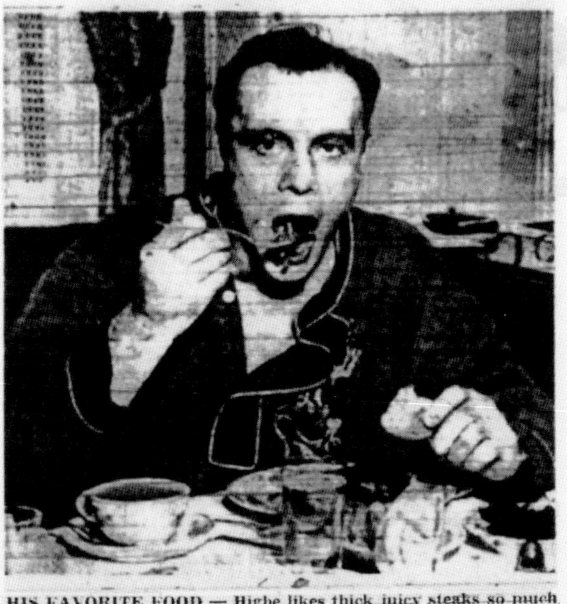

HIS FAVORITE FOOD — Higbe likes thick juicy steaks so much he eats them for breakfast. Here he is shown stowing away "a bite." Havana provides nothing like this," he says.

Fear of flying and loneliness were not Higbe's only issues with Cuba. "The food and water there made me a sick man," he told the papers. While still in Miami, "Kirby was a little disappointed that MacPhail didn't call him up last night," the *Herald-Tribune* reported. "He thinks the least Larry could have done was to have inquired if he'd enjoyed his dinner."

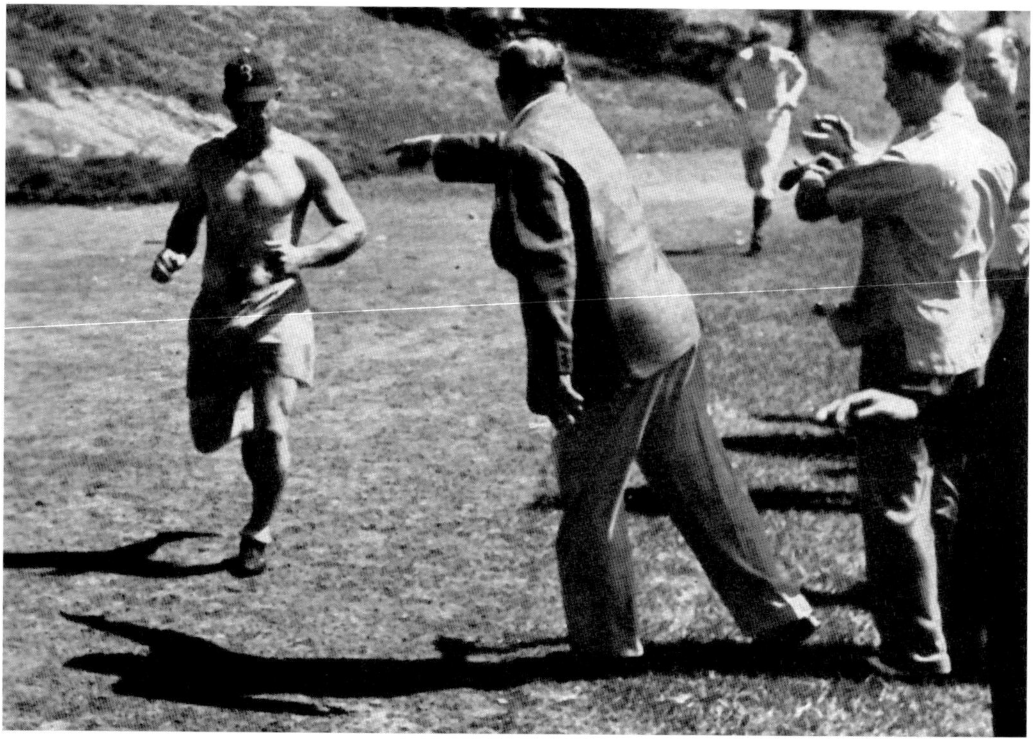

The Dodgers staged a mile-and-a-half team race in 1942, and owner Larry MacPhail offered $100 in prize money. The reporters had fun with it, covering the event as if it was a horse race for the papers back in the states. Mickey Owen won the "*handicapio*" by "seven lengths," the *Trib* kidded.

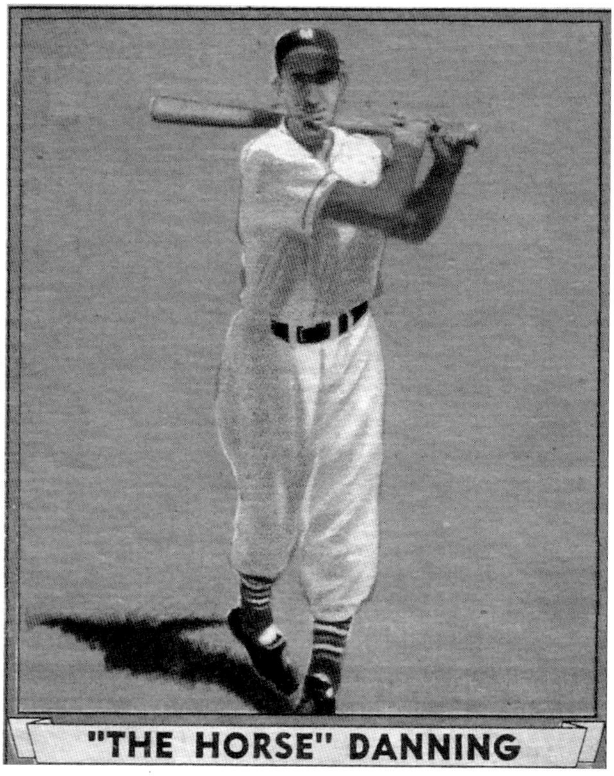

Despite all the wartime fears, the Giants brought their racehorses for the scheduled series. At the opener, the Dodgers beat their guests 6-3; player-manager Mel Ott and Johnny Mize got hits for New York, and Harry "the Horse" Danning smacked a triple.

After the Giants left, the Dodgers took 11 innings to beat the locals 6-4. "In the ninth," the *Herald-Tribune* reported, "Pollo (Little Chicken) Rodriguez cut across the plate while bunting. Out stormed Durocher, claiming the batter was out for leaving the box. He and (umpire Amado) Maestri argued chest-to-chest, although neither could understand what the other was talking about."

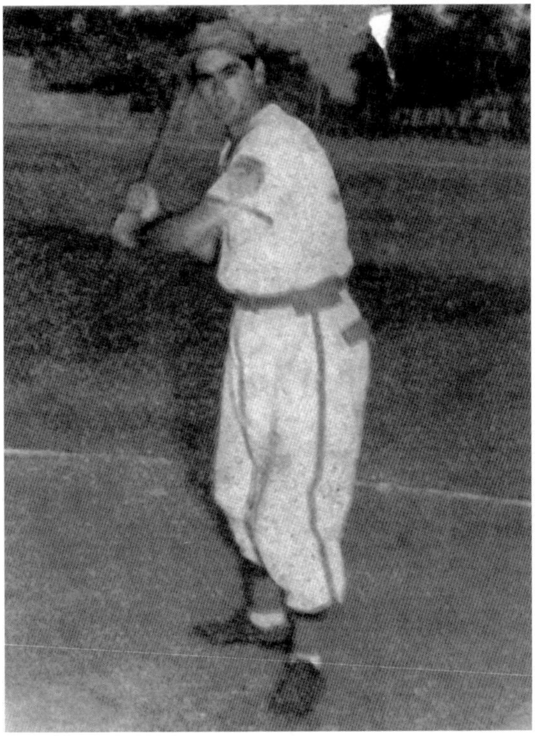

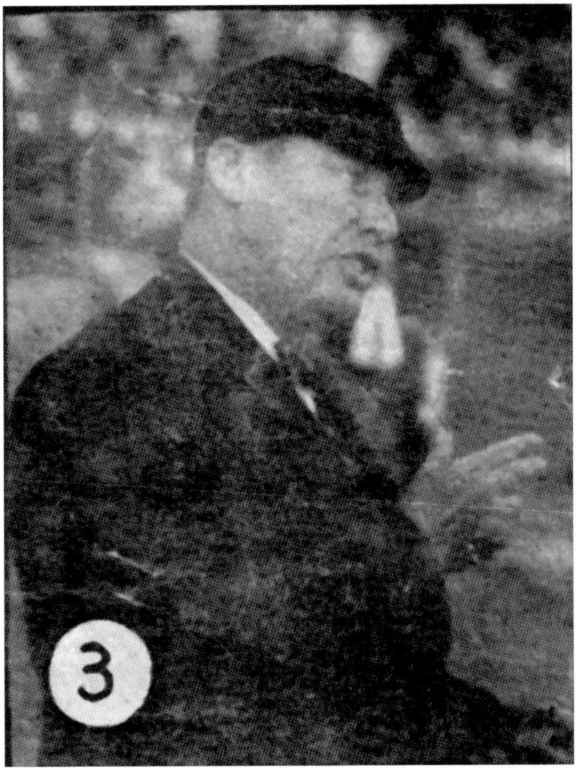

Leo Durocher and Amado Maestri "shoved each other around considerably," the paper continued. Durocher "called on young Monchy de Arcos, who works out with the club, and shouted at Maestri through him. Apparently de Arcos was a better interpreter than a diplomat. Finally, Jocko Conlan, a big-league arbiter, prevailed upon Durocher to leave. Peace was restored and the Dodgers won in the 11th. It looks like a great season for the umpires in Brooklyn."

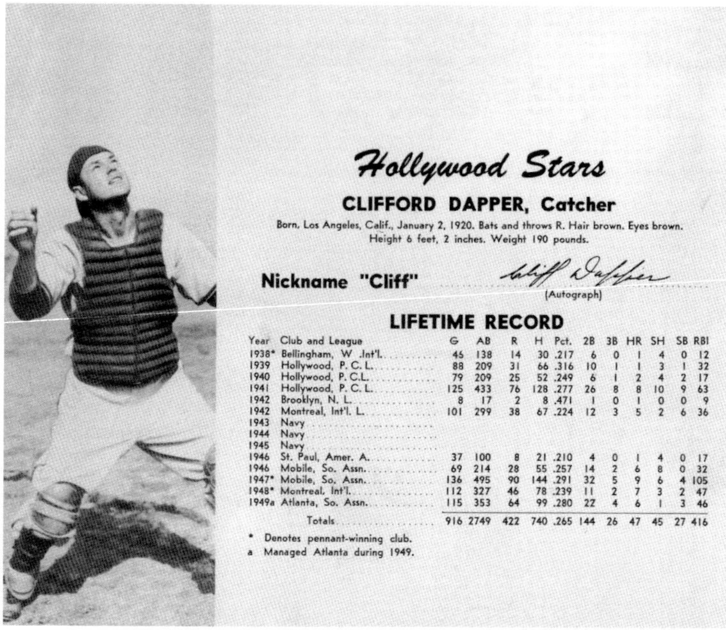

Hollywood Stars

CLIFFORD DAPPER, Catcher

Born, Los Angeles, Calif., January 2, 1920. Bats and throws R. Hair brown. Eyes brown. Height 6 feet, 2 inches. Weight 190 pounds.

Nickname "Cliff" (Autograph)

LIFETIME RECORD

Year	Club and League	G	AB	R	H	Pct.	2B	3B	HR	SH	SB	RBI
1938*	Bellingham, W .Int'l.	46	138	14	30	.217	6	0	1	4	0	12
1939	Hollywood, P. C. L.	88	209	31	66	.316	10	1	1	3	1	32
1940	Hollywood, P. C.L.	79	209	25	52	.249	6	1	2	4	2	17
1941	Hollywood, P. C. L.	125	433	76	128	.277	26	8	8	10	9	63
1942	Brooklyn, N. L.	8	17	2	8	.471	1	0	1	0	0	9
1942	Montreal, Int'l. L.	101	299	38	67	.224	12	3	5	2	6	36
1943	Navy											
1944	Navy											
1945	Navy											
1946	St. Paul, Amer. A.	37	100	8	21	.210	4	0	1	4	0	17
1946	Mobile, So. Assn.	69	214	28	55	.257	14	2	6	8	0	32
1947*	Mobile, So. Assn.	136	495	90	144	.291	32	5	9	6	4	105
1948*	Montreal, Int'l.	112	327	46	78	.239	11	2	7	3	2	47
1949a	Atlanta, So. Assn.	115	353	64	99	.280	22	4	6	1	3	46
	Totals	916	2749	422	740	.265	144	26	47	45	27	416

* Denotes pennant-winning club.
a Managed Atlanta during 1949.

Catcher Cliff Dapper "always dreamed of gettin' to the big leagues." He made the most of his 17 at-bats, swatting a double, homer, and six other hits for a lifetime .471 average. "I was in Brooklyn until April," Cliff says, "then the South Pacific." He never made it back to the show, playing for several minor-league teams. He later farmed an avocado orchard with Duke Snider.

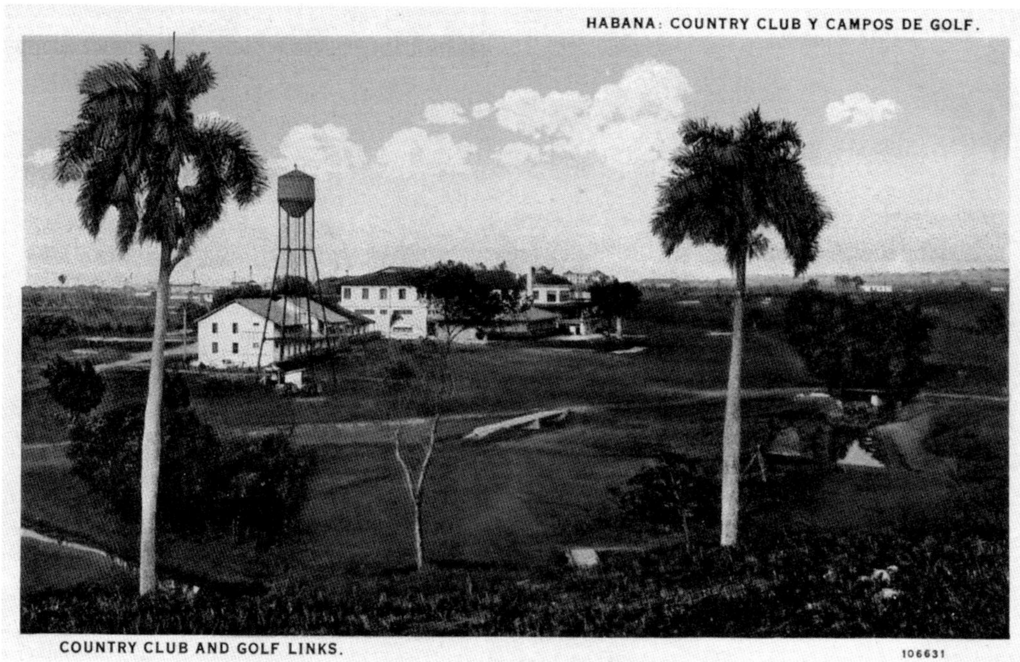

Havana was ideal for golf as well. In the *New York Times* the following was reported: "Can Reese and I play golf?" asked Kirby Higbe. "Do you make your living with these things?" asked Leo, picking up baseball shoes. "Yeah," said Higbe, "but you don't give me enough work; I need to get in shape." Retorted Leo: "I'll take care of that. If you can golf after I get through with you, all right."

5

1947

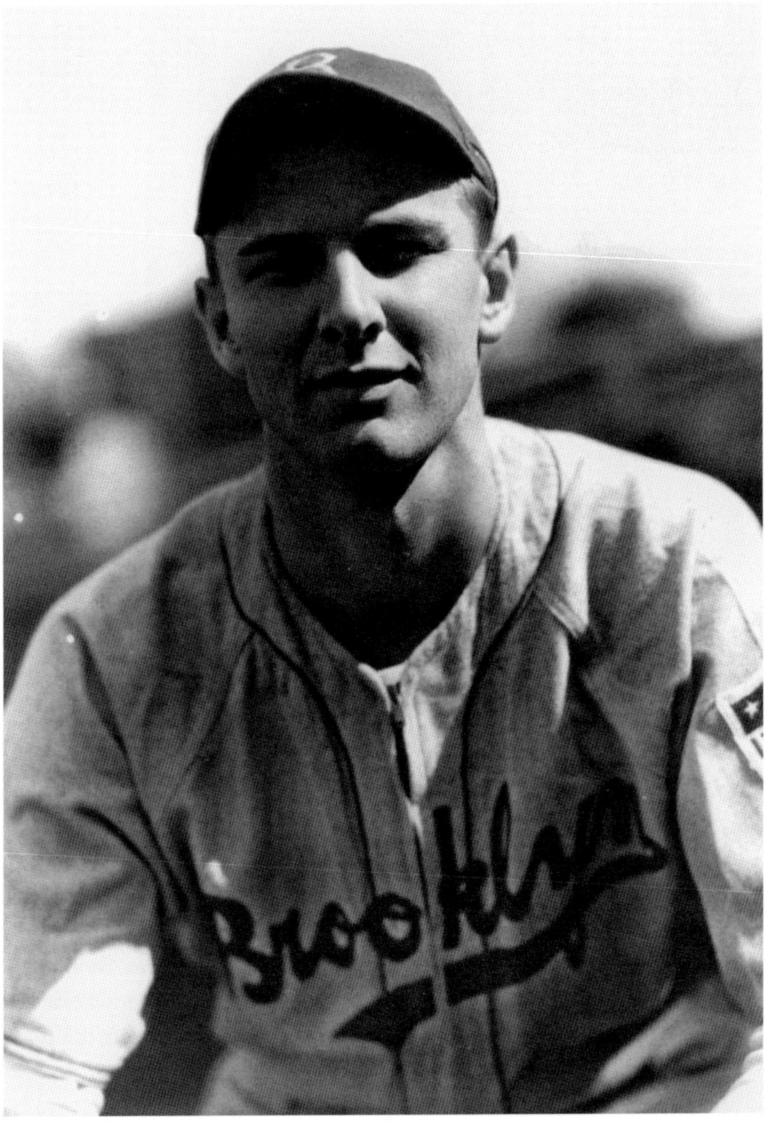

In 1947, the Dodgers returned to their beloved Cuba. Jackie Robinson was breaking down the color barrier. Manager Leo Durocher would be suspended for the season, yet Brooklyn managed to make the World Series. Branch Rickey brought the Montreal Royals along; Robinson was on the Royal roster to generate less controversy. Of the latecomers, one had a good excuse: a note from his NBA coach. Howie "Stretch" Schultz, a 6-foot, 6-inch-tall power forward for the Lakers, was contending with Jackie for the position at first base.

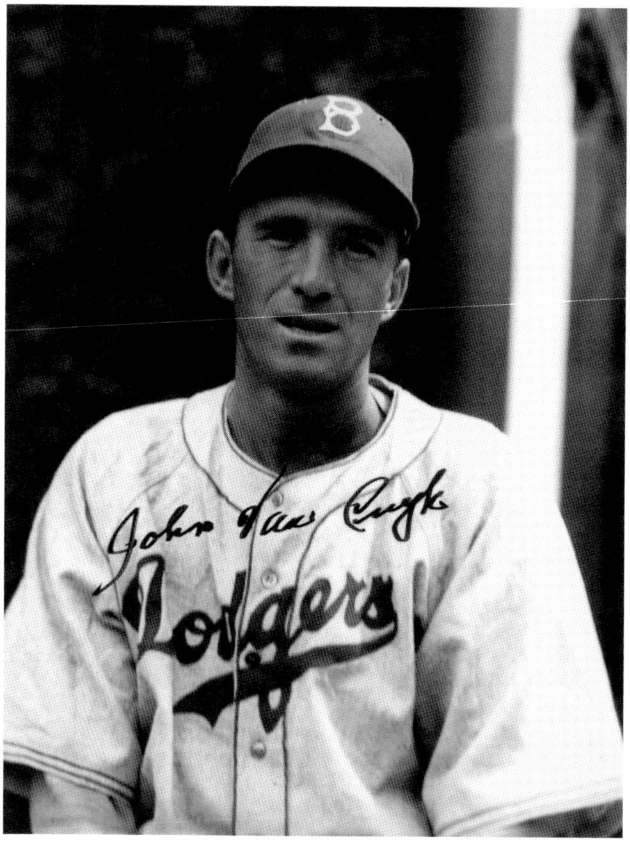

The pitching staff was overloaded. "John Van Cuyk is part of Rickey's growing financial pains," said the *Tribune*. "Like his associates, Van Cuyk never had a flare for existing on bread and water. And it looks as though Van Cuyk is here to stay. Rickey is actually proud to be providing for Van Cuyk because the latter will be providing for Rickey if minor league pedigrees are worth anything."

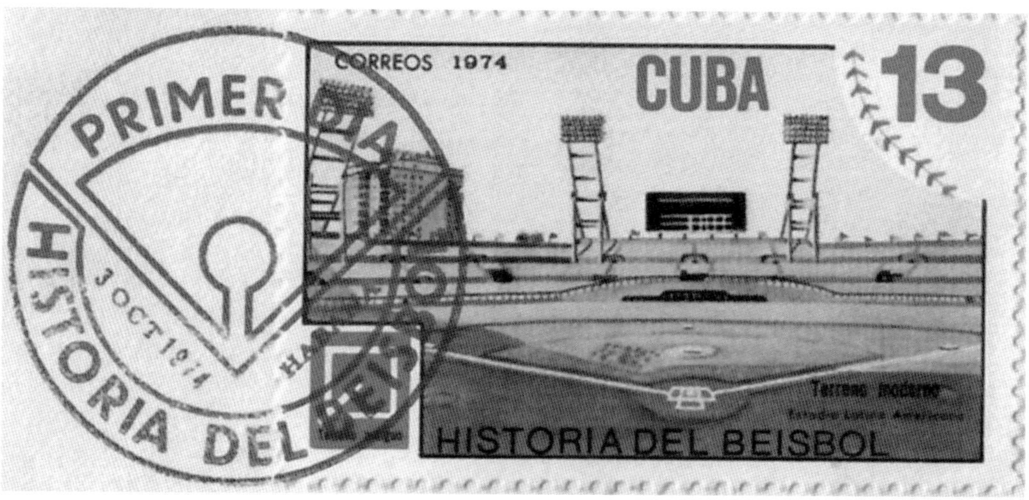

"The Brooks opened conditioning at spacious, new Gran Stadium," according to the *Daily News*. "Even as the Brooks worked out, laborers busily continued construction, which will accommodate 35,000. Gene Hermanski's line drive over right field wall was first Brook homer of the year." It was indeed called Gran Estadio, and it is still in use today, more than 60 seasons later, as the Estadio Latinoamericano.

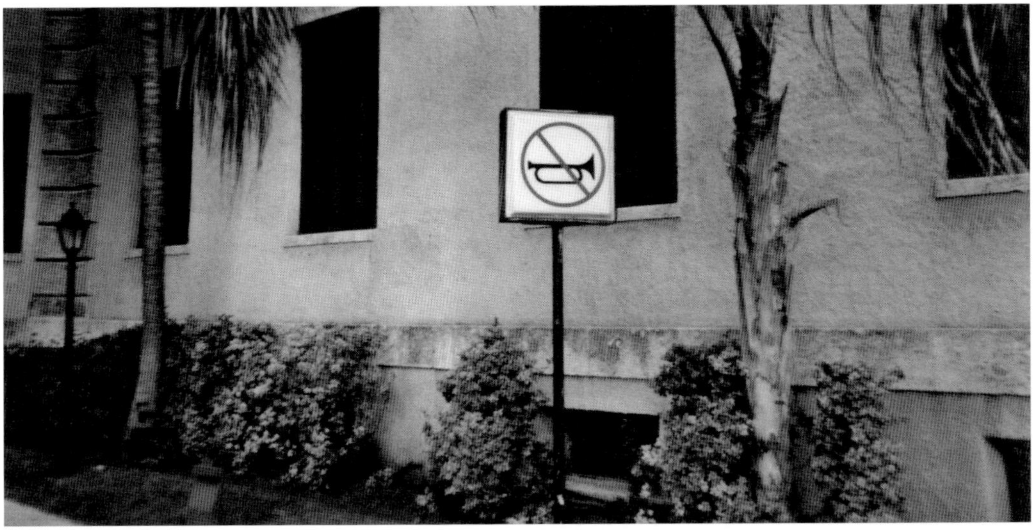

The trek to the park could be interesting. "The people would toot their horns out in traffic, all the time; beep-beep-beep, every day!" Gene Hermanski says. After all these years, the proprietors of the Hotel Nacional are still quite sensitive to the local horn-blowing custom, as evidenced by this sign in front of the main entrance.

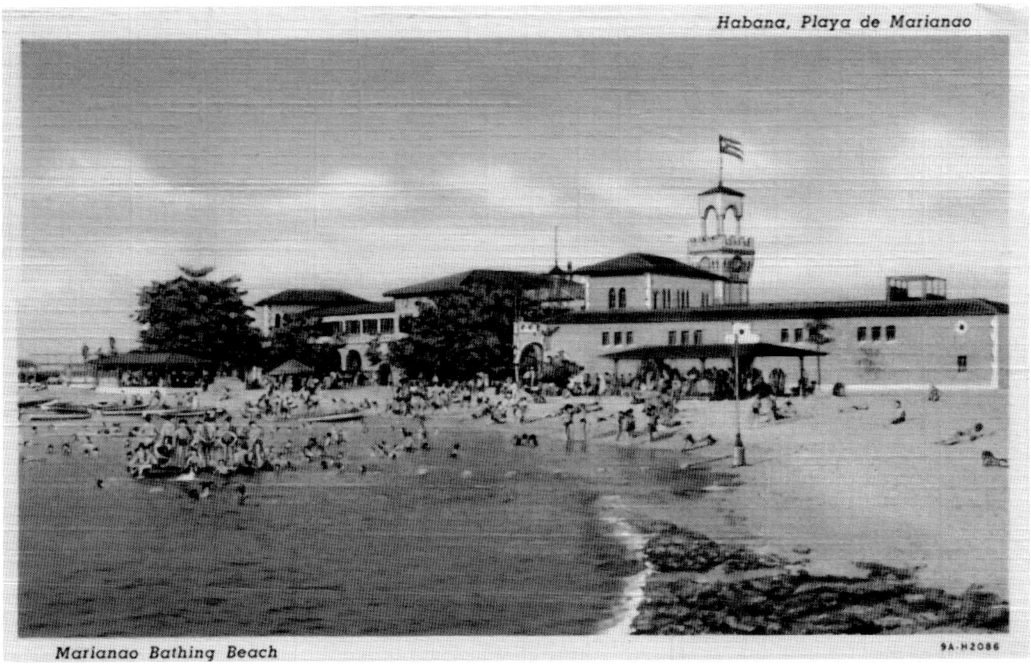

Rookie Gene Mauch had a near-career-ending swimming experience. "I went to Marianao Beach and I was swimming out to this little boat," says Gene, "and this fella on the pier was jumping up and down and screaming, 'Get outta the water!' There was a school of barracuda trailing me, and I didn't have any idea! The water is so clear and beautiful, they can still see from the pier. I wasn't really a strong swimmer, but I got stronger at that moment!"

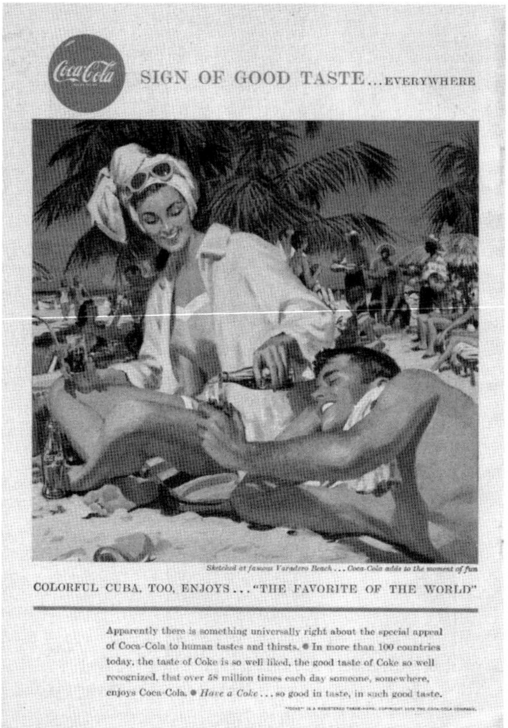

Before Cuba became closed to American business, its beaches were famous in the United States, as well as other ports, and beckoned *turistas* on a regular basis.

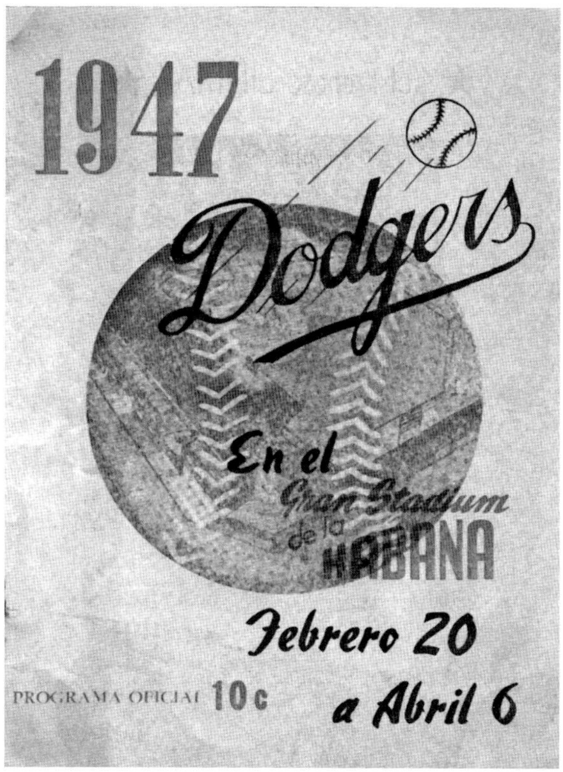

After their long wartime absence, the Dodgers were glad to be back, and so were the local fans. The team made sure plenty of souvenirs were available, like this scorecard, to keep everyone involved.

Most of the rookies abided by the rules and stayed out of trouble. "I didn't run around much, not at night," remembers Pat McGlothin. "That just wasn't my place to jingle. I didn't speak enough Spanish to communicate. I didn't enjoy working with what Branch Rickey called 'fire escape ballplayers,' the guys who'd sneak down the fire escape at night."

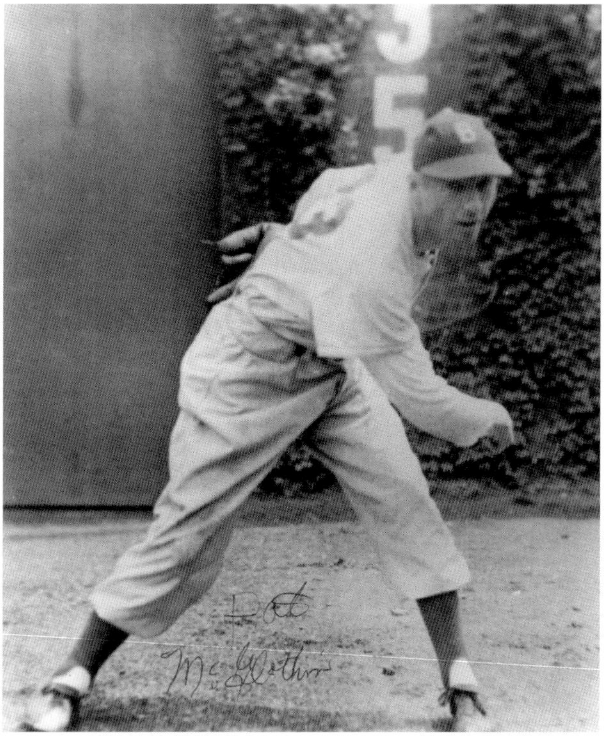

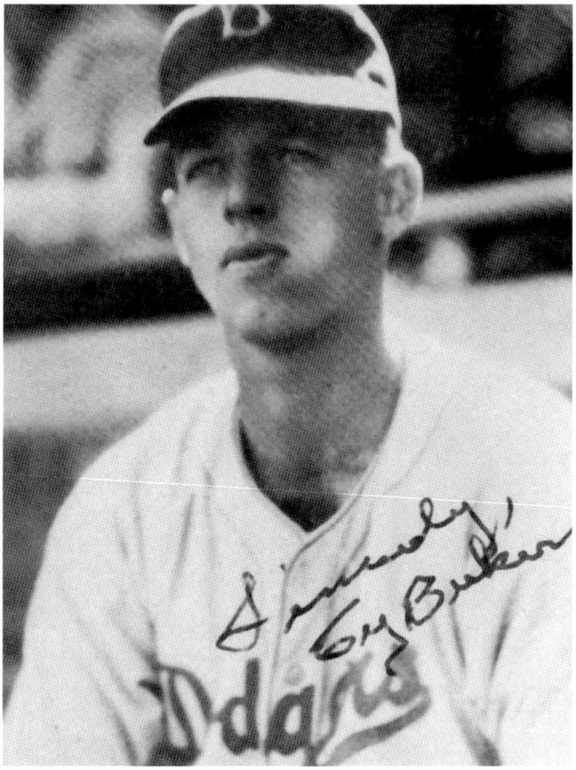

"Guys like Higbe and Casey played practical jokes all the time," says rookie Cy Buker. "You know, the usual: they'd nail your shoes to the floor, or tie knots in your stockings so you couldn't get 'em on. You had to watch everything, or they'd put it in the shower; they like to get your shoes all wet, especially if you had a new pair."

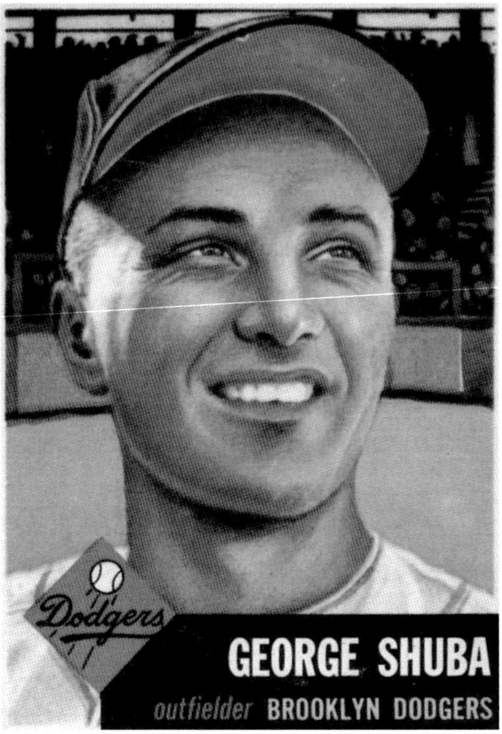

"Every once in a while, we'd go into the city to play an exhibition game; sometimes we'd go in at night," George "Shotgun" Shuba recalls. "Did you do anything interesting?" Mrs. Shuba wonders. "No," Shotgun says. "He says no," Mrs. Shuba clarifies, "but maybe they did and he doesn't want to tell you!"

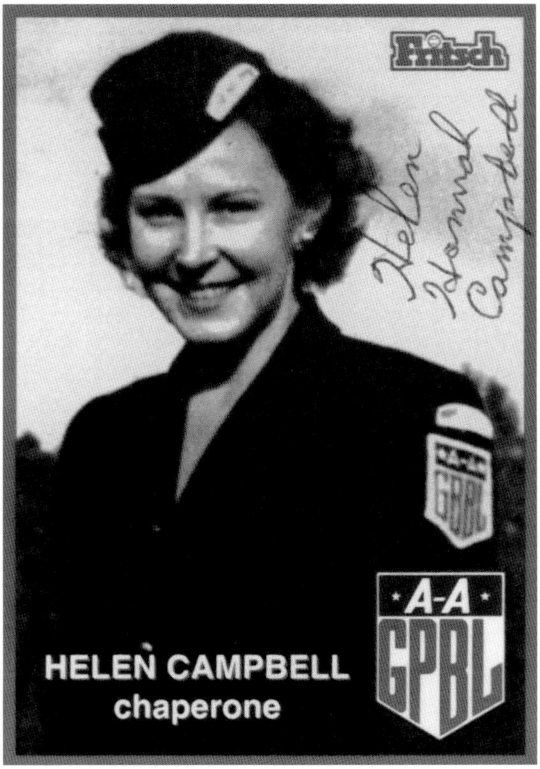

The All-American Girls' Professional Baseball League (AAGBL), immortalized by Madonna and Tom "There's No Crying in Baseball" Hanks in *A League of their Own*, also sent a contingent to Cuba that spring for some exhibition games. Helen Hannah Campbell, daughter of 1918–1920 Yankees catcher Truck Hannah, went along as a chaperone for the Muskegon Lassies. "The natives fell in love with blue-eyed blondes who could throw a ball 90 feet!" Helen remembers.

"I was on the Montreal roster," Don Lund recalls. "I had a good spring. I hit 12 home runs. So instead of being in Syracuse on Opening Day, I was in Philadelphia." Lund also played for the Browns and Tigers before becoming the baseball coach at the University of Michigan (UM), where his Wolverines won the 1962 NCAA championship. Coincidentally, Branch Rickey had also been a UM baseball coach from 1910 to 1913.

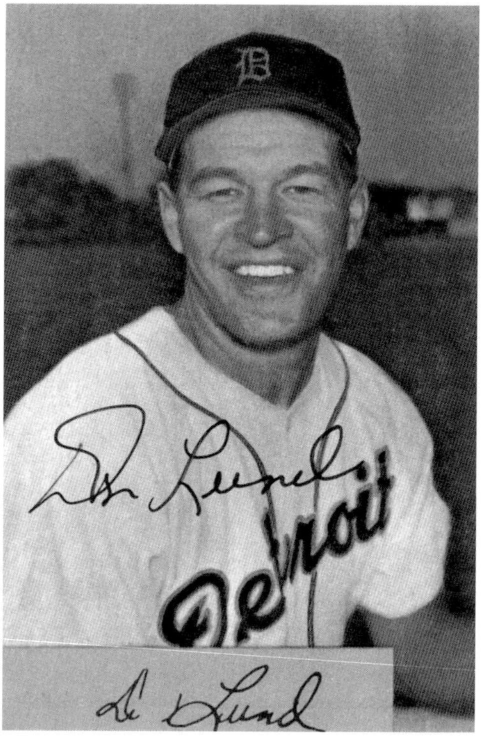

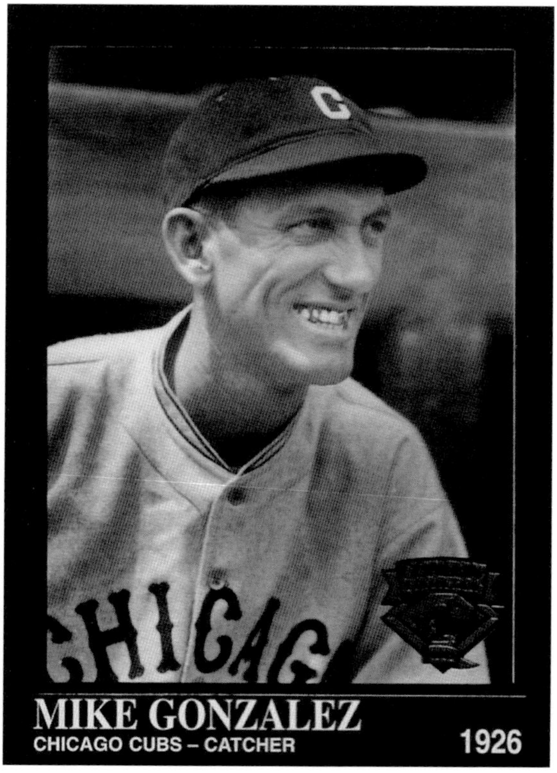

"It wouldn't be a Dodger game without a rhubarb with an umpire," said the *Brooklyn Eagle*. "The Dodgers grew hot over a decision at third by one of the local arbiters. Durocher charged out of the dugout to the transplanted Bronx cheers of the 3,000 fans." Mike Gonzalez, a longtime National League star and Cuban hero who was managing the Havana team at the time, was also in the discussion. "The Brooklyn manager wouldn't discuss what transpired, but it is safe to say they weren't wasting time talking about Havana politics."

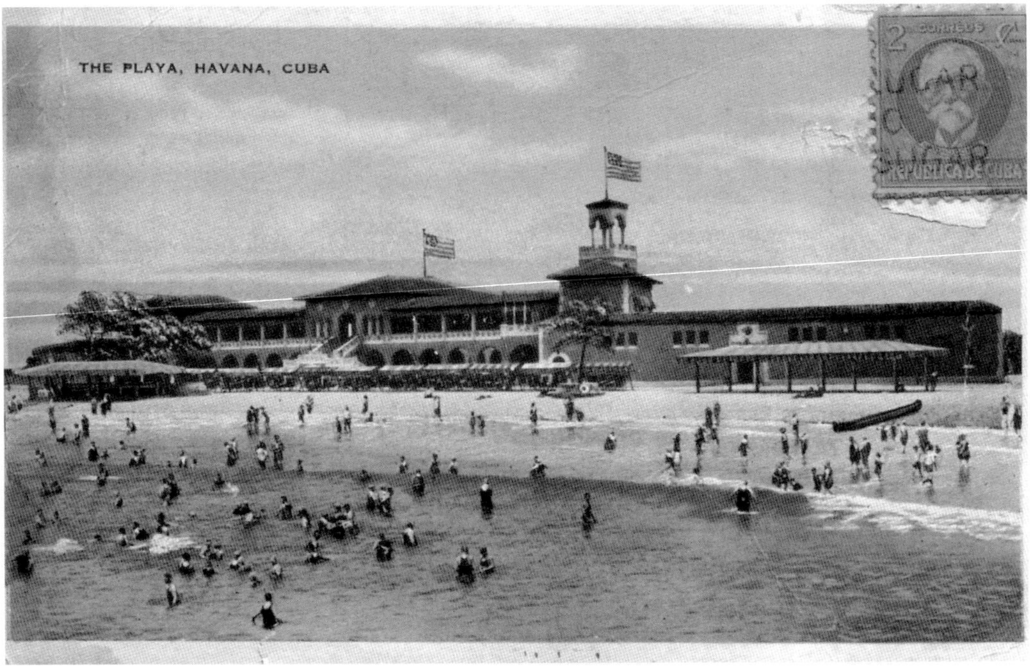

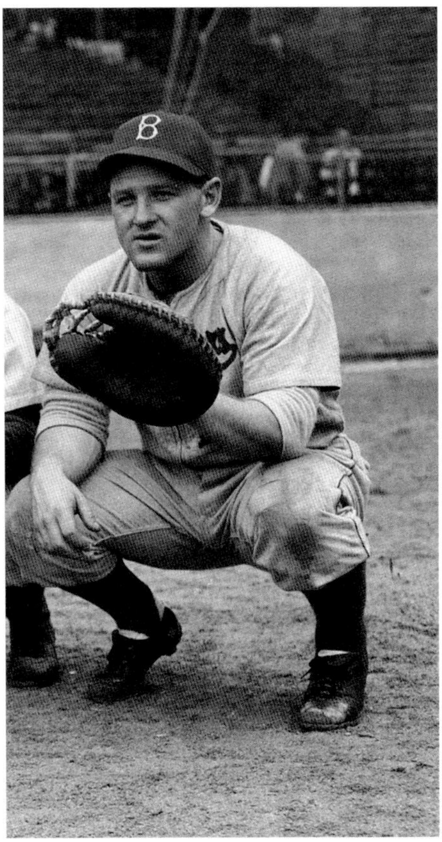

Harold Parrott was the team's traveling secretary. In 1947, his family came along. "We didn't have a lot to do in Havana," says Harold's son Lynn, who was seven at the time. "We'd go swimming at Veradero. We were from Rockaway in Queens, so we were comfortable with swimming in the ocean. The diving board was in pretty bad shape. They had a chain-link fence off the end of the pier to keep the sharks from eating the bathers."

Of course, too much of that glorious Caribbean sunshine can be a bad thing. "Bruce Edwards, regular Brooklyn catcher, wasn't in uniform," the *Post* said. "He overdid a siesta in the sun yesterday and looks like a piece of rare roast beef. The temperature was 85 today so Edwards remained indoors instead of making an effort to resemble an outside cut."

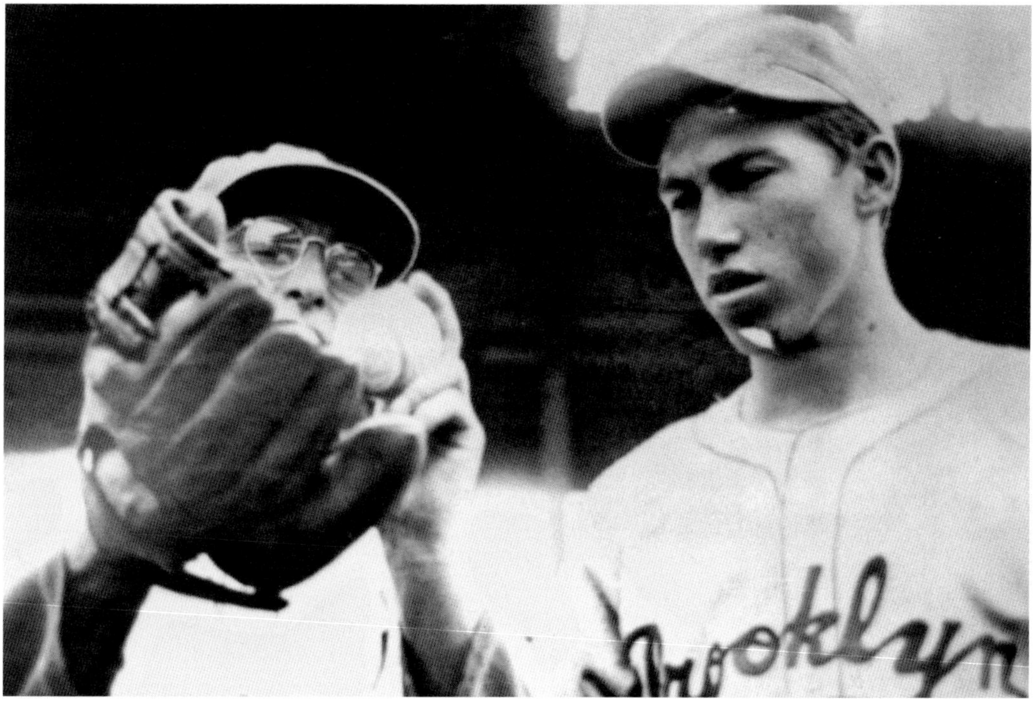

In 1925, the same year Cal McLish was born, Paul Waner hit .401 for San Francisco. Later the grizzled veteran and fresh-faced rookie attended camp together. "I didn't have a pitching coach," McLish says. "You had to learn on your own. Paul told me I should develop a change-up. I'd started with fastballs, trying to cross-seam everything, to be like Feller. I needed to be the kind of pitcher I should have been."

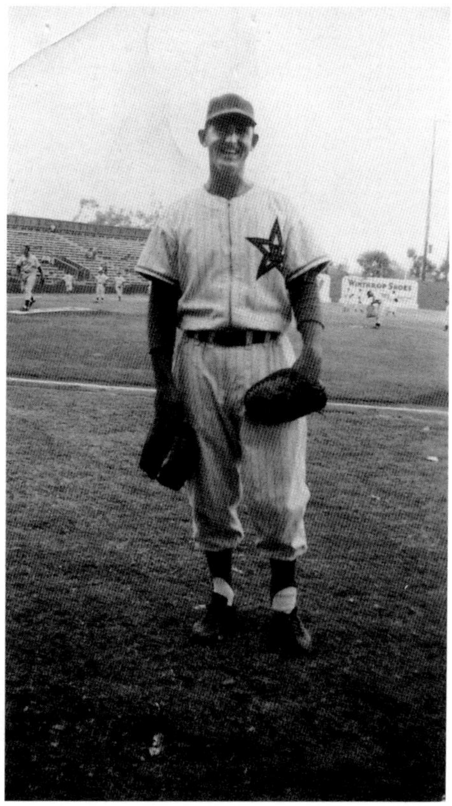

Jack Paepke pitched and caught during his 15-year minor-league career, but he never made the show. After that, he managed in the minors and coached for the Angels from 1961 to 1966. One side trip in the spring of 1947 proven eventful. "They had us in this big room on those fold-up bunks," Jack says. "All at once, there was this loud explosion, and I was on the floor. So was everyone else. It was five in the morning! They fired a cannon, 'cause it was an army base."

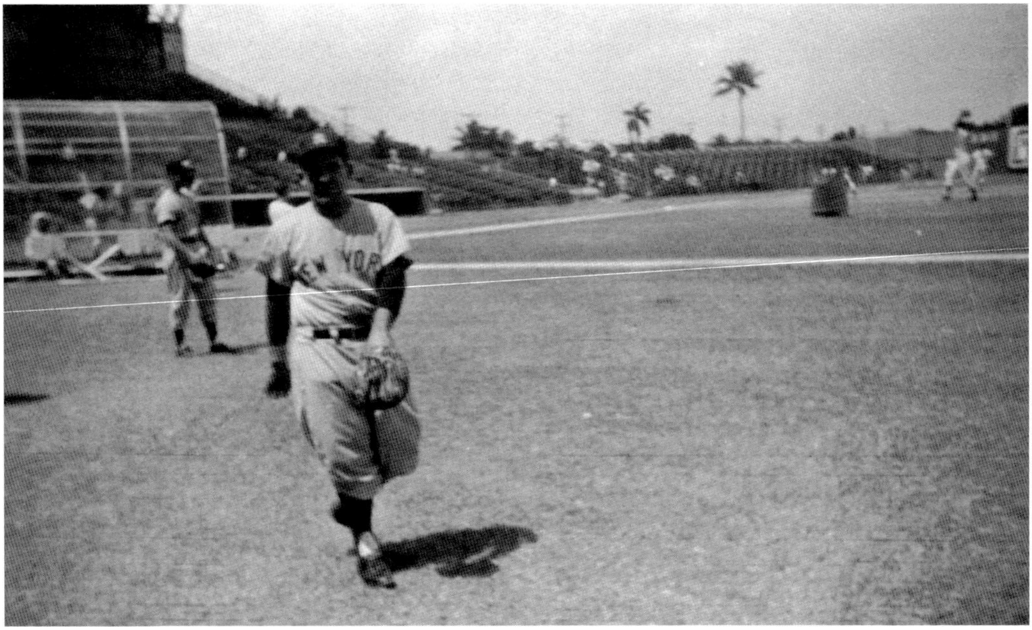

The Dodgers played 22 exhibition games in 1947; they finished 14-5-3 against the New York Yankees, Boston Braves, Montreal Royals, and numerous All-Star teams from Cuba, Puerto Rico, Venezuela, and Panama. Joe DiMaggio came to Cuba before flying off for surgery to remove the bone spurs Hemingway wrote about, but he never played. Before the world knew about Larry "Yogi" Berra, the *Daily News* aptly introduced the diminutive rookie by referring to him as a "contagious little gnome."

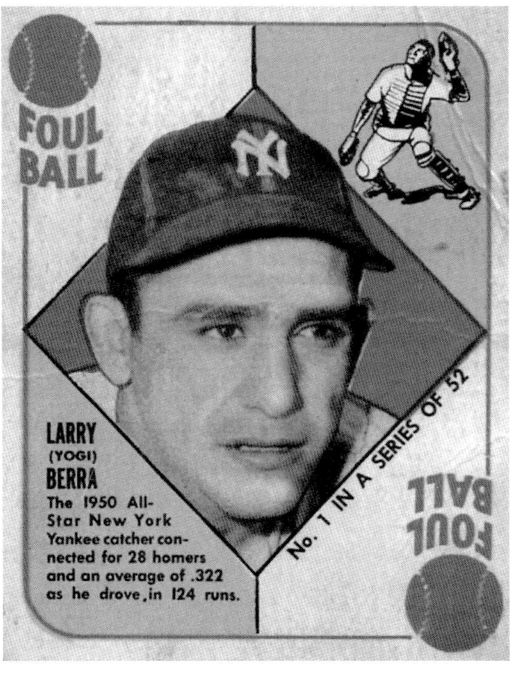

"Larry Berra, rookie catcher, started with a bang," the *Herald-Tribune* said. "He reached forward with his head and George Stirnweiss clipped him with a bat. Berra tried to be dizzy, but he is that way normally so he couldn't do it." But Yogi got the last laugh, because in the final Dodger game, the Yankees won 17-6 as Berra hit three doubles and played right field rather than catching.

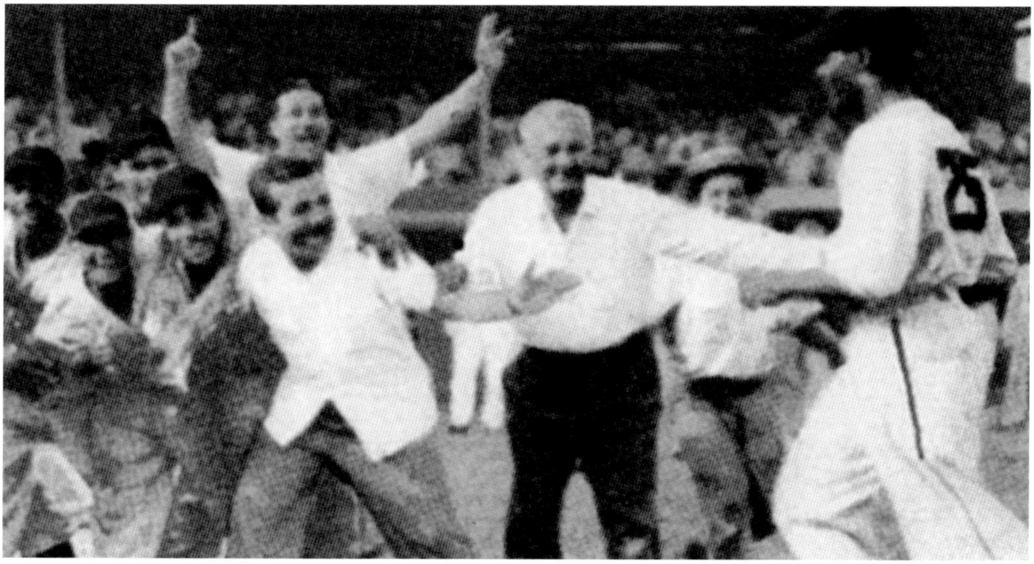

The Yanks also wandered off to Puerto Rico, playing against the local Ponce team. The game was tied in the sixth when a Puerto Rican player's home run tore it open. "The homer sent the crowd into a paroxysm of joy," the *Herald-Tribune* said. "The entire Ponce team gathered at the plate to welcome [Fernando] Pedroso. Pedroso then made a running collection tour of the boxes. The fans thrust money into his hands. He collected $70. It is a pleasant Puerto Rican custom."

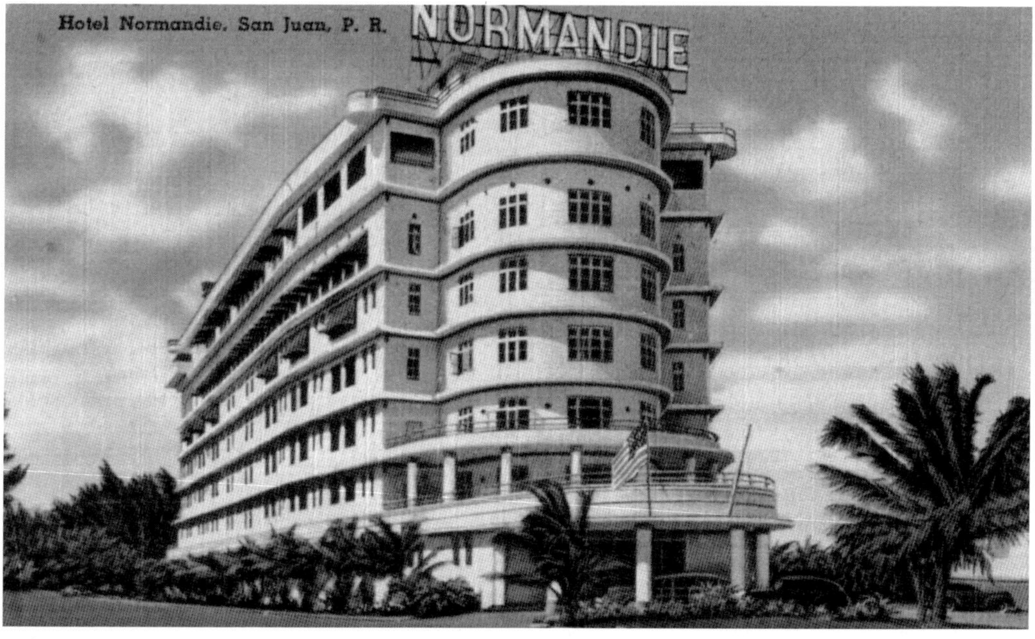

While in Puerto Rico, the Yanquis (Yankees) set up shop at the Hotel Normandie. "Hospitality was rampant," according to the *Tribune*. "A case of Don Q rum was placed in every writer's room. The rooms, incidentally, have little breakfast nooks looking out on the ocean. It is a shame to have to work."

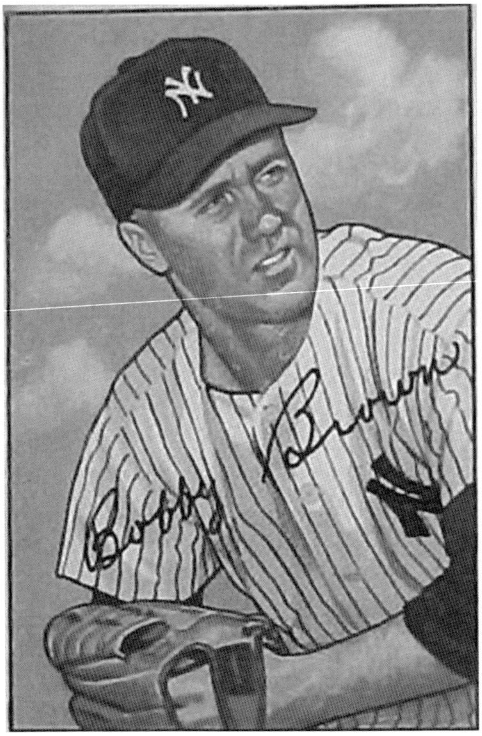

In Cuba, the Yanks also enjoyed their spare time. "We went to a cock fight," recalls Bobby Brown. "There was a lot of betting, but none of us knew which rooster to bet on. These weren't in back alleys; they had regular places, with a pit in the center, and several hundred people at these!" Brown hit .300 that season, went on to be a physician, and then president of the American League.

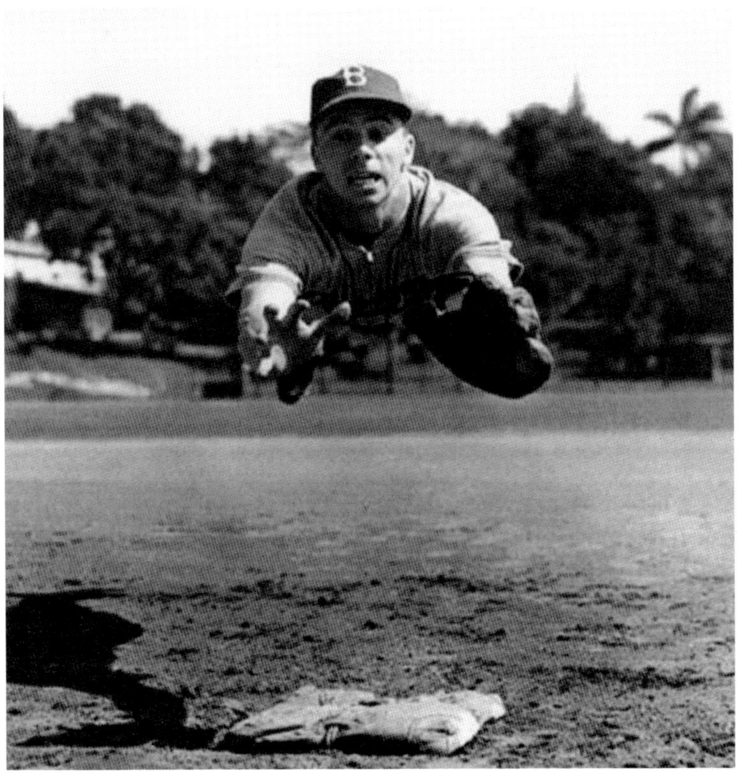

Pee Wee Reese gave his all in Cuba, as well as everywhere else he played. An all-time Dodger fan-favorite, the 5-foot, 9-inch-tall infielder hustled his way into the Hall of Fame after a stellar 16-year Brooklyn-to-Los Angeles career.

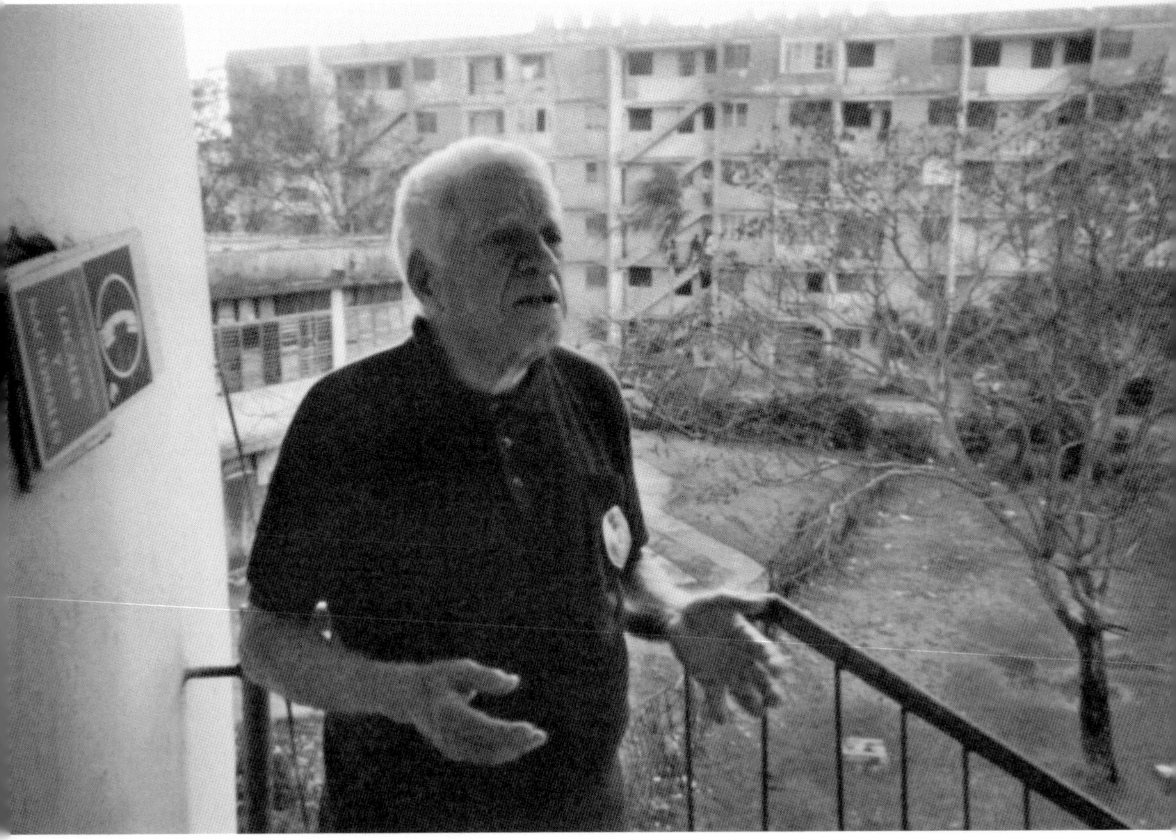

The local kids followed their semi-adopted teams with interest. "We listened to the radio," recalls Havana resident Pedro Alfonso, a youngster at the time who went on to a career in Cuban broadcasting. "Definitely people gathered in the house to listen, but in Parque Central [Central Park] they put up a board during the World Series and there was an announcer narrating the game, live, on the radio, and a little puppet moved when there was a hit: 1st base, 2nd base."

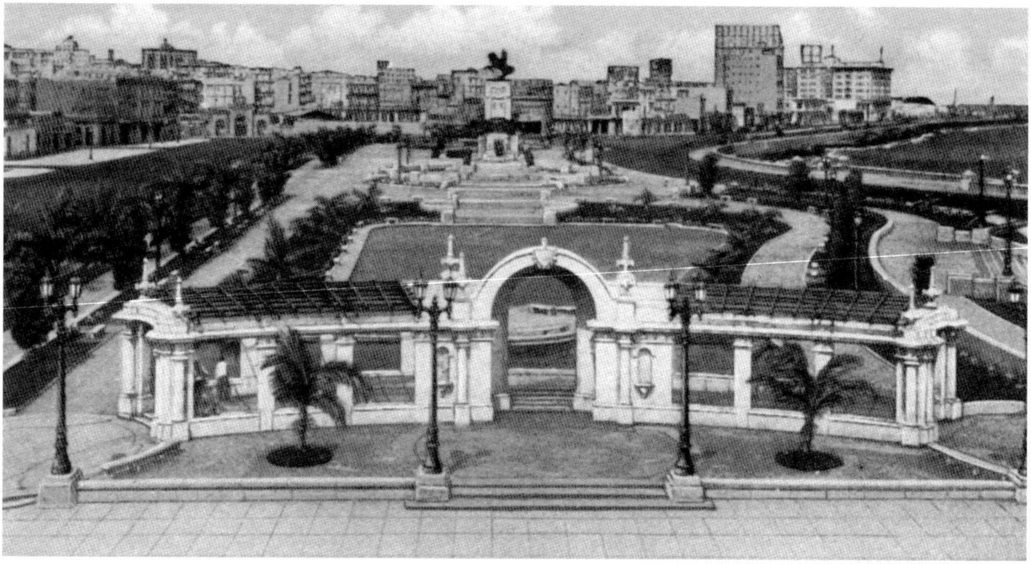

Havana also offered plenty of fancier sites, funded in part by visiting ballclubs. "For what it is costing the Brooks here," the *Daily News* said, "Rickey could have financed a juicy revolution and wound up owning the place."

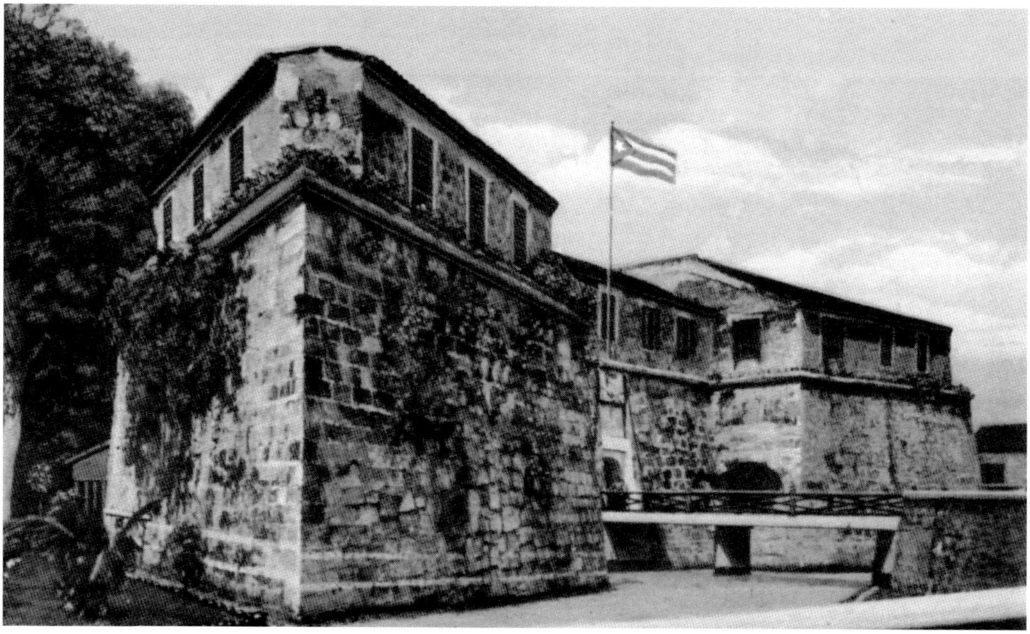

Forts and dungeons and ancient jails also abounded within walking distance of the hotel . . . with good reason. Cuban sportswriter Pepe Conte was attacked in a bar by a local player. "All I wrote was that this fellow was a lousy shortstop," he said. "He averages two errors a game and he could not hit the size of his sombrero. He read my article in his favorite hangout one night and thumped his chest, shouting, '*Tengo mucho honor.*' So he went after me, and I shot him. We later became good friends. Now, even he admits he was a lousy shortstop."

There were some less rowdy ballplayers around, fortunately. Le Roy Pfund had a stipulation in his contract (handwritten by Rickey) about his Christian beliefs. "Not playing on Sundays was a conviction I had," he says, "since I became a Christian at an early age." Pfund went on to coach baseball at Billy Graham's alma mater, Wheaton College, from 1949 to 1975; he also headed the basketball team for 24 years and led the first NCAA Division II champs in 1957. The school now hosts an annual Lee Pfund Classic tournament.

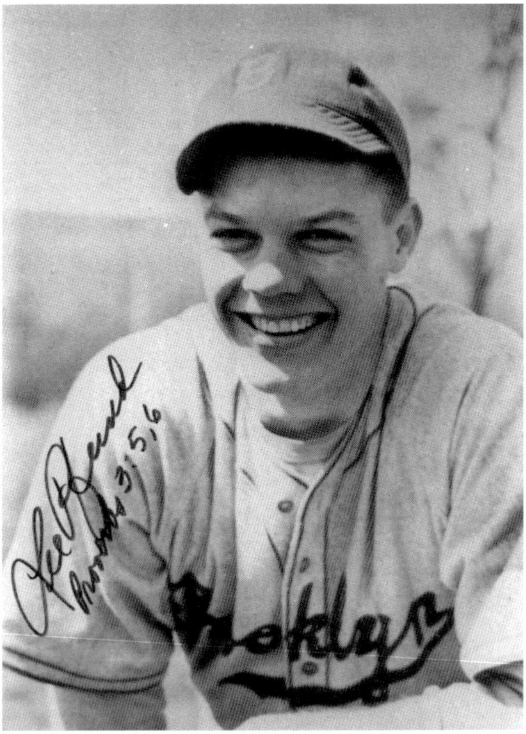

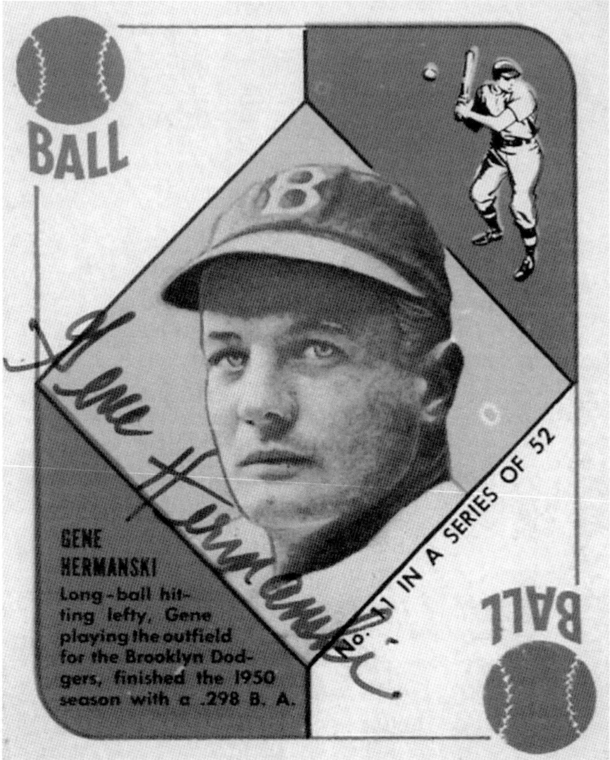

Not all rookies fared as well. "Mr. Rickey kinda liked me," Gene Hermanski recalls. "But the old man gave ya' trouble. Money. So ya' take it gracefully." Then, "if you made a bad play, he'd give you some 'constructive criticism,' " he adds.

TOMMY HOLMES

Clinical Notes On the Isthmus

Balboa C. Z., March 17

When a big Pan-American plane set us er. at the Albrook Field airport and the be greeted by army brass of varying xpression on the face of Kirby Higbe

nbled the uninhibited pitcher, "that I life for good. I never wanted to even

t Clayton has passed and even the out- otten his instinctive G. I. gripe, which it took ol' Hig to realize that the bugle m.

se, a vast difference between the in- you want to call them, and honored t, which the Dodgers have been. This n a luxurious life but the kindness and by the officers and the enlisted men isfactory.

CHER—The players are quartered in he heart of the camp. They live con- -hall, where you can get along very t on such items as steaks, roast beef, am, etc., etc.

ook out and see the skipper out in his th the movie camera that his bride way present from California.

have heard, this, indeed, seems to be is camera occupies his idle moments venings are devoted to, of all things, a ery, out of a volume which also is a ay. He aims to know as much about e learned about Hoyle.

right. The playing cards that once diversion after dinner now are re- as a device of the devil. Not even lay cards for money so that Leo can ance of what some consider evil.

table off the mess hall and the skip- iest dilettante manipulators of a cue Durocher won't go near it.

," he observed to Larry Goetz, the uld say that I was running a book

ow path that would be approved by Leo's native New England will do it, ill, avoid being dipped into the tubful nmissioner Happy Chandler is pop- ep ready for him.

it getting back to life as it is lived as this one transportation is neces- ation is here. A jeep or a staff car ace. I haven't yet made a trip to the ping for a minute to watch a fairly raflores locks, an important part of ssroads of the world.

e post for those that want it, tennis Trips have been planned and ex- bout the country. We have fished ay and in the Pacific.

people are picturesque and colorful. ed most of their exhibitions here at erally, Olympic Stadium). That is e Pacific side and a part of the Re- e adjacent American (Canal Zone) ust cross the street to go from one

"—The ball park is peculiarly con- ecause there are no seats whatever

Robinson May Be Dodgers' 1st Sacker After Royal Series

Negro Star to Display Talents Against Parent Club Starting Today

By HAROLD C. BURR

Balboa, Canal Zone, March 17—This is the day this town has been awaiting all Winter. It isn't just the anniversary of the driving of the snakes out of Ireland by the good St. Patrick. Jackie Robinson is making his debut at Olympic Stadium for Montreal against the Dodgers in the first of a three-game series and the betting is all in favor of his becoming the regular Brooklyn first baseman. The Negro population is expected to storm the gates to pay homage to the first member of their race to play professional ball since Newark tried the experiment back in the 1880s and John McGraw attempted to sneak in a Negro second baseman with straight hair against the Cubs, whom the crafty manager of the Giants swore was an Indian.

Manager Leo Durocher isn't going to be present at the unveiling of his new meteor "I've never seen Robinson play," said the Lip, who left on the morning plane for California on private business. He refused to discuss Robinson, but Coach Jack Pitler raves about him. Jake's been watching him for a week working out with the Royals in Havana.

"I'm leaving the team in charge of Ray Blades and should return to Cuba either Wednesday or Thursday at the latest," declared Durocher.

Jake stood behind everything Leo said.

"It would be a crime not to bring this boy up because of his color," said Pitler. "You ought to see him play first base. He's as much at home on the bag as if he had played it all his life. At bat Jackie always gets a piece of the ball. He won't get many home runs for you, but he hits for extra bases between the outfielders and he can run and bunt, too."

It's the belief that the Lip's mystery mission to California is to bring his bride, Laraine Day, back to Cuba with him. Miss Day is shy about journeying to a foreign country alone, which carries with it the annoyance of going through the customs. In addition there are one or two things in connection with the Los Angeles court mess the pepperpot manager thinks that he will be able to clear up.

Jackie Clouts Homer

Robinson warmed up across the isthmus yesterday at Mount Hope, Cristobal, against General Electric champions of the Panama professional league, the lone non-major league team to beat the Dodgers. Montreal won the ball game, 9 to 5, Robinson connecting for a single and a homer in four times at bat.

Roy Campanella, another colored Dodger farmhand from Nassau, got a double and a home run for a perfect day at the dish. However, the overflow crowd of 4,149 fans came out to cheer for Jackie, their idol.

Meanwhile, the Dodgers had to

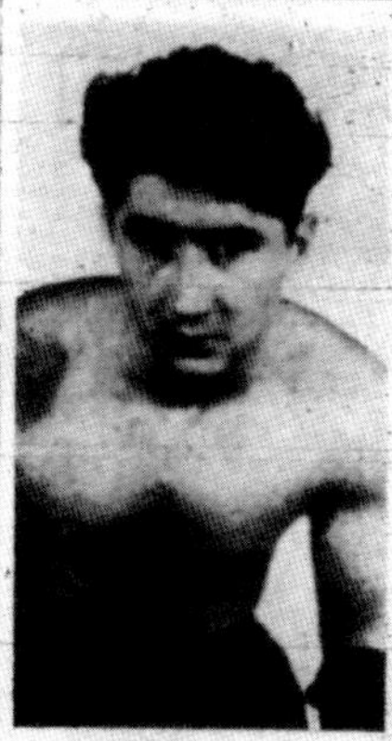

Leo Milito

Milito Risks Long Ring Skein In Warren Tiff

What shapes up as possibly the best card the Broadway Arena has offered this season in a season studded with excellent bouts, is on tap tomorrow night when unbeaten Leo Milito of the East Side seeks to carve out his 31st successive victory at the expense of Jimmy Warren, Bushwick lightweight, in the main eight-rounder.

This fight was a particularly tough one for Promoter Max Joss to make and don't think that a matchmaker doesn't take pride in matching two promising fighters like this in a small club ring. The Garden could have done a lot worse than grab these two fighters who keep the customers on the edge of their seats every time they climb through the ropes.

Jimmy will scale in holding a

RANGERS' CUP CHANCES FADE AMID RIOT

Casualties Run High As Injured Reardon Skulls a Spectator

By RALPH TROST

"Reardon, you bum, you were begging for it."

With those kind words, balm to the wounds of Kenny Reardon, Les Canadiens defenseman who was on his way to Dr. Nardiello's hemstitching emporium (the Rangers' dressing room), the biggest and best Donnybrook staged in Madison Square Garden in many a long year broke out.

The bloody, but unbowed Reardon, later to get six stitches sewed in his upper lip, turned and let go with his stick at the suspected customer who passed the crack. A bald-headed customer arose, pointed a long finger and said some hard words—and whoppo, he was rendered hors de combat with a considerable hole in his roof.

Fists flew and sticks flew. Bill Juzda and Maurice (The Rocket) Richard had a special fight. Bill Moe, shoulder separation and all, squared off with goalie Bill Durnan. The only absentee in the whole two squads was Nobbe Warwick. He was inside with ice bags packed around his thigh, suffering from a charley-horse.

At last count Hal Laycoe had an ice bag against a big bump alongside his eye; Ab DeMarco had a bleeding something about the size of a small onion on his cheek and a subsequent challenge to fight Nosdell; Edgar Laprade had a trickle of blood; Herb O'Connor was reported to have a broken jaw, and Emile (Butch) Bouchard had a couple of nobs. Those were the visible wounds.

Bentley Leads Scorers

Losing 4—3, their second one-goal loss to the Habitants in successive nights, the Rangers dropped everything but the remotest of hopes of getting into the Stanley Cup playoffs. If they win their remaining three and Detroit drops three, the Rangers are in. Otherwise it's all over for another year.

Atop all this the Canadiens got a bad physical beating, and Maurice Richard, who got a mere assist last night, slipped behind Chicago's Max Bentley in the race for individual scoring honors, Max picking up two goals and an assist even though the Blackhawks lost, 10—6.

This affair last night was no hangover from a battle in Canada Saturday night. That was a quiet game. But a brawl was in the making right from the start last night. The game was only a few minutes old before Allen was caught working on Cooper. Then Referee Hayes spotted Hextall retaliating for a little roughing by Reardon. Later Ken Mozdell intrigued Juzda into making violent gestures—and getting caught. Before long Chuck Rayner was squawking that every

L. I. Up

Duques In Othe Court T

By GEORGE

We're takii with the E flying agains that has the cats swallov Island Birds in quesne meets U invitation base at the Garden

Back in 1941 rate with West and Ohio Univ the experts fig Si Lobello, Saul ders, Sol S c h Schechtman gli pionship with

Now, five ye Islanders once to squeeze int while Kentucky ent, is rated tl the country, a Wildcats have

We're not say team should But the Birds give Adolph Ru toughest eveni experienced.

As in all the this battle can decided under much will depe Bob Smith a one of whom maa, a freshma still may be tl ning.

Blackbirds Con

There is on Blackbirds that are more confi tucky than th taking L. I. U. ever accused Rupp of not be wise men of Island U.'s Bee self, far above to analyzing tl then selecting cagers to dull points and tak weak spots. T dence in Bee's ity.

When the champions bea in the season big Harry Bo Redmen were smart basketb in the season.

The wide di Gray Tribe's p Saturday night in front of No the early half. late stanza. during the ea the Redmen They couldn't so they

Branch Rickey's great semi-secret experiment was progressing nicely; Jackie Robinson was still on the Montreal Royals roster, not Brooklyn's, and word began to leak out about his chances with the big club. Jackie helped his cause by dazzling everyone on the field. "He can do everything but stay at the Waldorf," observed Montreal secretary Mel Jones.

6

JACKIE

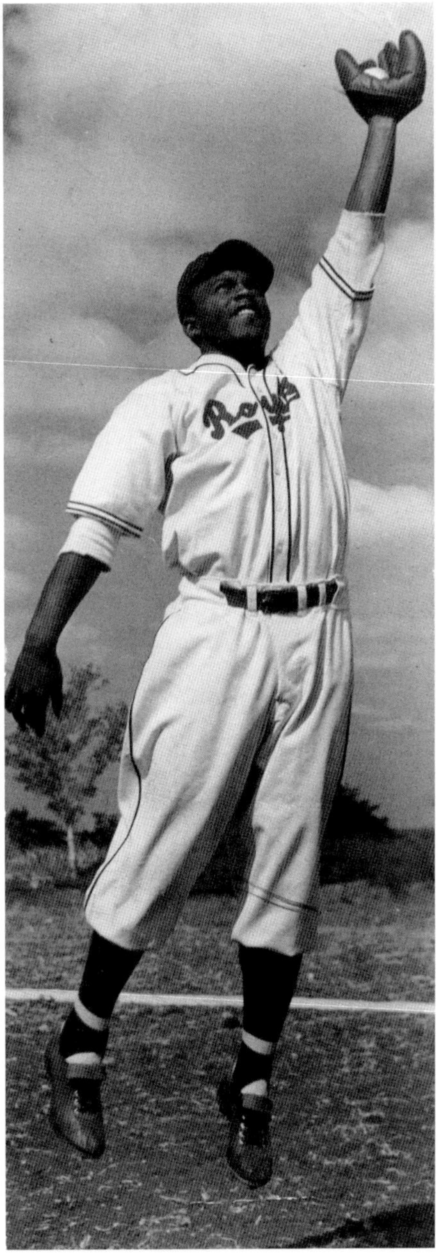

When Jackie Robinson broke the major-league color barrier in 1947, he still had to eat in the team bus because he was not allowed in whites-only restaurants; he had to stay at ratty hotels, as he was not allowed in the team's luxurious quarters; and he was yelled at, thrown at, cursed at, spiked at, and was the target of many death threats. He had debuted with the Montreal Royals in 1946, leading the league at .349, and Rickey planned for both clubs to train in Cuba; Robinson was assigned to Montreal to keep the profile low.

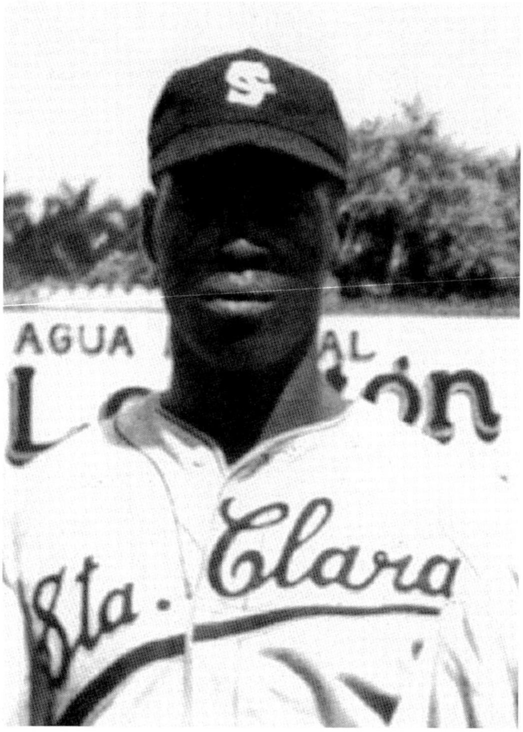

Roy Partlow was part of that historic 1947 experiment too; along with Don Newcombe and Roy Campanella, he was also assigned to the Montreal camp. A fiery pitcher, he had gone 12-1 in the minors in 1946, finishing with Montreal 2-0. In the Negro Leagues, he pitched for the fabled Homestead Grays, tossed a no-hitter at the Chicago American Giants in 1942, and whipped a Cuban All-Star team. In Cuba, Roy led Santa Clara in wins during the winter of 1939–1940.

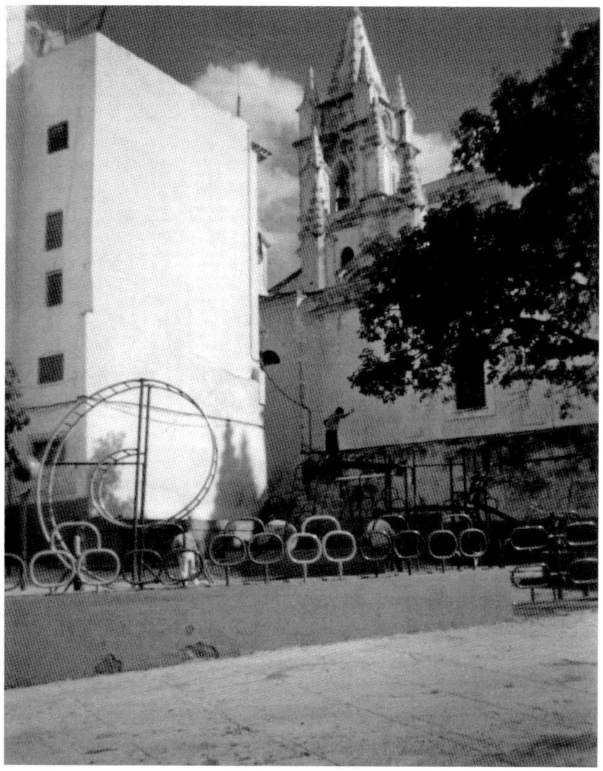

The four ballplayers could not stay at the Nacional. They bunked at the ratty Hotel Boston in Havana, which is no more; it was leveled to make way for a multiracial Cuban playground. Yet this innocuous spot is the site where Jackie and his segregated cohorts spent many sleepless nights in 1947.

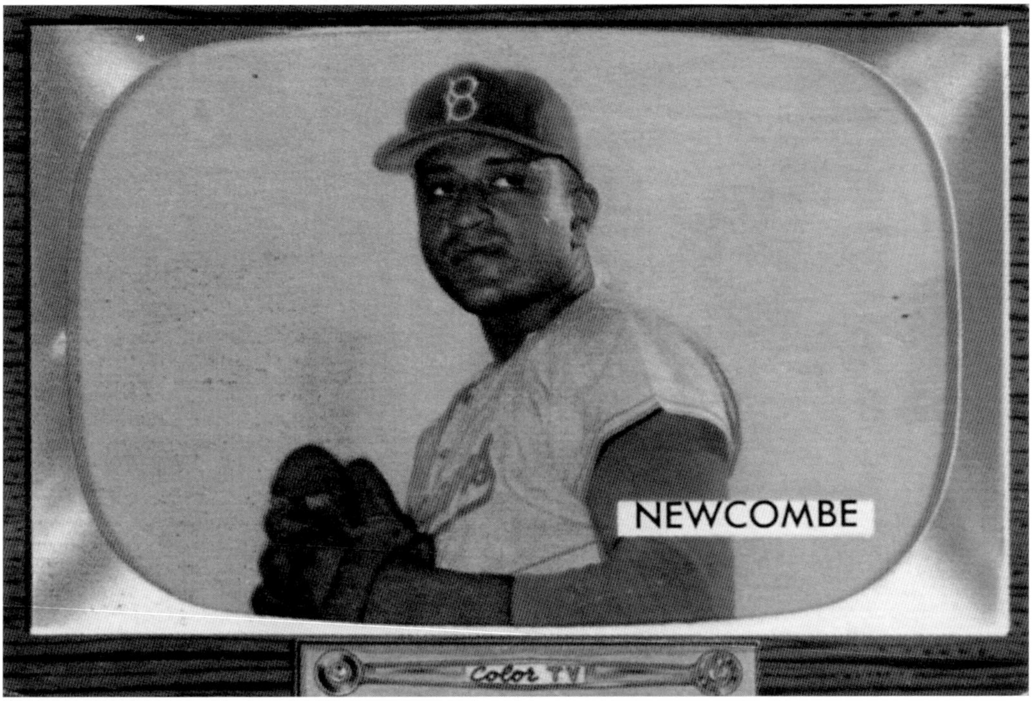

They were on their own for cheap dining, too. "One night," Newcombe says, "I sat in the restaurant next to the hotel eating a bowl of soup. I stirred the soup, and a cockroach came up out of it. I got so weak I could hardly swell your lip if I hit you with a fastball."

"After the first game, in the clubhouse, everybody was taking a shower," Eddie Stevens remembers. "Campanella was standing in the corner, holding his toothbrush, his washrag, and his soap. So I asked him, 'Roy, whatcha waitin' on?' " He says, 'Oh, Mister Eddie, I'll wait for everybody else, then I'll take mine.' But I told him, 'Roy, you're one of us—there ain't none of that.' "

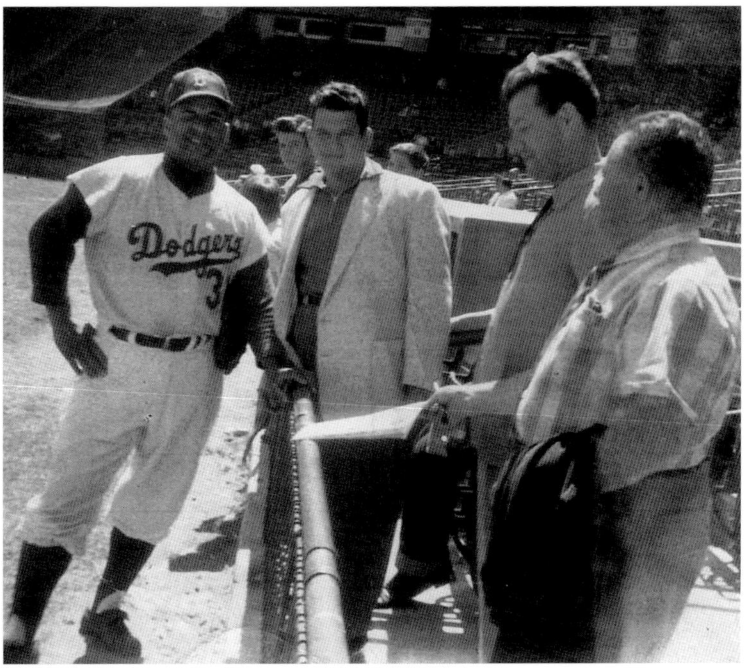

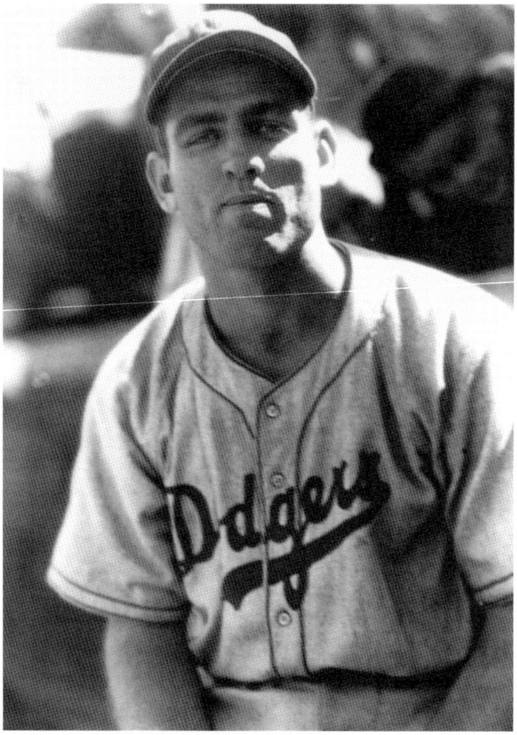

Eddie Stevens is a forgotten footnote to history. He was the Dodgers' starting first baseman in 1946 but lost his job to Robinson, as Rickey had moved Robbie to first to avoid promises made by some Southern ballplayers—who pledged to slide into second with their cleats high. "In the end, he was usin' me to spell Jackie," Eddie says. "He'd play six innings, and they'd let me finish. But it was decided from the top, he was gonna play the whole season."

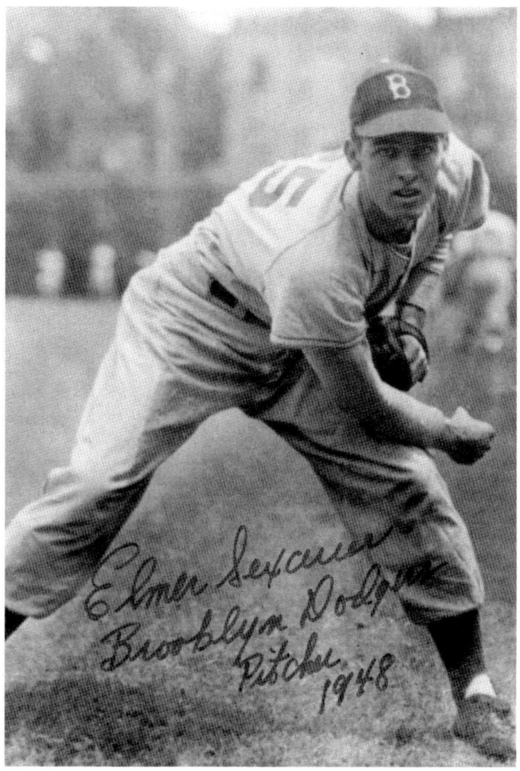

"I was pitching in a spring game and Jackie made an error behind me," recalls Elmer Sexauer. "He came in to the mound and apologized. Not too many guys did that. He was a real nice guy."

At right is an illustration of Robinson swinging away, thanks in great part to Pee Wee Reese's courage. Reese had grown up in segregated Kentucky, but he played a key role. "Pee Wee literally stepped to Jackie's defense, early in the season," Duke Snider wrote in his autobiography, "when he went over to Jackie, put his arm around Jackie's shoulders, and stared into our opponents' dugout. The message was clear."

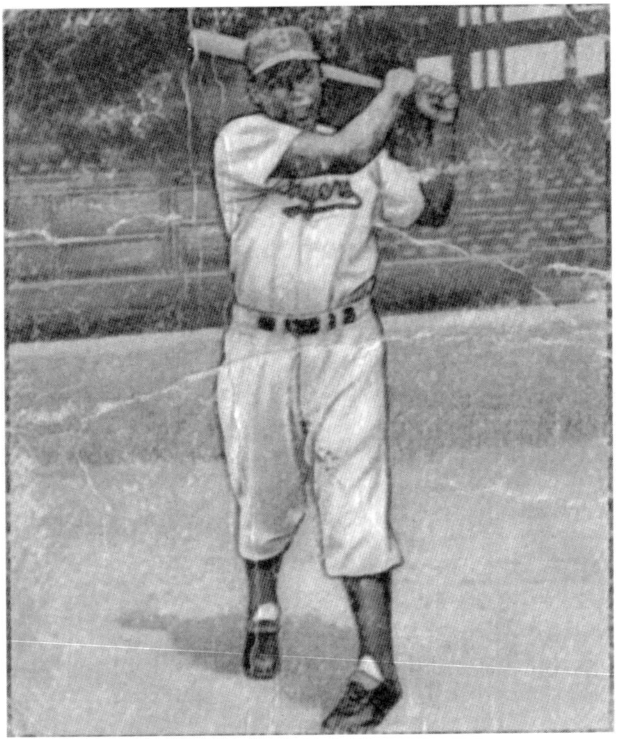

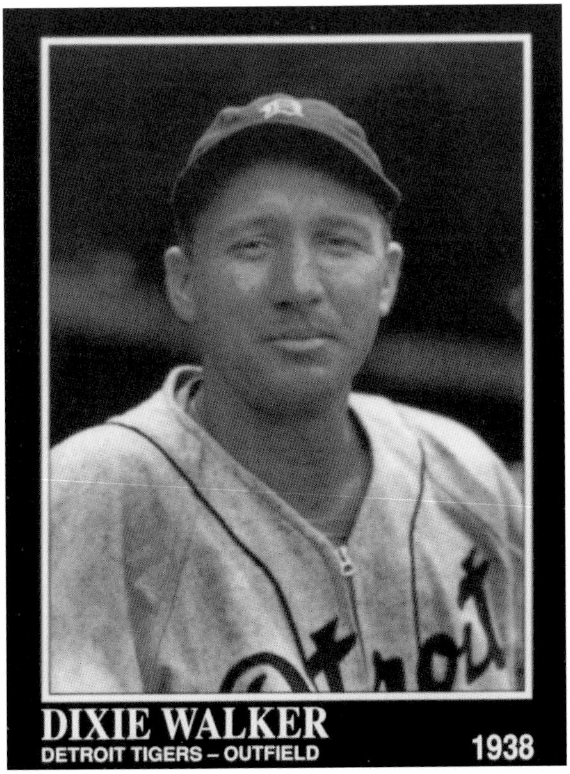

Dixie Walker fed the other end of the spectrum. A few of the Southern ballplayers started a petition to stand against integrating their team, and rumor had it that Dixie was the point guy. "Kirby Higbe had too many beers one night," Robinson wrote later, "and he began feeling uncomfortable about the conspiracy. He revealed the plot to one of Mr. Rickey's aides."

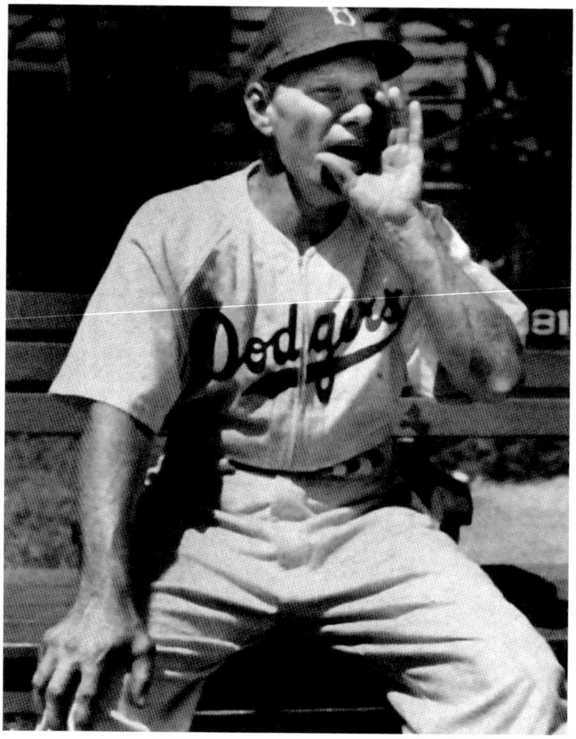

One evening, Leo Durocher could not sleep, so he leapt up and told the coaches to gather the boys in the hotel kitchen. "I said, 'I hear some of you don't want to play with Robinson and have a petition. You know what you can do with that petition. I'm interested in one thing. Winning. I'll play an elephant if he can do the job, and to make room for him I'll send my own brother home. This fellow is a great ballplayer. He's going to win pennants for us. He's going to put money in your pockets and mine. So, I don't want to see your petition, and I don't want to hear anything more about it. The meeting is over; go back to bed.' "

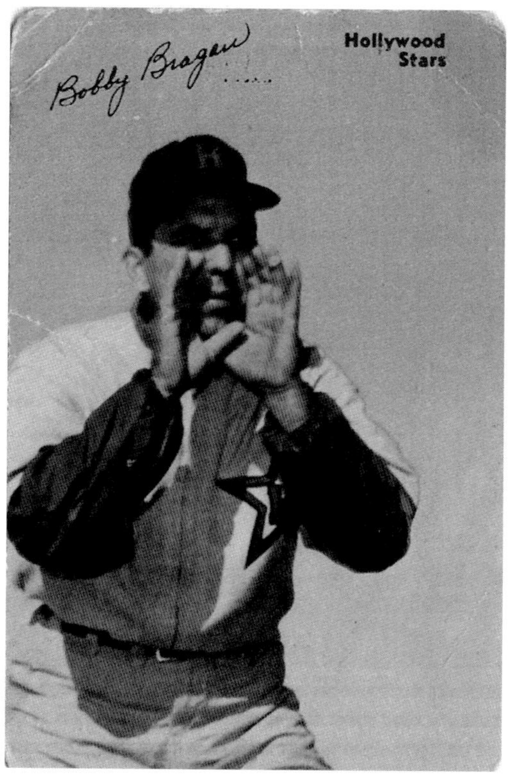

Southern heads rolled. Rickey unloaded Dixie Walker, Ed Stevens, Dixie Howell, Hugh Casey, and Kirby Higbe to Pittsburgh. Ed Head was sold to Fort Worth of the Texas League, although he had pitched a no-hitter for Brooklyn the year before. Bobby Bragan technically remained but was relegated to minor-league duty, and Eddie Stanky was sent to the Braves, freeing up second base for Robinson.

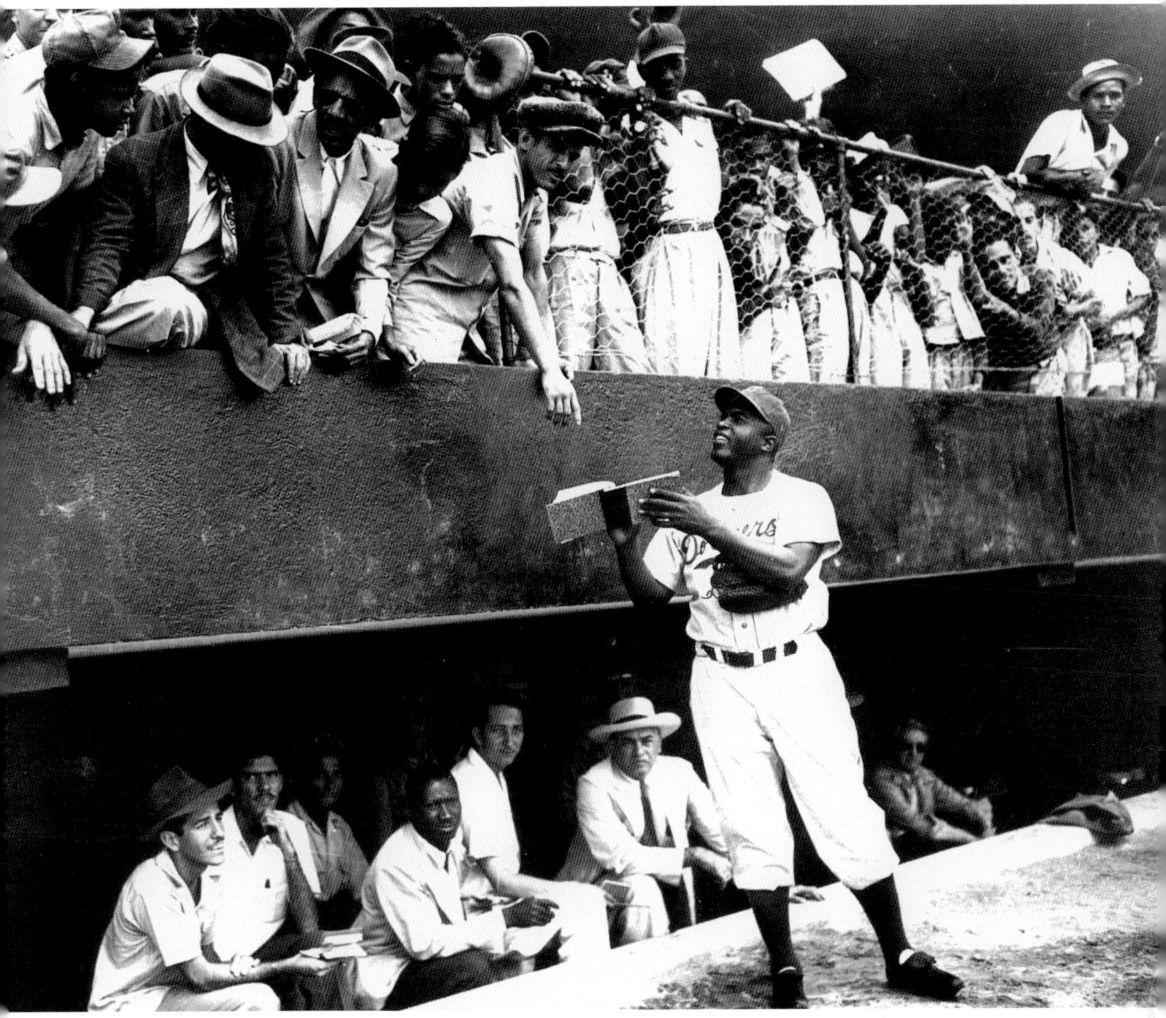

Cuban fans, color blind for nearly half a century by then, accepted Jackie with ease in 1947. Although he was officially a minor-league player that spring, he was already a major-league hero in Havana.

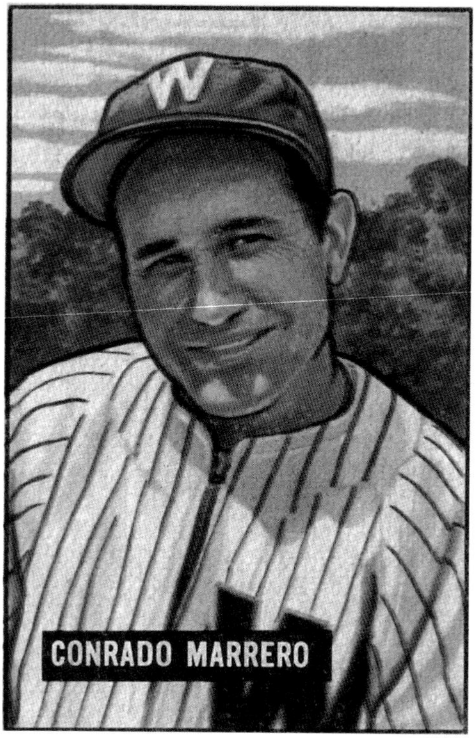

"I was pitching against Montreal," says Conrado Marrero. "Robinson got a hit and stole second. But not on me, on the catcher!" Marrero was an All-Star in his homeland that season before becoming a major-league All-Star with Washington. Besides facing Robinson, he also battled hitters like the Great DiMaggio. "I pitched to DiMaggio twice, late in his career, when he was so-so. I punched him out," Marrero recalls.

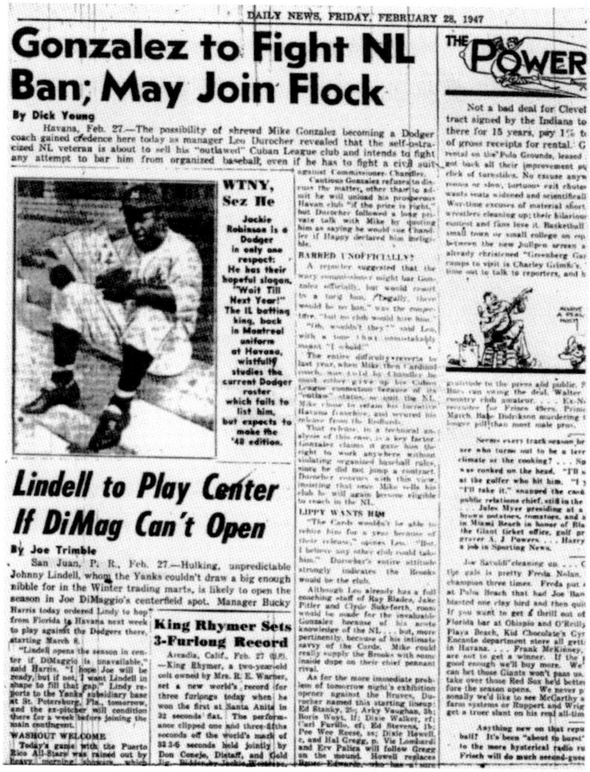

DAILY NEWS, FRIDAY, FEBRUARY 28, 1947

Gonzalez to Fight NL Ban; May Join Flock

By Dick Young

Havana, Feb. 27.—The possibility of shrewd Mike Gonzalez becoming a Dodger coach gained credence here today as manager Leo Durocher revealed that the self-ostracized NL veteran is about to sell his "outlawed" Cuban League club and intends to fight any attempt to bar him from organized baseball, even if he has to fight a civil suit against Commissioner Chandler.

WTNY, Sez He

Jackie Robinson is a Dodger in only one respect: He has their hopeful slogan, "Wait Till Next Year!" The IL batting king, back in Montreal uniform at Havana, wistfully studies the current Dodger roster which fails to list him, but expects to make the '48 edition.

Cautious Gonzalez refuses to discuss the matter, other than to admit he will unload his prosperous Havana club "if the price is right," but Durocher followed a long private talk with Mike by quoting him as saying he would sue Chandler if Happy declared him ineligible.

BARRED UNOFFICIALLY?

A reporter suggested that the wary commissioner might bar Gonzalez officially, but would resort to a tacit ban. "Legally, there would be no ban," was the conjecture, "but no club would hire him."

"Oh, wouldn't they?" said Leo, with a tone that unmistakably meant "I would."

The entire difficulty reverts to last year, when Mike, then Cardinal coach, was told by Chandler he must either give up his Cuban League connection because of its "outlaw" status, or quit the NL. Mike chose to retain his lucrative Havana franchise, and secured his release from the Redbirds.

That release, in a technical analysis of this case, is a key factor. Gonzalez claims it gave him the right to work anywhere without violating organized baseball rules, since he did not jump a contract. Durocher concurs with this view, insisting that once Mike sells his club he will again become eligible to coach in the NL.

LIPPY WANTS HIM

"The Cards wouldn't be able to rehire him for a year because of their release," opines Leo. "But I believe any other club could take him." Durocher's entire attitude strongly indicates the Brooks would be the club.

Although Leo already has a full coaching staff of Ray Blades, Jake Pitler and Clyde Sukeforth, room would be made for the invaluable Gonzalez because of his acute knowledge of the NL . . . but, more pertinently, because of his intimate savvy of the Cards. Mike could really supply the Brooks with some inside dope on their chief pennant rival.

As for the more immediate problem of tomorrow night's exhibition opener against the Braves, Durocher named this starting lineup: Ed Stanky, 2b; Arky Vaughan, 3b; Boris Woyt, lf; Dixie Walker, rf; Carl Furillo, cf; Ed Stevens, 1b; Pee Wee Reese, ss; Dixie Howell, c, and Hal Gregg, p. Vic Lombardi and Erv Palica will follow Gregg on the mound. Howell replaces [illegible]

Lindell to Play Center If DiMag Can't Open

By Joe Trimble

San Juan, P. R., Feb. 27.—Hulking, unpredictable Johnny Lindell, whom the Yanks couldn't draw a big enough nibble for in the Winter trading marts, is likely to open the season in Joe DiMaggio's centerfield spot. Manager Bucky Harris today ordered Lindy to hop from Florida to Havana next week to play against the Dodgers there, starting March 8.

"Lindell opens the season in center if DiMaggio is unavailable," said Harris. "I hope Joe will be ready, but if not, I want Lindell in shape to fill that gap." Lindy reports to the Yanks' subsidiary base at St. Petersburg, Fla., tomorrow, and the ex-pitcher will condition there for a week before joining the main contingent.

WASHOUT WELCOME

Today's game with the Puerto Rico All-Stars was rained out by heavy morning showers, which [illegible]

King Rhymer Sets 3-Furlong Record

Arcadia, Calif., Feb. 27 (UP).—King Rhymer, a two-year-old colt owned by Mrs. R. E. Warner, set a new world's record for three furlongs today when he won the first at Santa Anita in 32 seconds flat. The performance clipped one and three-fifths seconds off the world's mark of 33 3-5 seconds held jointly by Don Conejo, Distaff, and Gold Jig. [illegible]

THE POWER

Not a bad deal for Cleveland [illegible] tract signed by the Indians [illegible] there for 15 years, pay [illegible] of gross receipts for rental. [illegible]

Rickey's Montreal strategy worked wonders with the press; since Jackie was practicing with the Royals and the papers were covering Brooklyn rather than Montreal, he was under the radar. "Robinson is a Dodger in only one respect," the AP wirephoto cutline said, "He has their hopeful slogan, 'Wait 'Til Next Year!' The I.L. batting king, back in Montreal uniform in Havana, wistfully studies the current Dodger roster which fails to list him, but expects to make the '48 edition."

Clyde Sukeforth, not Durocher, was Jackie Robinson's color barrier-breaking manager during the first two games of the 1947 regular season. Leo found himself suspended for the year on charges technically unrelated to integration, so he had to watch from the stands (see the following chapter for details). Sukeforth, the interim skipper, finished 2-0 and was replaced by Burt Shotton for the duration.

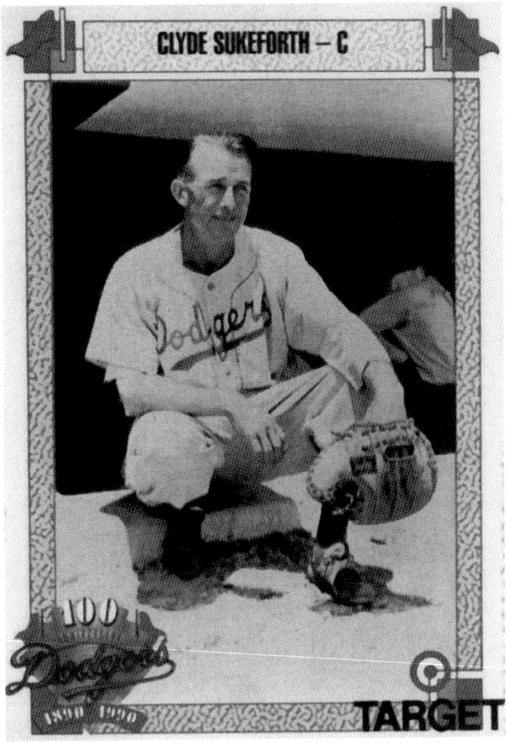

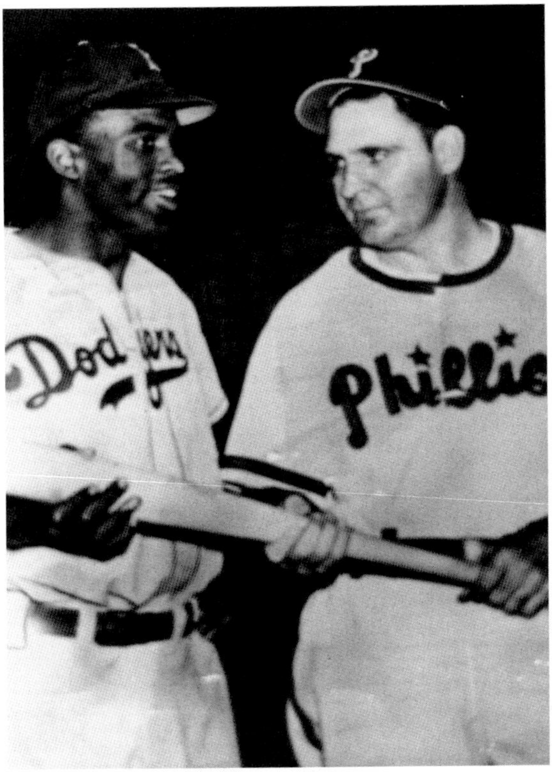

Robinson poses with Philadelphia manager Ben Chapman. "Jackie endured what no other mere mortal could or should," Duke Snider recalled. "The opposing players and fans got on him without mercy and without letup. The Phillies were especially harsh, egged on by their manager, Chapman. Jackie made us closer because of his suffering. He helped to make us champions."

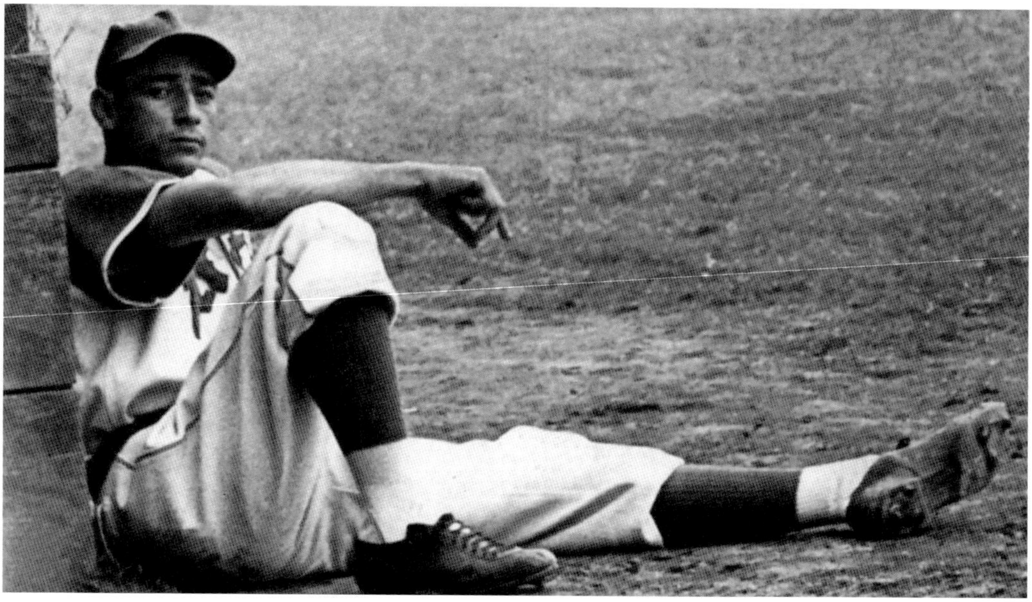

Luis Olmo played for the Dodgers in the 1940s and knew firsthand what Robinson faced. "I thought of a time playing in North Carolina," he says from his native Puerto Rico, "where some of my teammates tried not to talk to me." Olmo belted a homer in a 1949 World Series game for Brooklyn and has since been elected to the Caribbean Baseball Hall of Fame.

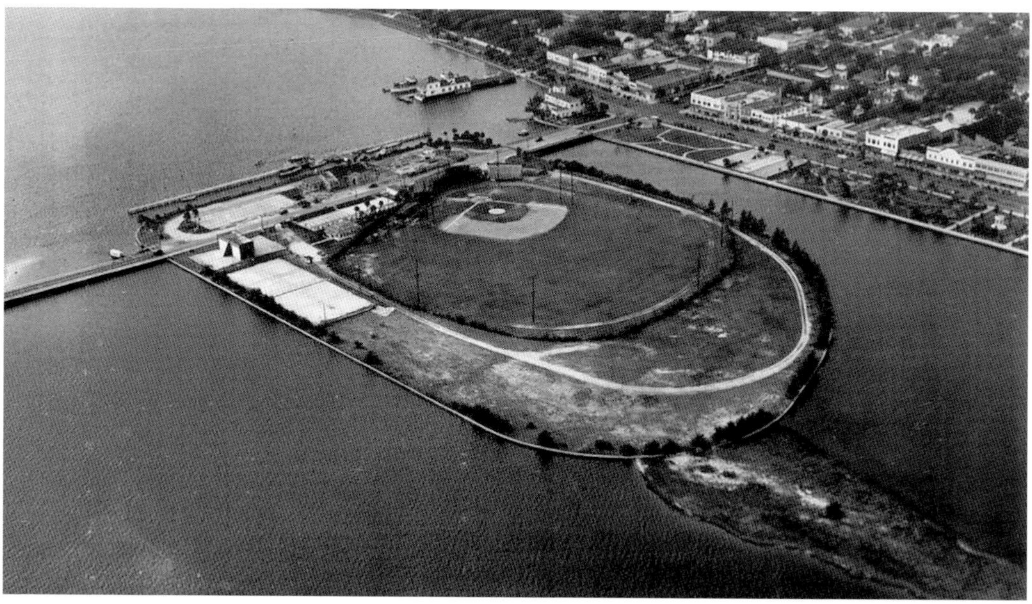

En route to Brooklyn from Cuba, Jackie and his mates played at City Island Ball Park (in Daytona Beach, Florida) that spring, when most other Florida cities refused to allow integrated games. It is now Jackie Robinson Ballpark, with an outdoor museum on the grounds. Like its Cuban counterparts, it is on an island. Built in 1914, the Daytona Cubs' home field is one of the oldest pro parks in the United States.

Rickey had pulled it off, but a new problem arose: what to do next spring? "Rickey had us train in the Dominican Republic," Rex Barney says. "Then, in places like Macon, we got letters that they were gonna kill us. Robinson and Campanella couldn't stay at the team hotel there. From their windows, they could see a charred KKK cross."

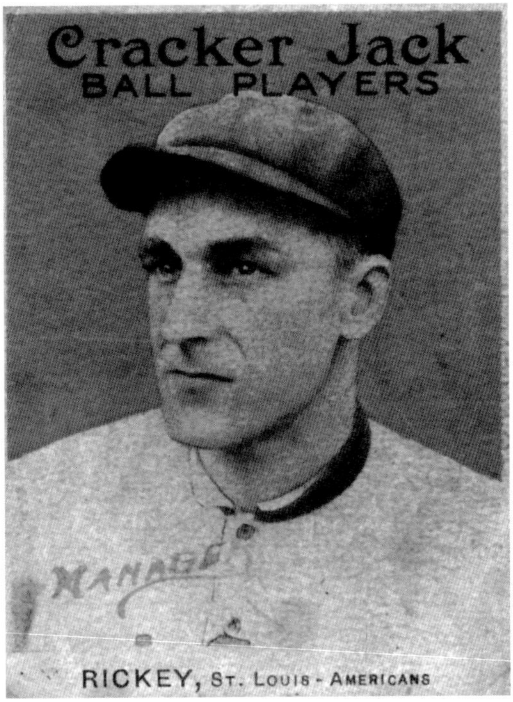

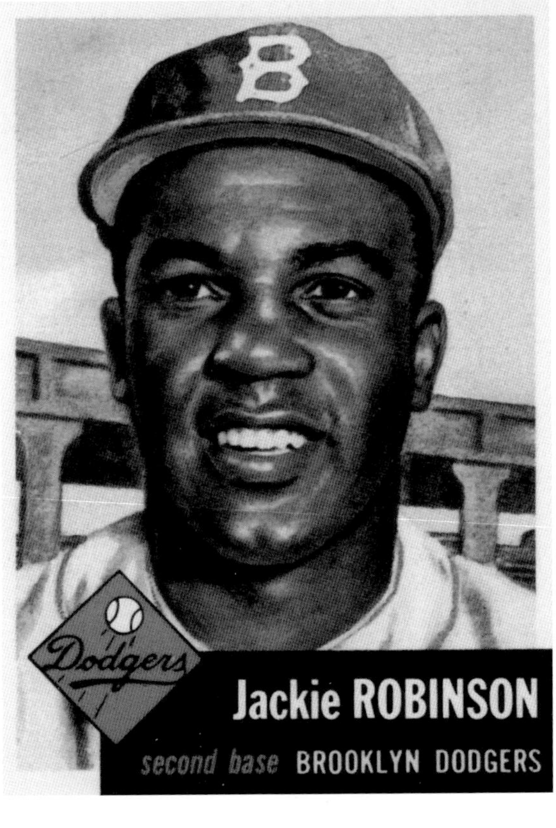

And the rest is history. Robinson led the league in steals, and Brooklyn won the National League title. Jackie was named Rookie of the Year, too. Barriers were broken, Jackie played out a fabulous Hall of Fame career, and he even helped an unlikely event unfold in Brooklyn: the 1955 World Championship.

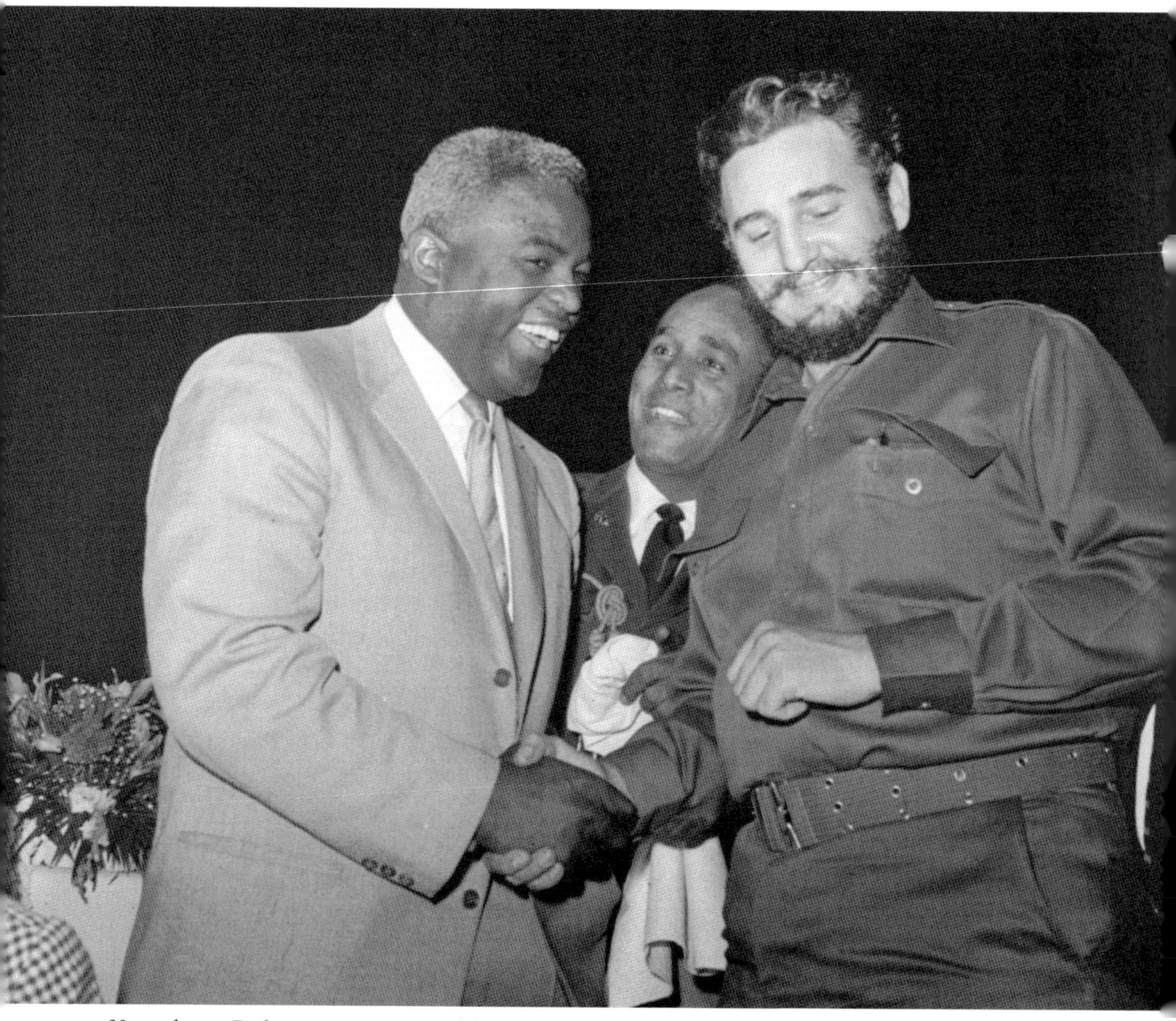

Years later, Robinson was invited back to Cuba to reminisce about the old Dodger days by the country's number one *fanatico*, Fidel Castro.

7

DUROCHER

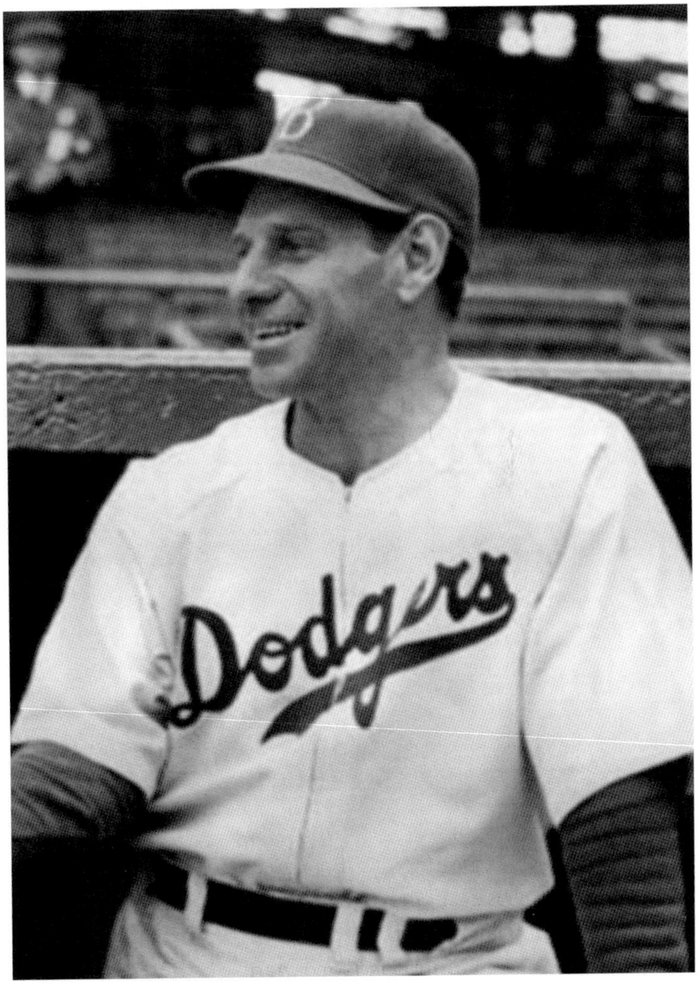

Leo "the Lip" Durocher, the Dodger manager from 1939 to 1948, was larger than life and remembered for his famous phrase, "Nice guys finish last." Also known as "Leo the Lion," the Lip's career spanned six decades, starting as a rookie teammate of Babe Ruth to managing the 1973 Astros. "Lippy" won three pennants and the 1954 World Series, and was finally elected to the Hall of Fame in 1994. "What the Lion left out of this," Pee Wee Reese said, referring to Durocher's autobiography, "would make a good book!"

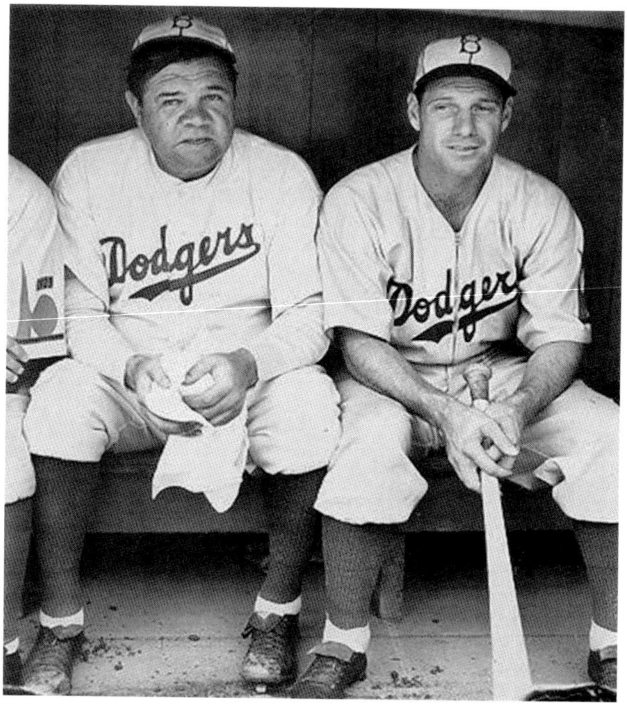

Durocher made a lot of enemies along the way, including Babe Ruth. Ruth accused him of stealing his watch, and the two endured a chilly relationship for years. However, rough-and-tumble literary figure Ernest Hemingway seemed to like him. "If Durocher had continued to come here each year," Santiago said to Manolin in *The Old Man and the Sea*, "your father would think him the greatest manager."

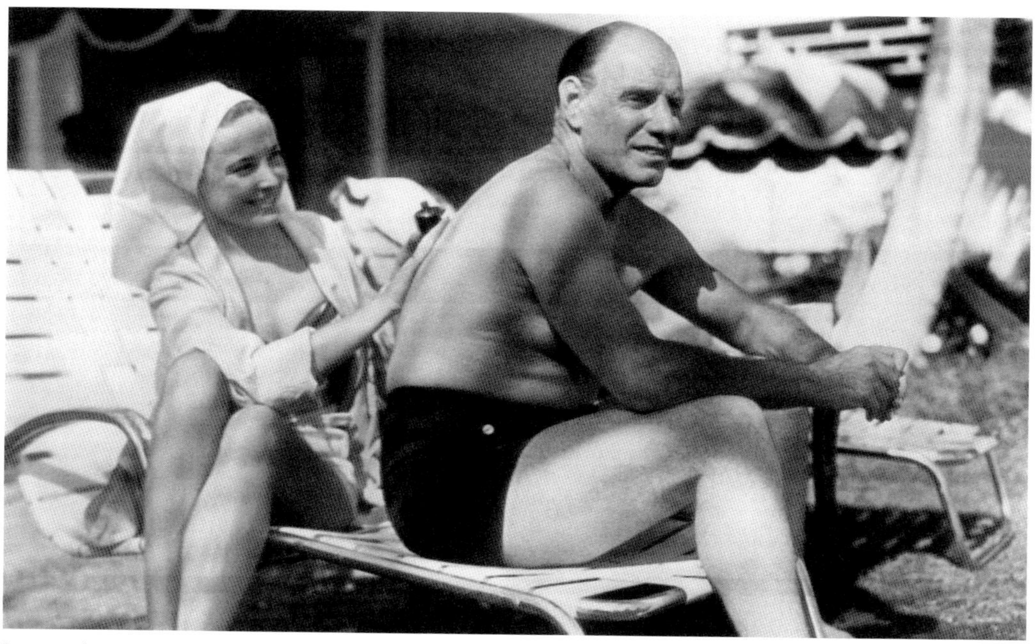

Leo and movie star Laraine Day got married during the 1947 Dodger trek to Havana. He had to bounce in and out of camp a few times, even missing Jackie Robinson's exhibition game debut, to adjust the paperwork. Once things were in order, Leo and Laraine turned their attention toward the honeymoon. Leo "spent more time rubbing suntan lotion on her than he spent at the ballpark!" "Stretch" Schultz recalls.

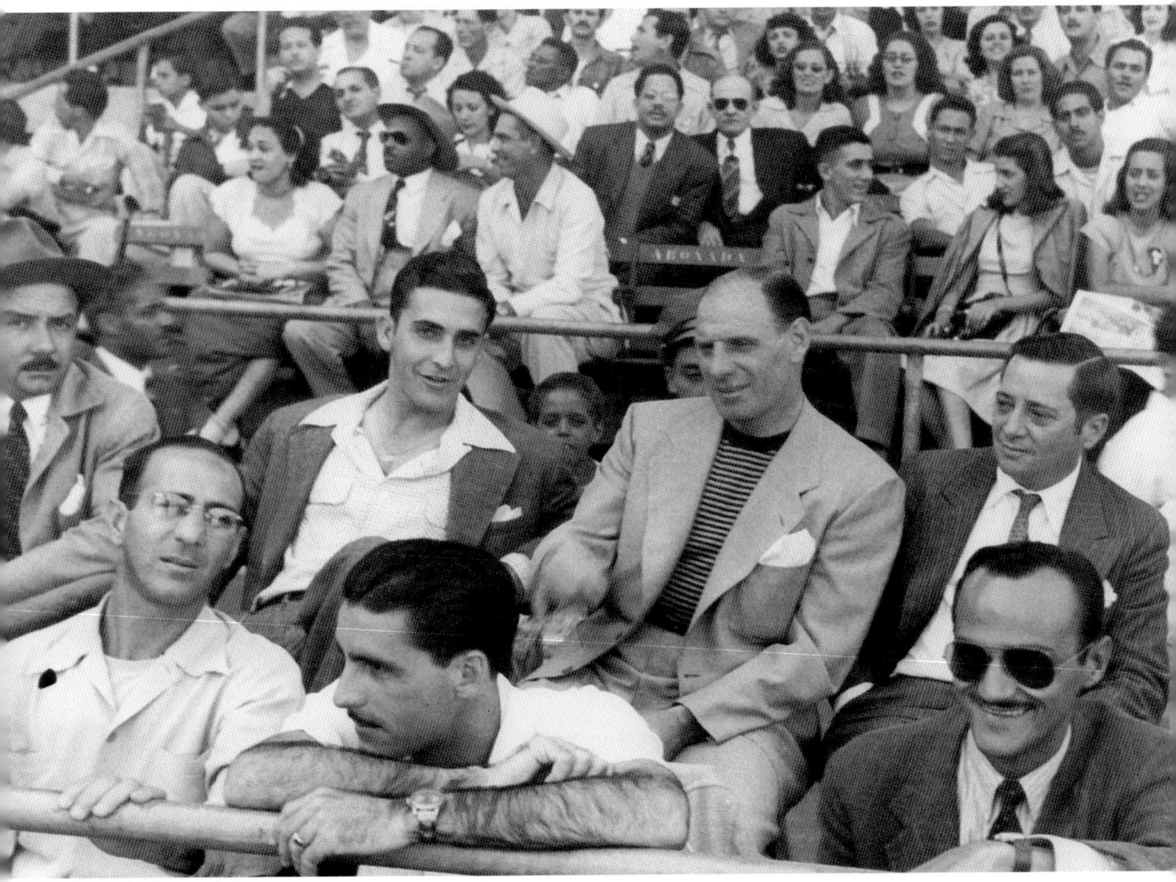

Leo enjoyed a Cuban game in the stands with Monchy de Arcos in the 1950s, but things were not so quiet during the 1941 Dodger camp. "Saturday was a rather trying day for me," Durocher wrote, "what with being escorted off the field by a squad of Batista's soldiers and all." He got into an argument with the Cuban umpire, who did not understand his colorful language. He hailed Monchy, with instruction to curse at him in Spanish. "The umpire took his mask off and started to hit me over the head with it. I started to take a punch at him. Here come Batista's soldiers with bayonets. The fans were yelling and the cushions were coming down. It took a squad of soldiers to get me out of there. The soldiers had to form a circle around me and march me to the clubhouse. After the game Batista told Larry MacPhail it was the greatest thing he had ever seen: 'Tell Durocher to do it again tomorrow.' He thought from everything he had heard about me that it was my act."

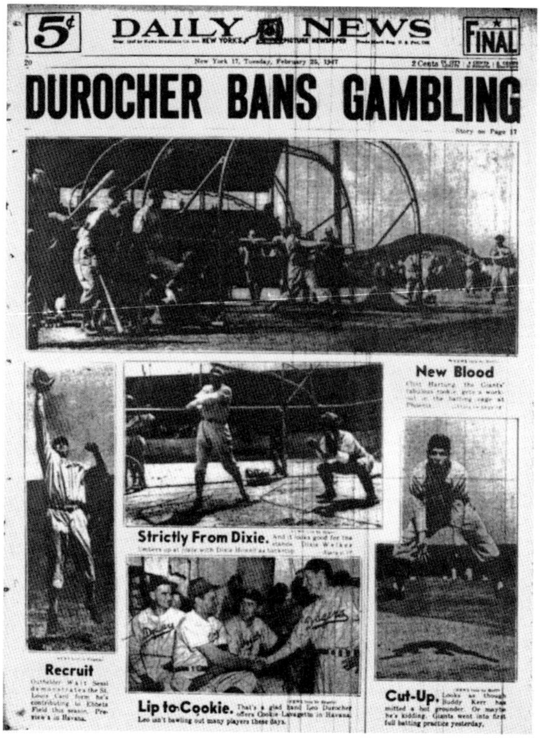
5¢ DAILY NEWS FINAL

New York 17, Tuesday, February 25, 1947

DUROCHER BANS GAMBLING

Story on Page 17

New Blood

Strictly From Dixie. And it looks good for the stands. Dixie Walker

Recruit

Outfielder Walt Sessi demonstrates the St. Louis Card form he's contributing to Ebbets Field this season. Preview's in Havana.

Lip to Cookie. That's a glad hand Leo Durocher offers Cookie Lavagetto in Havana. Leo isn't bawling out many players these days.

Cut-Up. Looks as though Buddy Kerr has mitted a hot grounder. Or maybe he's kidding. Giants went into first full batting practice yesterday.

The commissioner, "Happy" Chandler, was leaning on Durocher because of Leo's gambling ties, so he had to go the extra mile in dice-laden Havana. "The Dodger camp, which once resembled a buzzing Reno game room during off-field hours," said the *Daily News*, "has become a virtual monastery as a result of a stringent anti-gambling edict issued by manager Leo Durocher. Lippy, doubtless guided by Commissioner Happy Chandler's admonitions during winter meetings in Los Angeles, has enacted a rule barring card-playing."

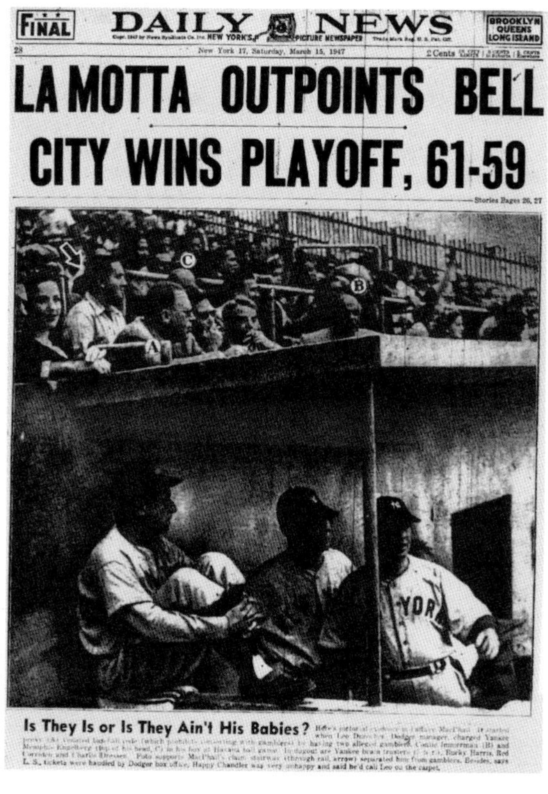
FINAL DAILY NEWS BROOKLYN QUEENS LONG ISLAND

New York 17, Saturday, March 15, 1947

LA MOTTA OUTPOINTS BELL
CITY WINS PLAYOFF, 61-59

Stories Pages 26, 27

Is They Is or Is They Ain't His Babies? ... when Leo Durocher, Dodger manager, charged Yankee ... having two alleged gamblers, Connie Immerman (B) and Memphis Engelberg (top of his head, C) in his box at Havana ball game. In dugout are Yankee brain trusters (l. to r.), Bucky Harris, Red Corriden and Charlie Dressen. Foto supports MacPhail's claim stairway (through rail, arrow) separated him from gamblers. Besides, says L. S., tickets were handled by Dodger box office. Happy Chandler was very unhappy and said he'd call Leo on the carpet.

A war of words erupted between Durocher and Yankees president Larry MacPhail, who had at one time been the president of the Dodgers. Each accused the other of hanging out with gamblers and other seedy sorts. When the papers printed photographs of MacPhail sitting next to the bad guys, Durocher publicly criticized MacPhail, but the commissioner, a good friend of Larry's, called Durocher on the carpet instead.

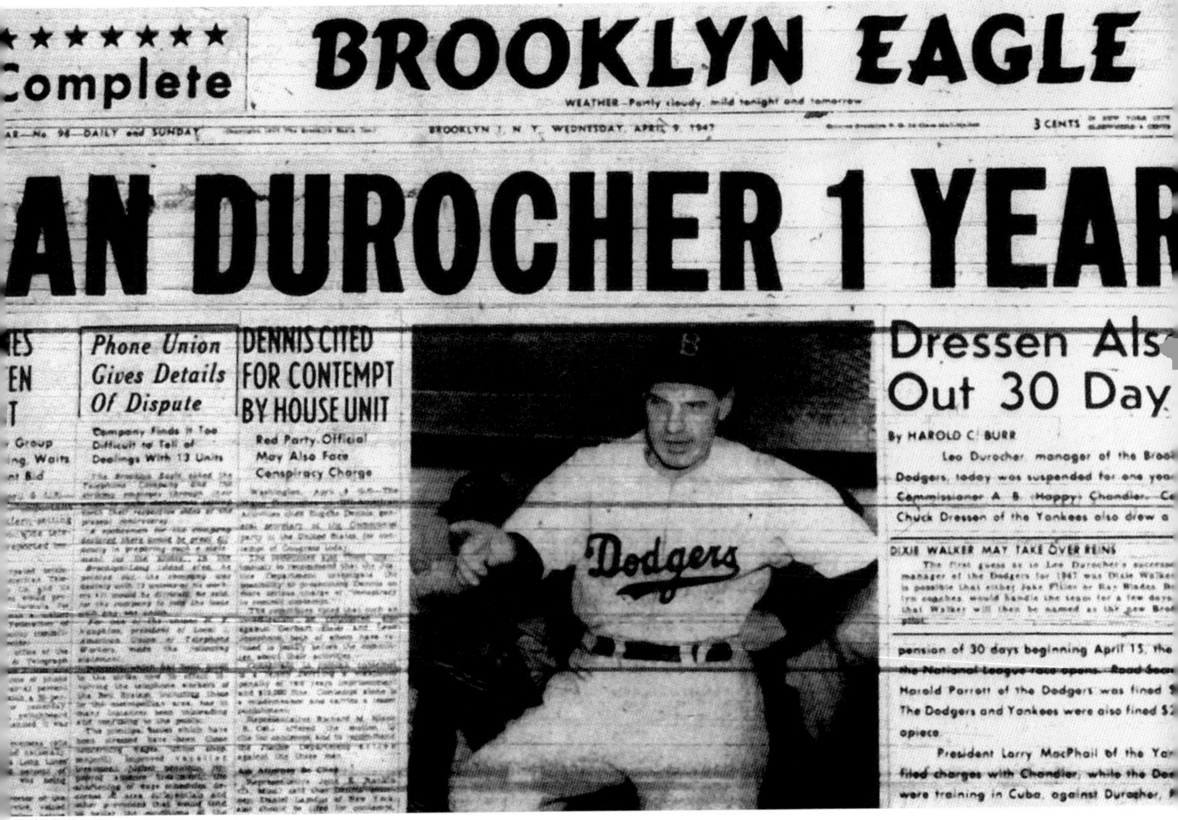
Complete

BROOKLYN EAGLE

WEATHER—Partly cloudy, mild tonight and tomorrow

DAILY and SUNDAY — BROOKLYN, N. Y., WEDNESDAY, APRIL 9, 1947 — 3 CENTS

AN DUROCHER 1 YEAR

Phone Union Gives Details Of Dispute

Company Finds It Too Difficult to Tell of Dealings With 13 Units

DENNIS CITED FOR CONTEMPT BY HOUSE UNIT

Red Party Official May Also Face Conspiracy Charge

Dressen Als Out 30 Day

By HAROLD C. BURR

Leo Durocher manager of the Broo Dodgers, today was suspended for one yea Commissioner A. B. (Happy) Chandler. Ca Chuck Dressen of the Yankees also drew a

DIXIE WALKER MAY TAKE OVER REINS

pension of 30 days beginning April 15, the the National League race opens. Road Sec Harold Parrott of the Dodgers was fined The Dodgers and Yankees were also fined $ apiece.

President Larry MacPhail of the Ya filed charges with Chandler, while the Do were training in Cuba, against Durocher,

Commissioner Chandler called for closed-door hearings to take place in Florida; 22 witnesses were subpoenaed, and Durocher was the first to testify. "Amid the bizarre setting of swaying palms and not far distance from the winter quarters of the Ringling Circus," *the New York Times* reported, "Commissioner Chandler today conducted his extraordinary hearing." When the mud settled, Durocher was suspended for one year, allegedly for conduct detrimental to the game, but most Dodgers felt it was the only way Chandler could slap Rickey's hand for integrating baseball that season.

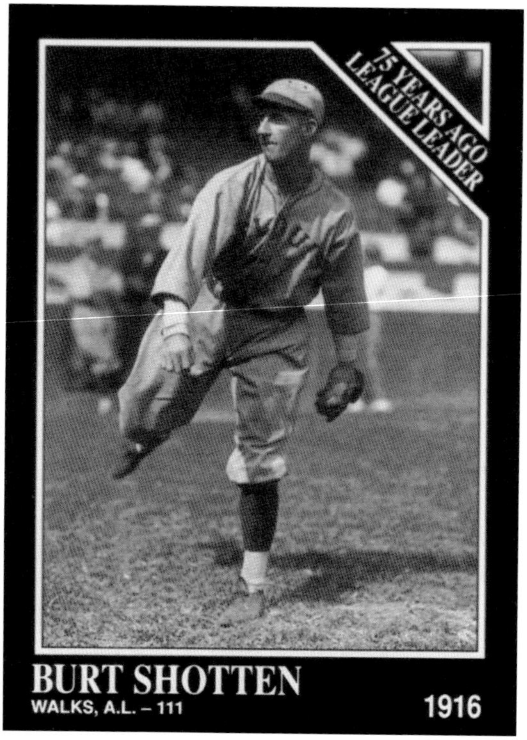

Burt Shotton took over as skipper through the turbulent waters of Jackie Robinson's rookie year, and his beloved Bums won the pennant. "It was a good thing Burt Shotton was already white-haired when he took over as manager of the 1947 Dodgers," legendary Brooklyn broadcaster "Red" Barber observed. "Otherwise what he had to contend with would have turned his head the color of new-fallen snow. Shotton was steady as a rock."

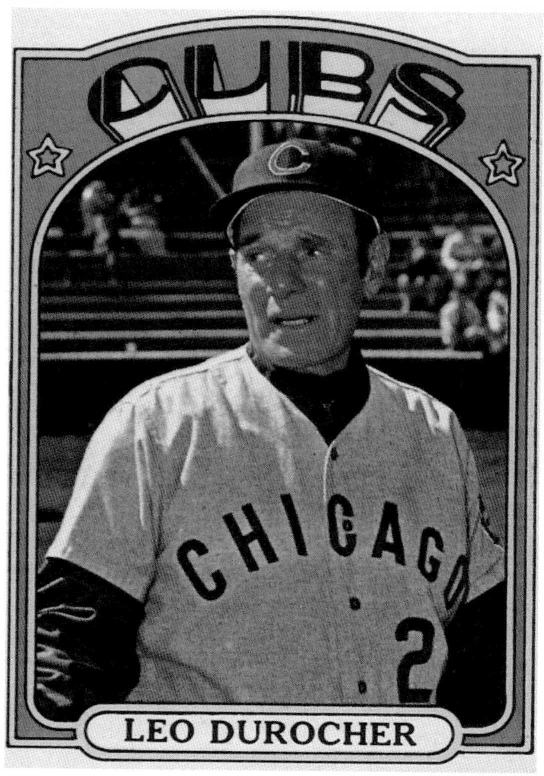

Leo Durocher returned in 1948 to dodge a bullet. "The vultures hovering nearly had some Dodger corpses to feed on," according to the *Daily News*. En route to their mountaintop hotel, "at a sharp turn the auto holding Durocher, secretary [Harold] Parrott, Gene Hermanski, and rookie Butch Woyt crashed. It missed catapulting down the 2,000-foot incline, thanks to a 3-foot-high barrier." Always the survivor, Leo was still managing decades later.

8

THE DOMINICAN REPUBLIC

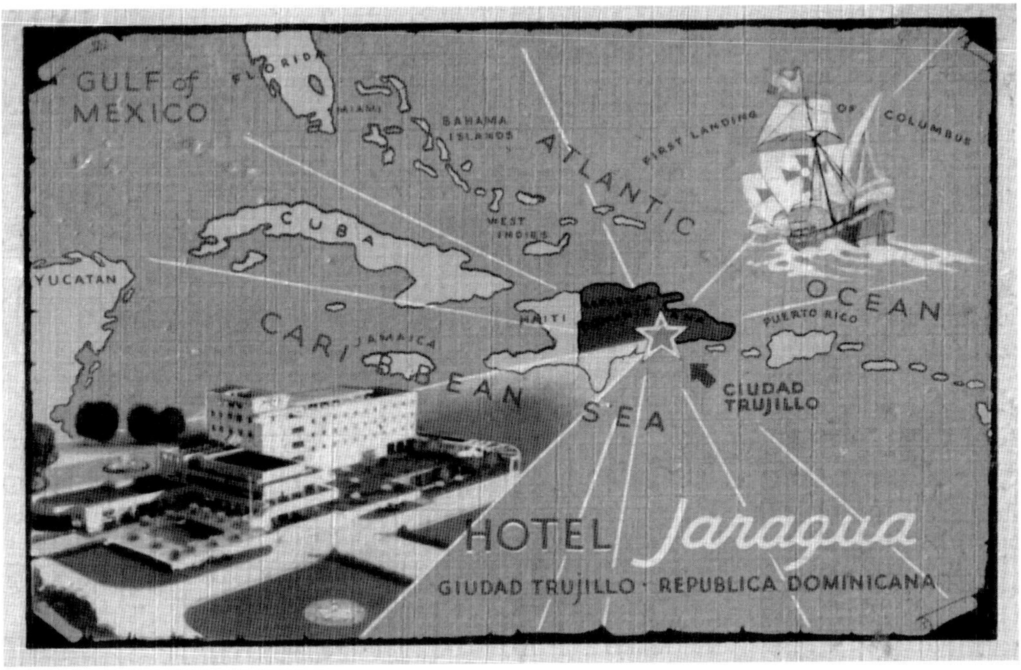

For 1948, the Dominican Republic outbid Cuba, so the Dodgers went to Ciudad Trujillo (which has since been renamed Santo Domingo). Rafael Trujillo was elected president of the Dominican Republic in 1930, winning 99 percent of the vote. He was assassinated in 1961. "The Brooks are headquartered in the Hotel Jaragua, which is slightly more impressive than the Taj Mahal," swooned *the New York Times*. "It gleams whitely in its setting among palm trees. A hundred yards beyond, the blue waters of the Caribbean curl against the beach. That's the kind of joint our Brooks have as their home. So far no one has complained."

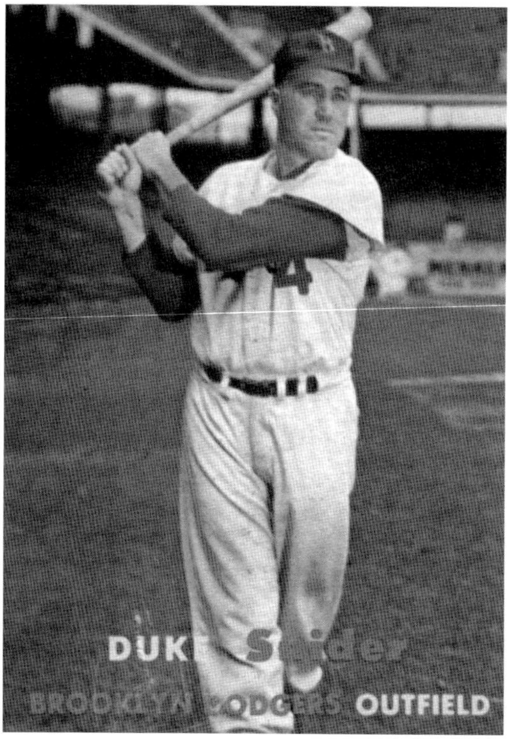

Hall of Famer Duke Snider went back to the minors in 1947 for more seasoning. "Snider," the *Times* said, "was looking for that strike zone. Asked whether he found it, he blushed and replied: 'I certainly hope so.' " His mark on the locals persists. "When the guys are playing domino," says Havana native Antonio Valdez, "if somebody wins with a 'two,' he doesn't shout, *Duque*, for 'deuce'—he shouts, *Duque Snider*!"

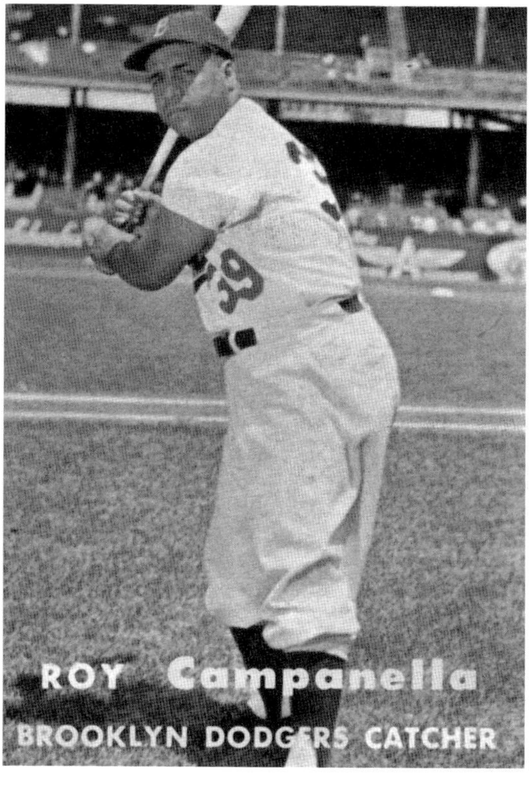

Once Robinson paved the way, Roy "Campy" Campanella could join the Dodgers in 1948. But spring training was still filled with racist peril, particularly on the trip through the South after the Caribbean camp. "We got a telegram from the wizard of the Ku Klux Klan," Campy said. "If you come to Atlanta, we'll kill you. We'll shoot you out on the field." The Klan's Grand Dragon called for a boycott, but the game sold out. Robbie stole home in the first inning.

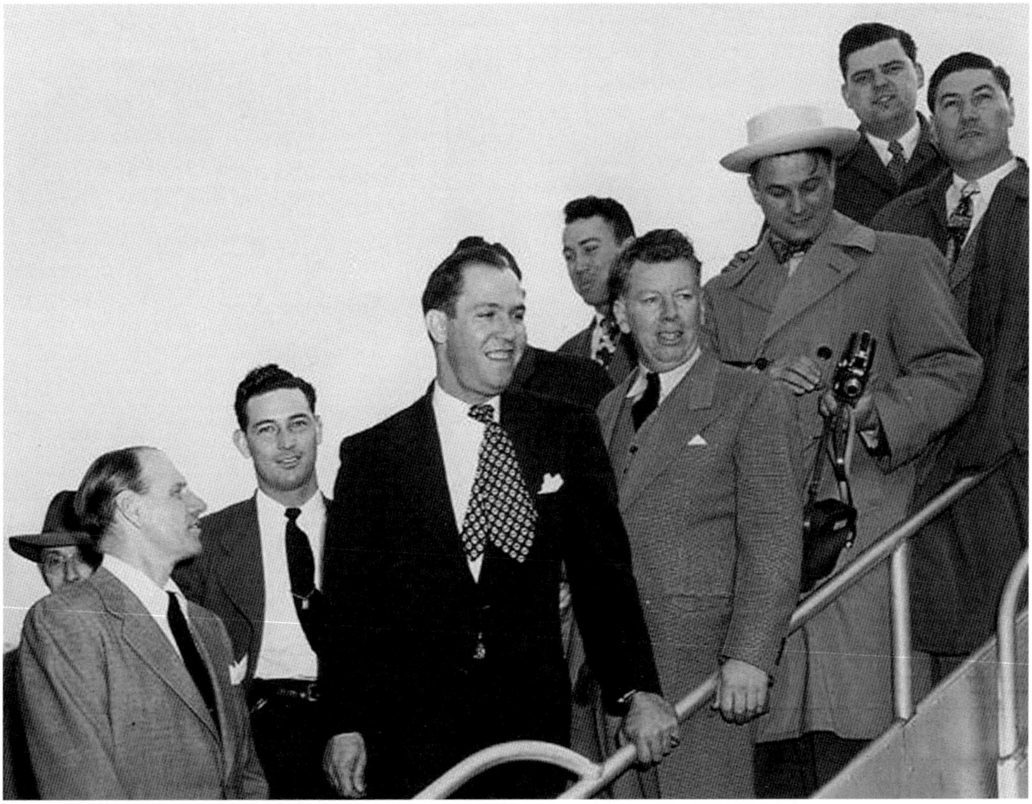

The 1948 Dodgers arrived in Santo Domingo aboard their Pan Am clipper ship. Seen here are, from left to right, manager Leo Durocher, Harry Taylor, Pete Reiser, club secretary Harold Parrott, Gene Hermanski, photographer Bill Wasilevich, and photographer Walter Kelleher.

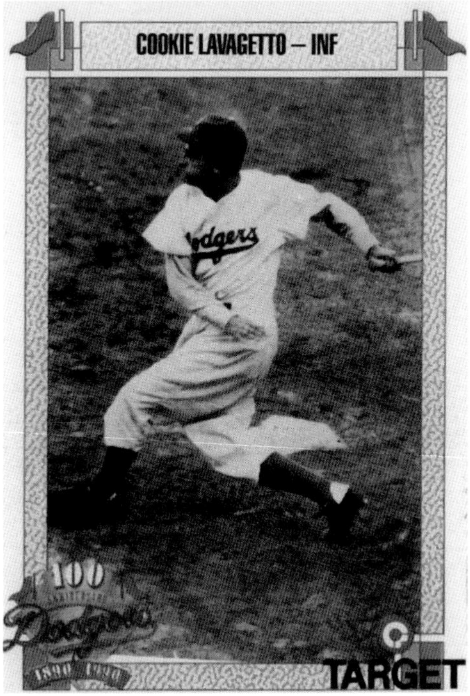

Latecomers straggled in. "Branca arrived by plane from Puerto Rico, after the boat he boarded at Mobile was held up by fog," said the *Times*. Also, "traveling by train from California, Arky Vaughan and Cookie Lavagetto spent twelve hours last night on the airways." Lavagetto was fresh from the 1947 World Series where his ninth-inning pinch-double ended a no-hitter and won the game, but after a bad spring, he was released.

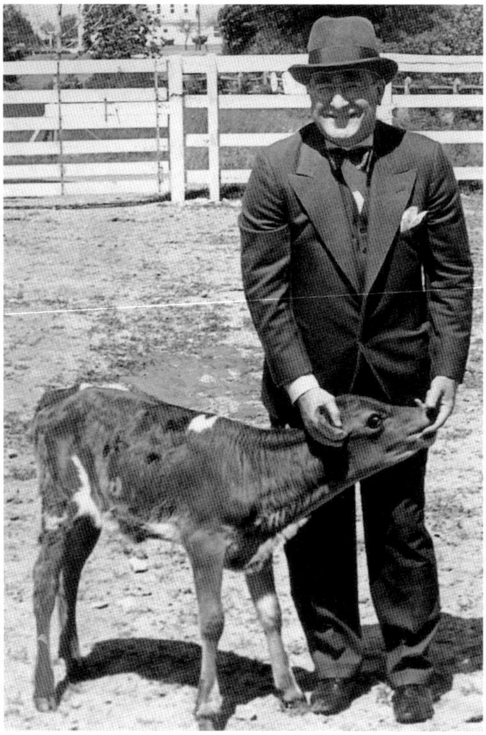

Rickey, here with a calf, tried to keep the boys well fed. "We stayed close to the hotel," Preacher Roe recalls, because "we had a hard time trying to find something to eat. They made chicken, and they tried beef, but . . . they didn't cook it like we did. They sauteed it in that butter, but it tasted like rotten eggs. They finally brought some T-bones in, but they put those in that butter too!"

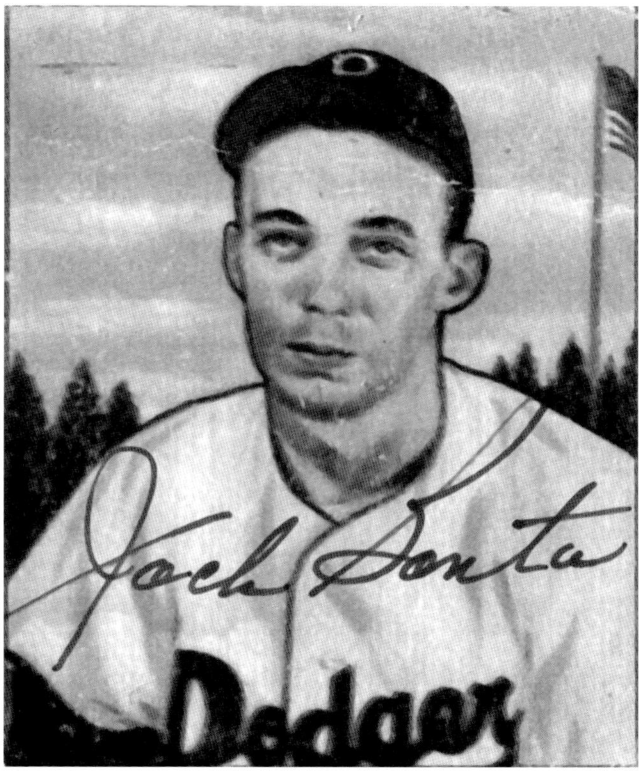

After finally downing a good steak, the boys had some free time. "I don't think we met any local gals," Jack Banta reflects. "We were pretty young and naive. We always talked about girls, but we didn't get much action." Jack did get some action in the 1949 World Series, pitching relief in three games after going 10-6 during the regular season.

Chuck Connors was a television and movie star, best remembered as *The Rifleman*, yet he also played in the NBA for the Boston Celtics, as well as briefly for the Brooklyn Dodgers and Chicago Cubs. "Yeah, Chuck Connors was there," says pitcher Lefty Martin. "What a character. There aren't many clean stories about Chuck!"

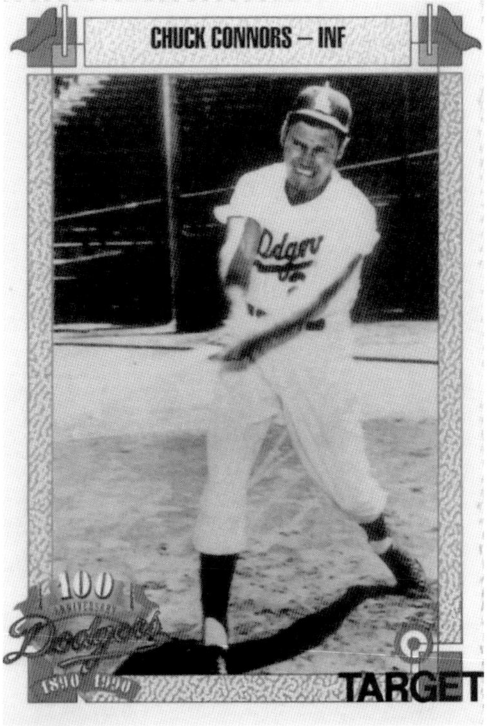

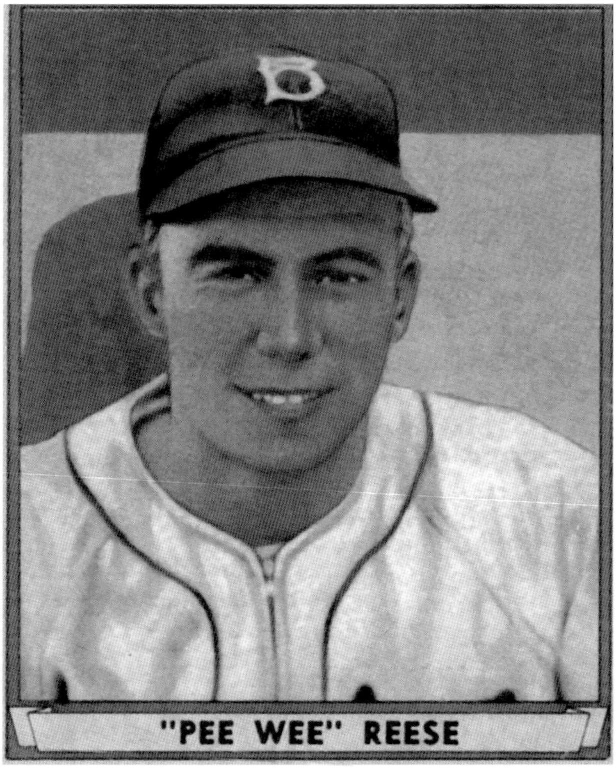

"Durocher solved the problem of no competition for the Dodgers today by forming two teams and turning them loose against each other," the *Times* reported. "Pee Wee Reese, still nursing his sore right wing, became manager for a day and piloted the losing team. While coaching at third Reese was roundly roasted by Durocher and many of his mates for sending in George Bradshaw to bat for pitcher Ole Olsen, a good hitter, in the final frame and then ordering a bunt."

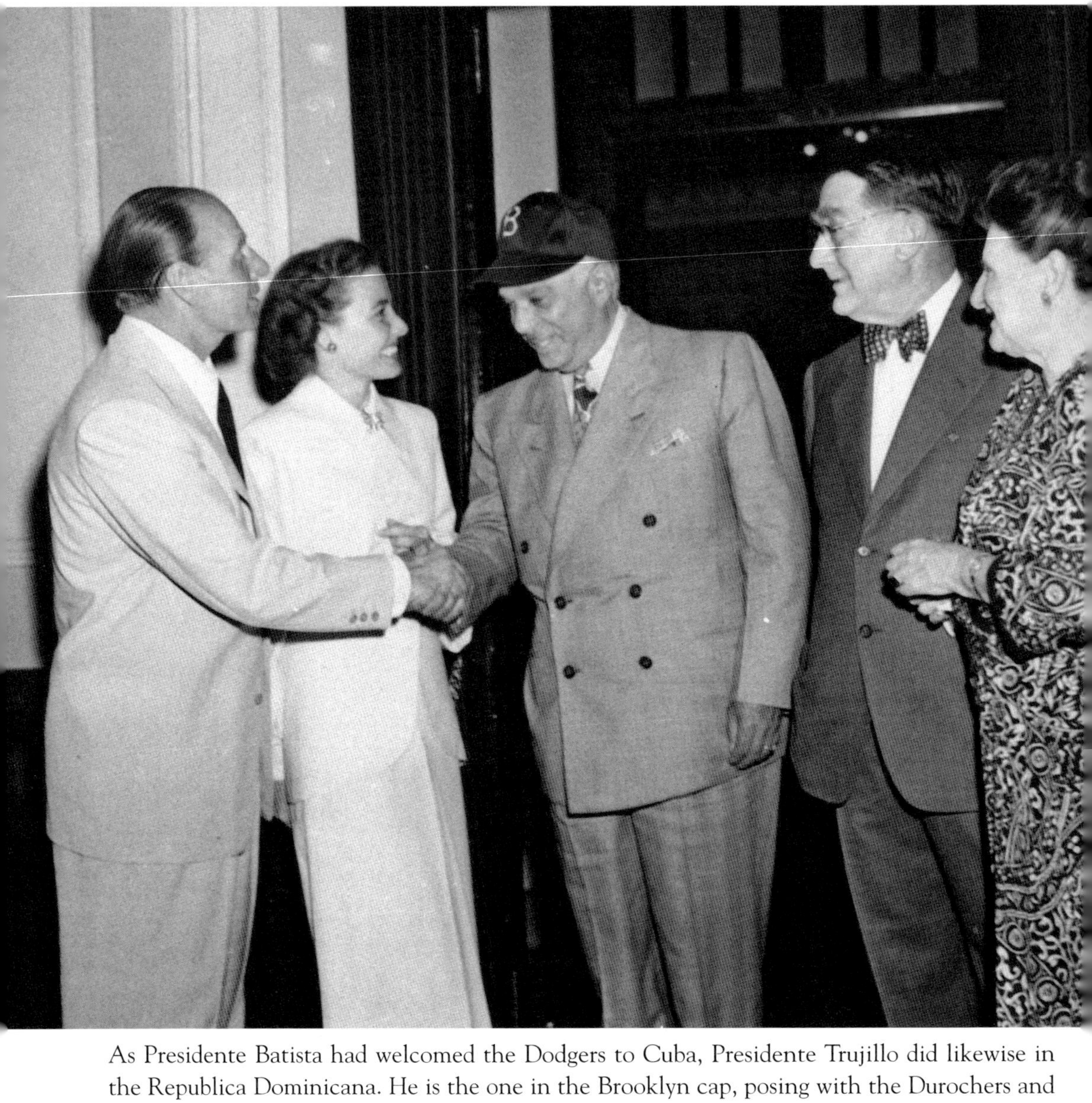

As Presidente Batista had welcomed the Dodgers to Cuba, Presidente Trujillo did likewise in the Republica Dominicana. He is the one in the Brooklyn cap, posing with the Durochers and the Rickeys.

One flight, Preacher Roe says, two engines failed. Above water, the pilot announced, " 'We may have to set down. Have something that floats. Don't worry, there's no sharks . . . but lotsa barracuda.' They foamed down the field, with fire trucks there. The engines burst into flames. The stewardesses did a job outa this world, goin' through the crowd, settin' on boys' laps, brushin' their hair back, tellin' em it'd be all right."

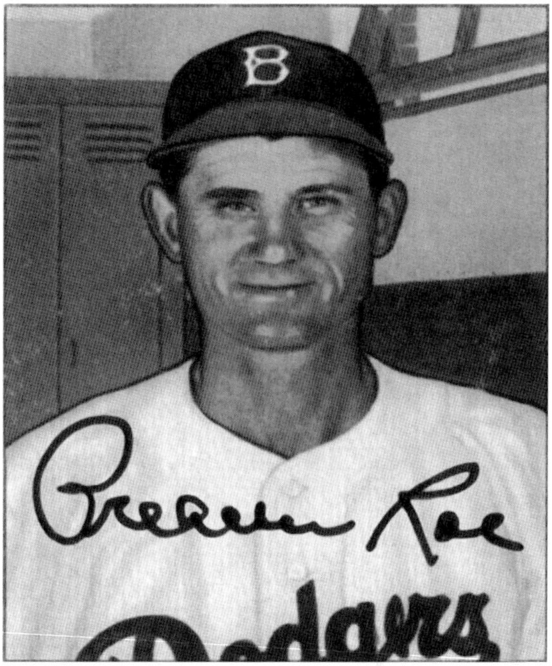

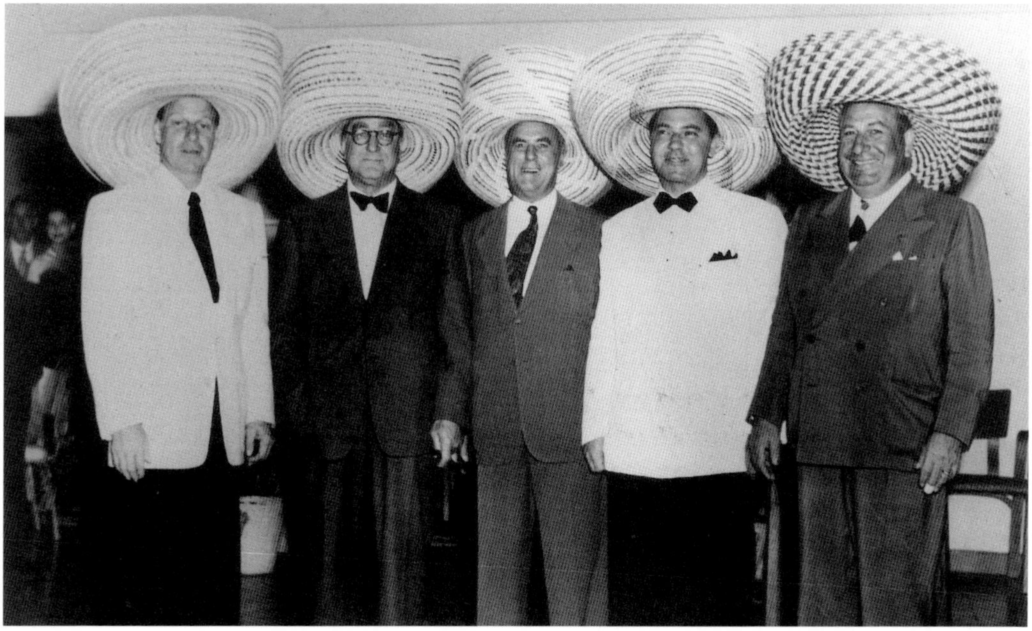

After the final game, the *Times* said, "The big Branch tossed an elaborate dinner party on the Hotel Jaragua roof, attended by representatives of Pres. Rafael Trujillo and virtually committed the Dodgers to returning here for training next year. Rickey told the gathering he hoped to come back and both he and Manager Durocher praised the climate, the hospitality, and everything else inordinately. It was a Dodger-Dominican love feast." Seen here on the roof are, from left to right, Durocher, Rickey, and hotel staffers George Wartman, Anthony Vaughan, and Charles Rochester.

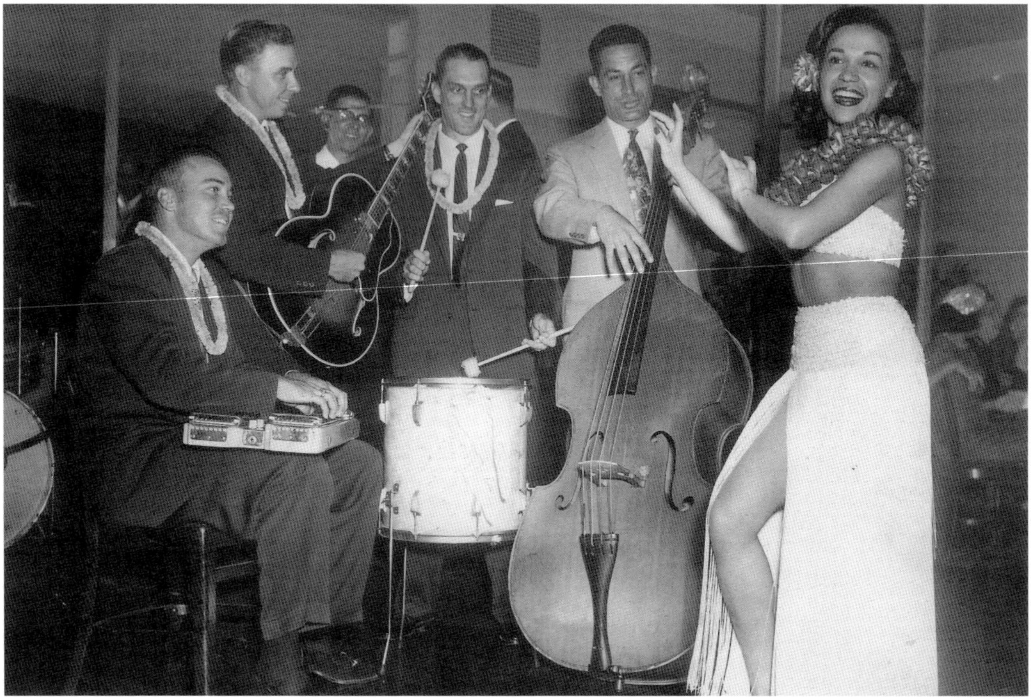

Before leaving the isle, Dodgers Duke Snider, Pee Wee Reese, Carl Erskine, and Carl Furillo (pictured above from left to right) got in a little extra evening exercise at the hotel after practice.

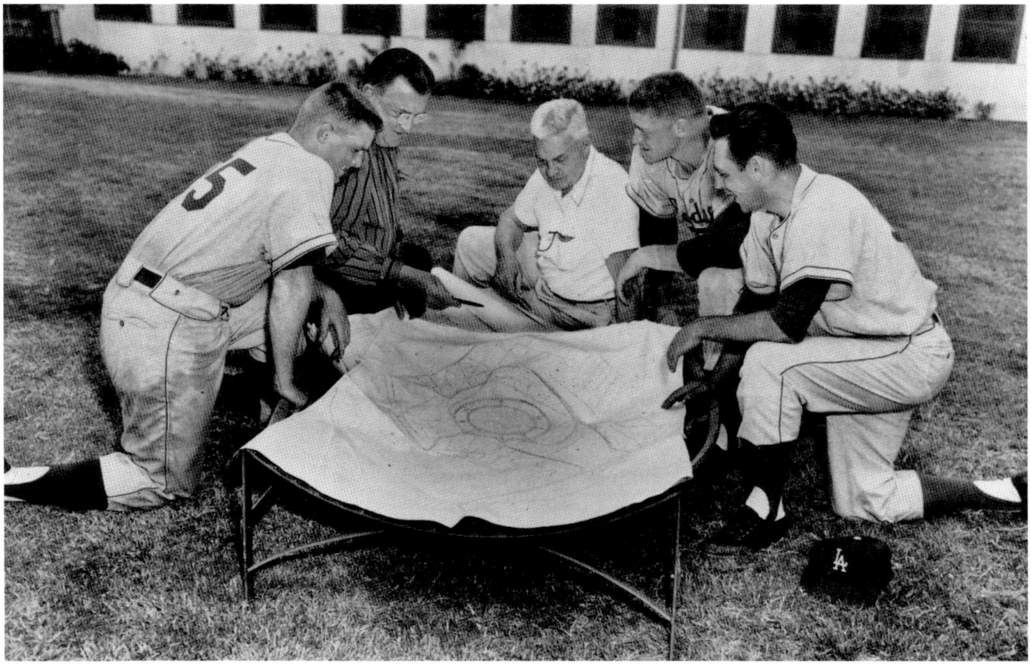

Once they finished camp and found a working plane, the team went to Vero Beach, Florida, for their first look at Dodgertown, which Rickey converted from a U.S. Navy Air Force base.

9

FIDEL

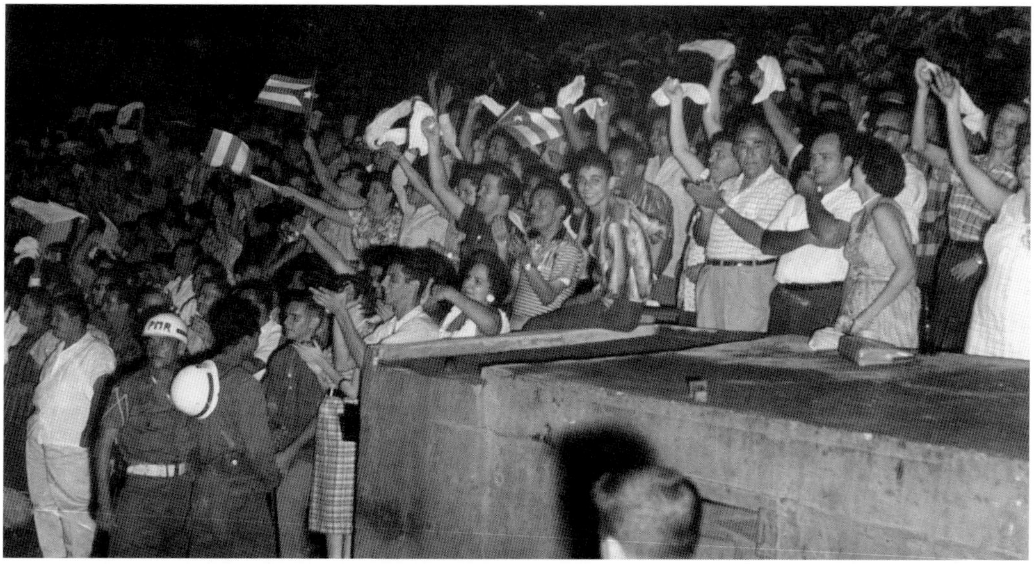

Fidel Castro has been on the world stage for more than half a century, surviving 11 U.S. presidencies. Legend says the Washington Senators offered him a tryout. This is not true, but he did pitch in school and has interacted with plenty of American ballplayers over the years. Castro seized power during the 1959 Winter League season, and heavily armed soldiers filled the stands and spilled out onto the fields. Castro would often appear, entering with great fanfare. Gene Mauch managed there and remembers, "There were 35,000 people at the ballpark every night, waving their handkerchiefs, chanting, 'Fi-del . . . *Feee*-del!' "

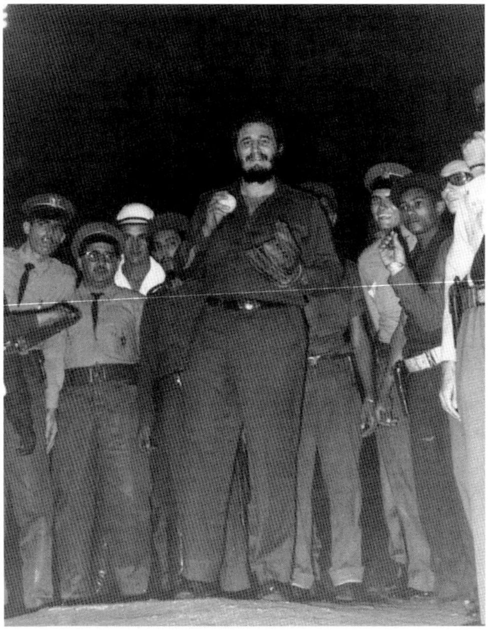

The newly self-elected president would wear his fatigues (complimented by a firearm) as he walked to the mound to throw out the first pitch. After the Winter Leagues wrapped up, the regular 1959 American season began; Havana still had an International League team, so nervous competitors flew in from U.S. cities like Buffalo, Columbus, Miami, Richmond, and Rochester, as well as Montreal and Toronto in Canada. There, Fidel would often take his entourage out to the ball game.

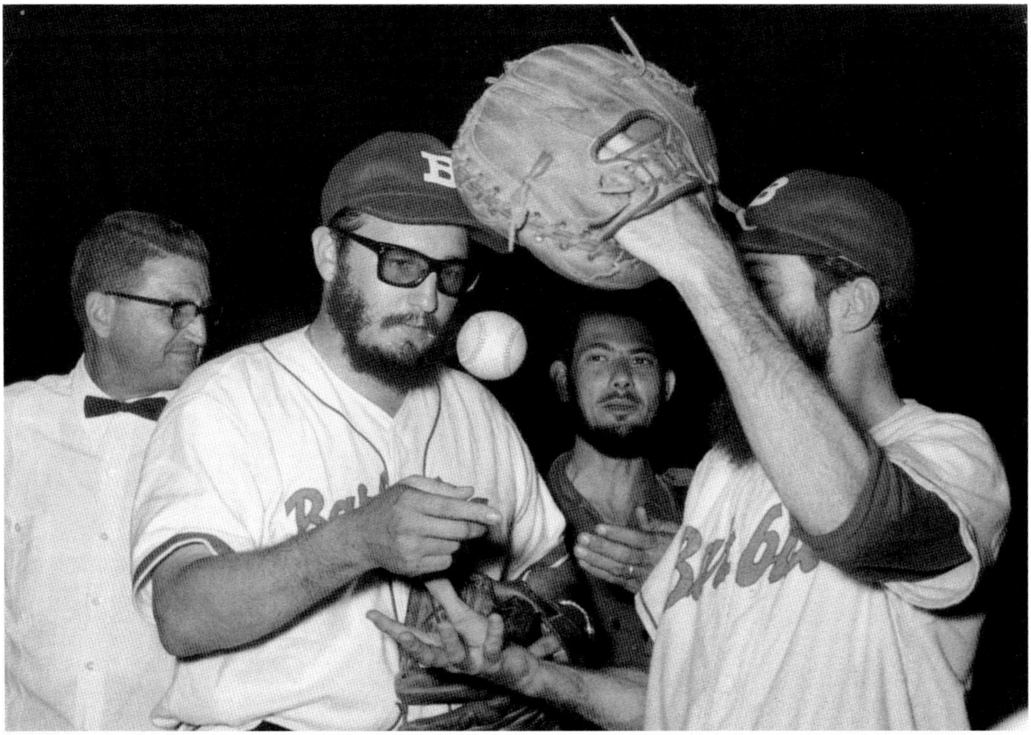

Castro organized his own team, the Barbudas, and barnstormed around the isle against regional teams. *Barbuda* translated as "bearded one," and it was considered a sign of honor. In theory, the longer the beard, the longer one had been holed up in the mountains, preparing to ambush Batista. Before fellow revolutionary Camilo Cienfuegos was killed, he often caught for Castro's team.

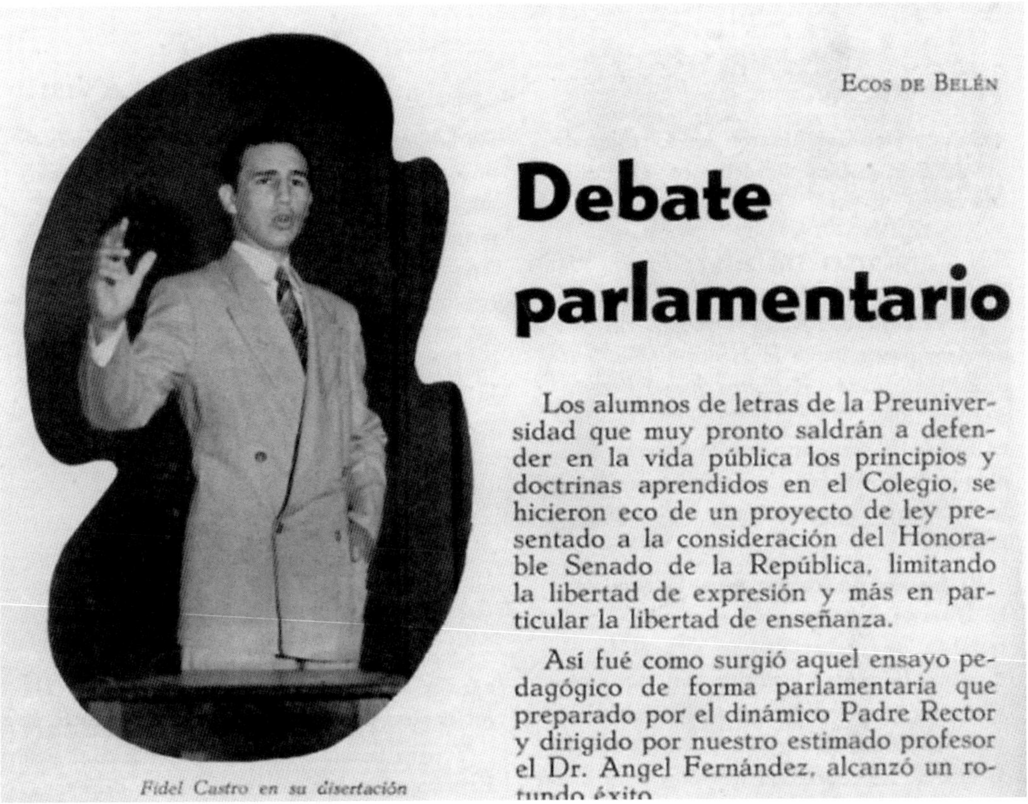

Ecos de Belén

Debate parlamentario

Los alumnos de letras de la Preuniversidad que muy pronto saldrán a defender en la vida pública los principios y doctrinas aprendidos en el Colegio, se hicieron eco de un proyecto de ley presentado a la consideración del Honorable Senado de la República, limitando la libertad de expresión y más en particular la libertad de enseñanza.

Así fué como surgió aquel ensayo pedagógico de forma parlamentaria que preparado por el dinámico Padre Rector y dirigido por nuestro estimado profesor el Dr. Angel Fernández, alcanzó un rotundo éxito.

Fidel Castro en su disertación

As a clean-shaven teen, Castro attended Belen Academy. Young Fidel practiced oratory to become a lawyer. After law school at the University of Havana, he sued the government when Batista canceled elections. Bastista dismissed the case, and in revolt, Castro gathered a band of armed guerrillas and staged a coup. After being released from jail, Fidel regrouped and overthrew Batista on January 1, 1959.

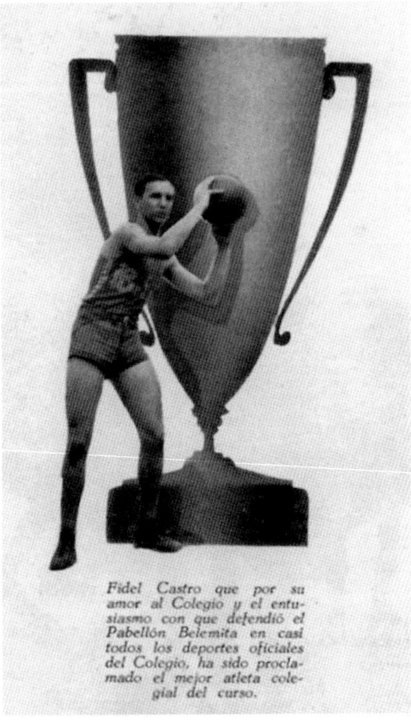

Fidel Castro que por su amor al Colegio y el entusiasmo con que defendió el Pabellón Belemita en casi todos los deportes oficiales del Colegio, ha sido proclamado el mejor atleta colegial del curso.

Quite the jock in school, Castro played basketball and baseball and was captain of the hiking team. The 1945 yearbook stated, "He has been a true athlete, defending with valor and pride the banner of our school."

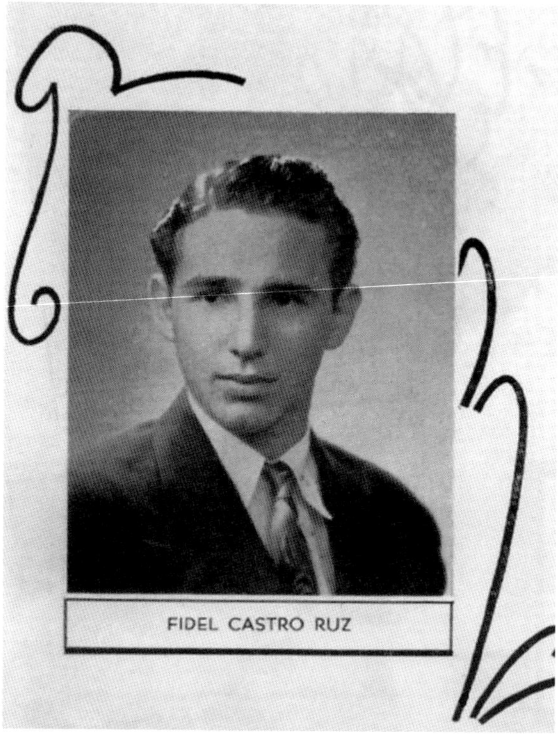

Conrado "Connie" Marrero, the longtime Cuban star who also pitched for the Washington Senators, recalls Castro as a young hopeful. "Yes, I saw him play once, by coincidence, when he was a pitcher," says Connie at age 93, living in Havana. After being asked if Castro was any good, he answered after a long pause with a wry grin, "I think Fidel liked to pitch. Yes, let us say he liked to pitch."

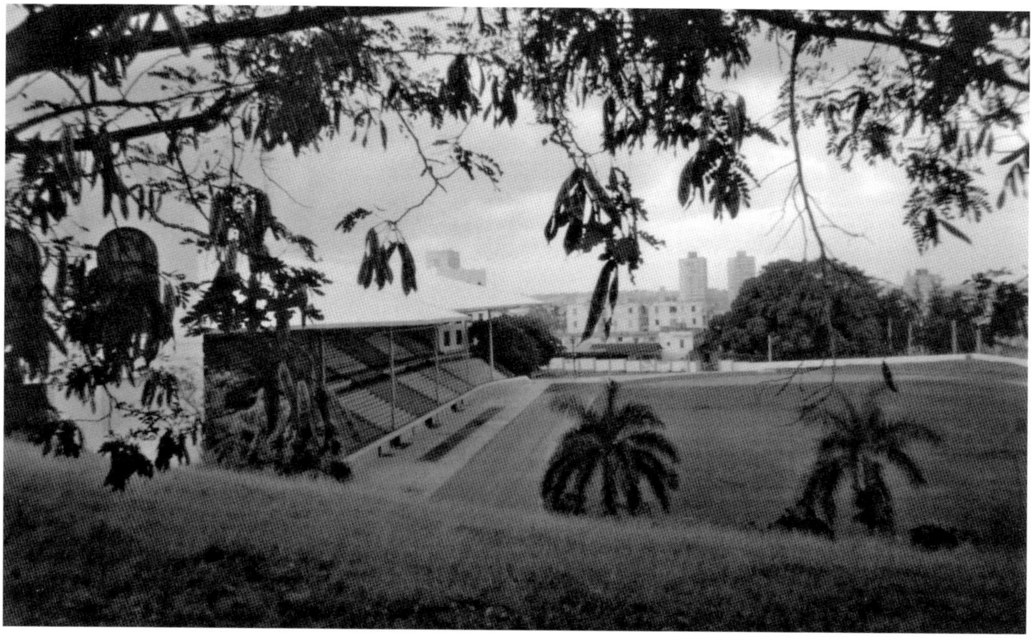

The University of Havana baseball stadium, where Fidel played in 1947, is still in use. Through his interpreter, Marrero adds some detail: "He wasn't very good. Then, he was very bad. But now, everyone would say he was very good. He didn't have anything—just a straight ball and a little bit of a screwball."

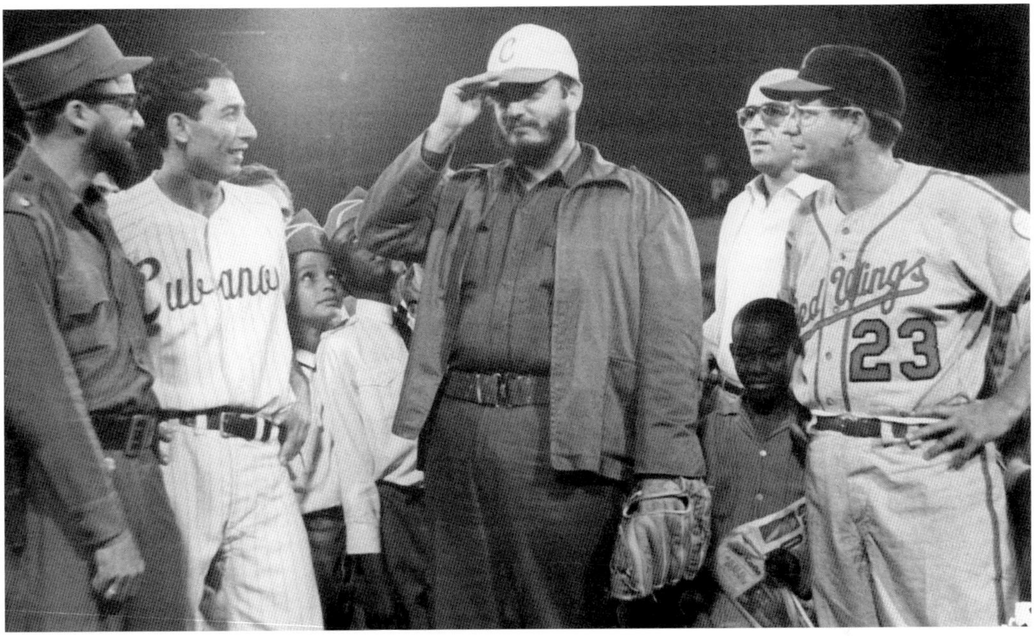

After training in Cuba as a Dodgers pitcher in 1947, Clyde King returned in the 1950s as manager of the Rochester Red Wings. On opening night in 1959, Castro threw out the first pitch. King recalls their pregame conversation on the mound: "He says, 'You rememmer peetching agaanst oonibersitee of habana?' And I nodded; we'd split squads and played against the college team. Then he said, 'You rememmer who you peetch agaanst? Eet was mee you peetch agaanst!' I laughed, and I asked if he remembered the score. He said he didn't, and I told him, 'It was 16-1!' And he says, 'Tha's why I no rememmer!' "

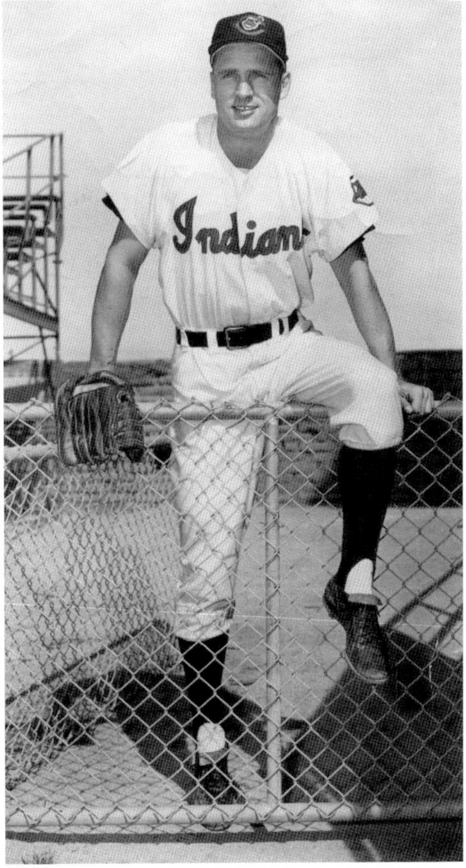

At the end of 1959, the Minneapolis Millers faced the Havana Sugar Kings in the Little World Series. Stu "Lefty" Locklin, with the Millers, had played for the Cleveland Indians. "Every night," Lefty says, "Castro came in. There were guys with bayonets around the dugout. One time, he came through the centerfield fence, and we were warming up the pitchers. He put his hand on his revolver and said, 'Tonight, we win!' in English. He laughed." Havana won.

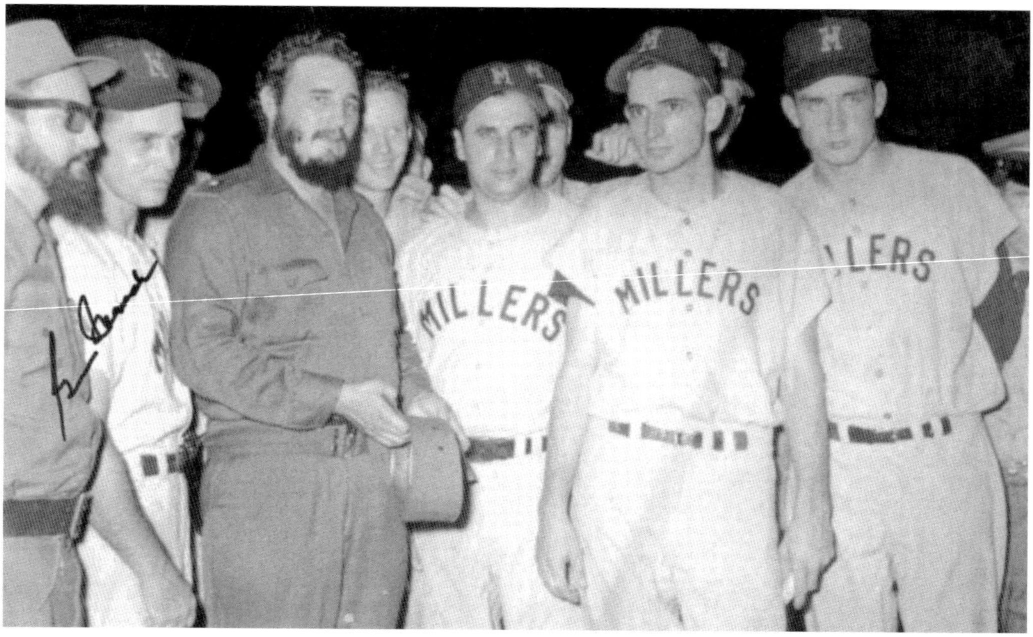

Second from left above, Gene Mauch, the Millers manager, along with members of his team, pose with Castro. "I knew Castro from 1950," Mauch explains, "from when I was playing winter ball down there. He was a reserve on our Cienfuegos team. He was not very good, but he thought he was. They paid him to throw batting practice. I saw him quite a bit in 1959; he'd come to the dugout. You know that cutthroat sign you can make with your forefinger? They were looking at us, holding their guns, and they'd make that sign."

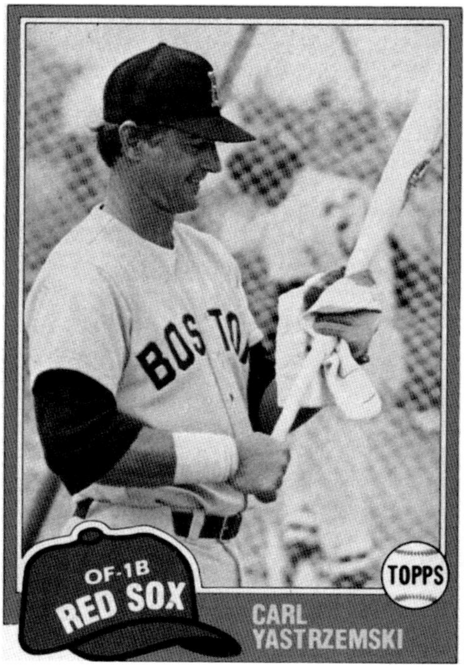

A young Carl Yastrzemski was with Minneapolis during the 1959 contest. The Millers lost, but "we were so overjoyed at going home we went crazy in the hotel. A platoon of soldiers suddenly appeared. They wanted to arrest us. 'Wait!' shouted Mauch. 'I'm going to call Castro.' The next thing we knew, there was Castro, shouting orders. The only command we were interested in, though, was to let us go."

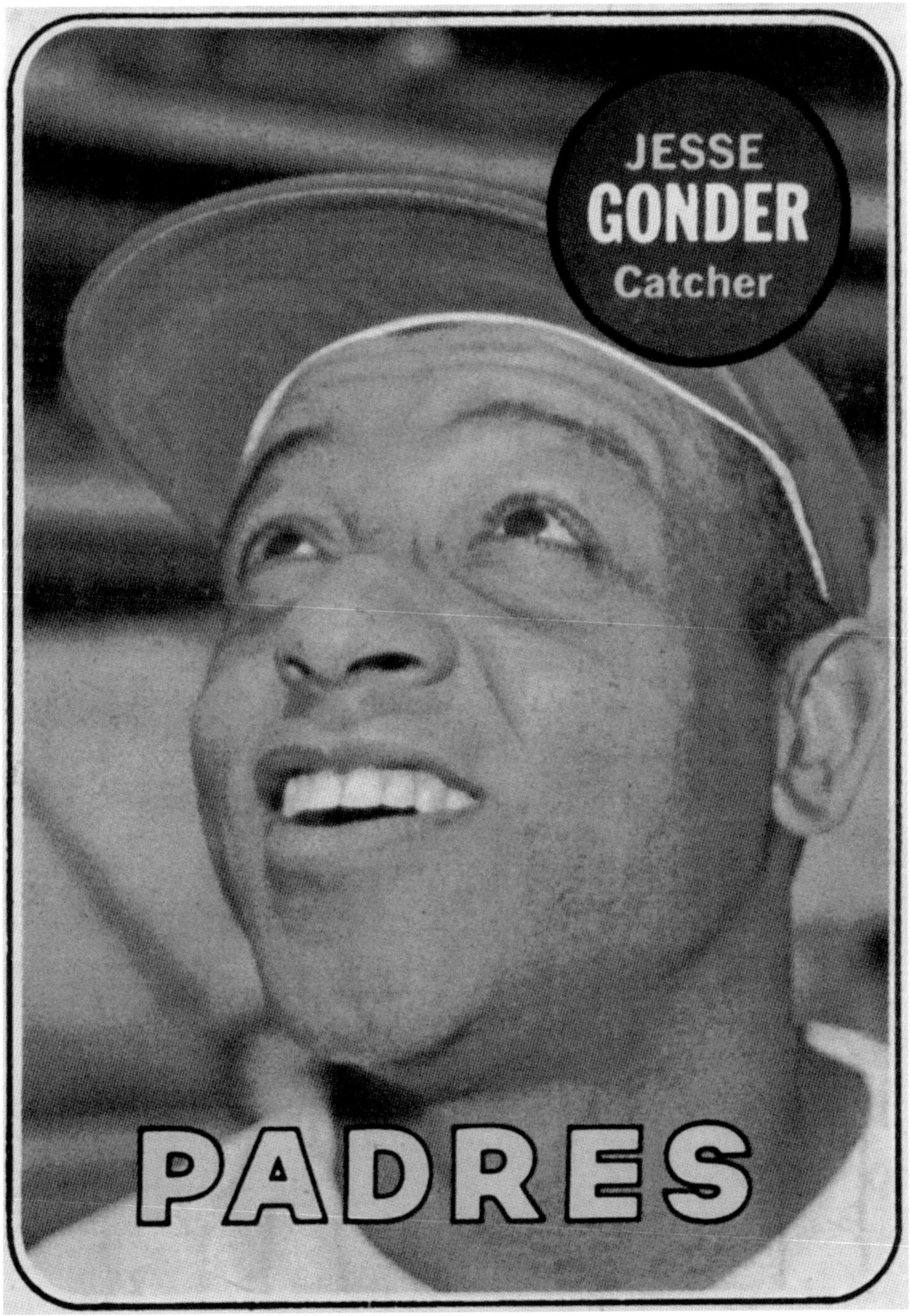

"It was like they showed up carrying bats, except with machine guns instead," Jesse Gondor recalls. He occasionally played catch with Castro. "He threw first pitches, and warm up. We'd talk baseball, how he loved the game, his wantin' to be a ballplayer. He asked, 'What you think of my pitching?' I say, 'You're throwin' pretty good.' I had to build his butt up; that's what the catcher's supposed to do. But he didn't have nothin'."

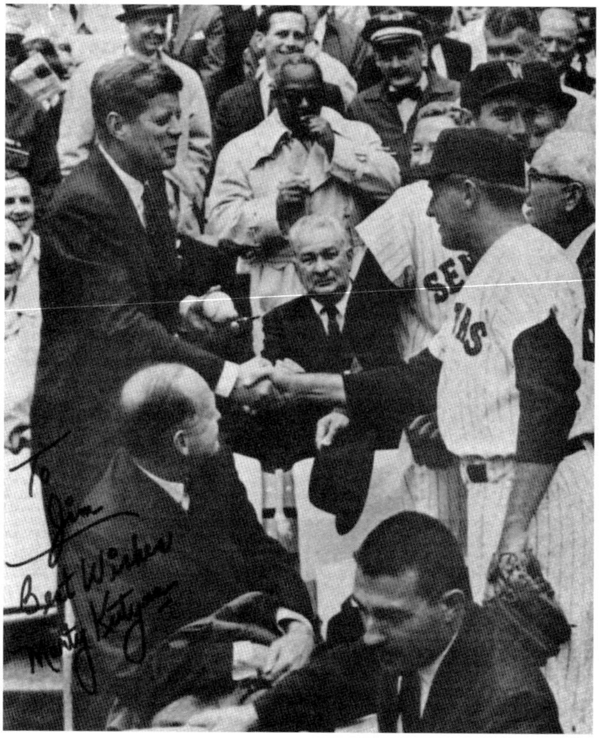

Marty Kutyna caught the first pitch from John F. Kennedy in 1962. In Cuba, "We stayed in a castle [with] 40 cots and one light bulb. Bats flew through the windows at night. In Cienfuegos, we played in a bullring! We heard sirens, and they pull up, carrying machine guns. Castro's wearing pearl .45s. He asks me, 'Can I pitch?' I said, 'Of course, Mr. President, sir,' handed him my glove, and he handed me the gunbelt. I started to take out the .45, and he says, 'No, no.' So I left it in the holster. He threw a few knuckleballs, gave me back the glove, put the belt back on, and took off. And there go the sirens again. I guess he was just in the neighborhood!"

Tommy Lasorda met Fidel, too. "Soon after Castro marched into Havana," Tommy recollects in his book, he was invited to Castro's suite in the Havana Hilton, "before anyone knew he was a Communist. It would not have made any difference—never argue with a dictator. Castro was wearing his jungle fatigues. We stayed about an hour talking baseball. However during the conversation I did not tell Castro that I'd met Batista."

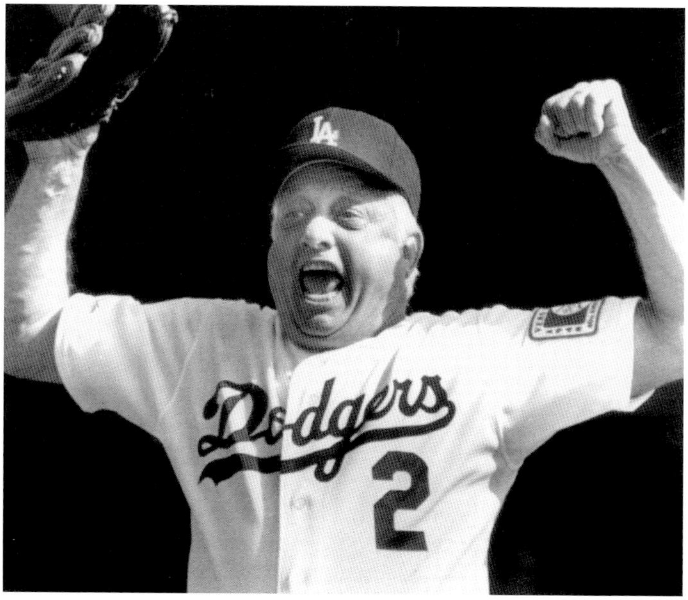

10

Since Then

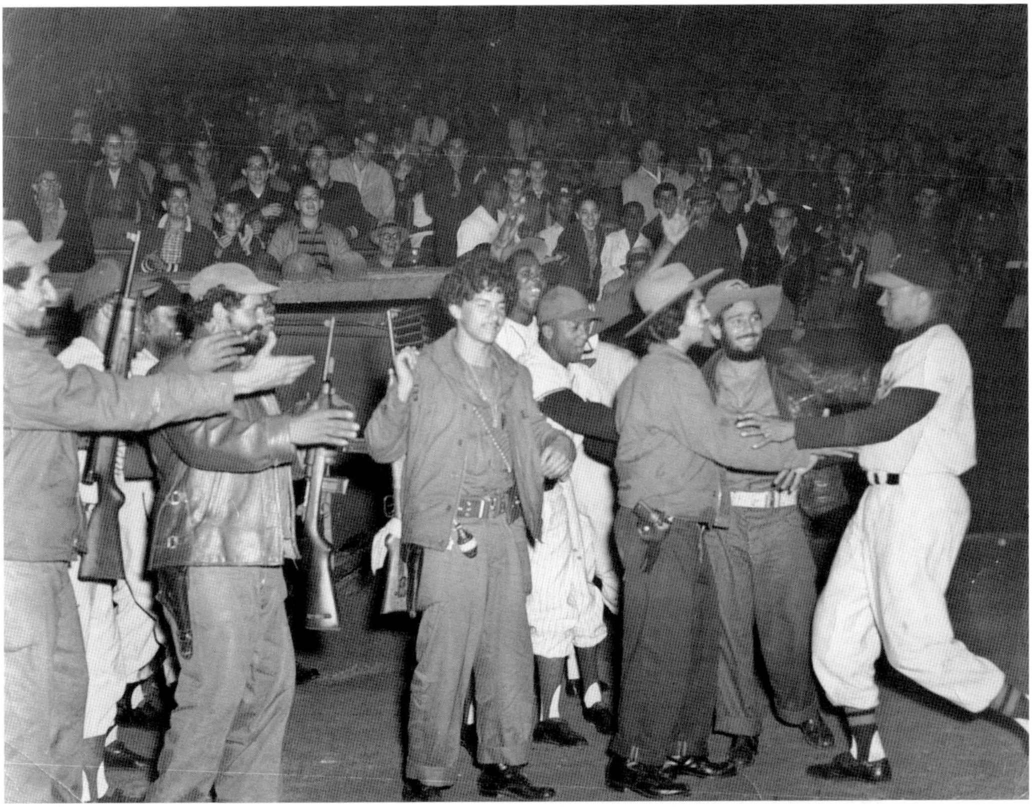

The Dodgers moved away from Brooklyn after the 1957 season. The United States and Cuba decided not to play together anymore. Leo Durocher, Branch Rickey, and Jackie Robinson are all gone now. But the Los Angeles Dodgers enjoy an enormous following, and their 2010 manager, Joe Torre, happens to be from Brooklyn. And baseball also went on in Cuba. Julio Becquer spent seven major-league seasons in the states; each winter, he also did some moonlighting for Marianao in his homeland, leading the league in homers one year. Here he is enthusiastically greeted after a game-winning play by his gun-toting proletariat Campesino amigos.

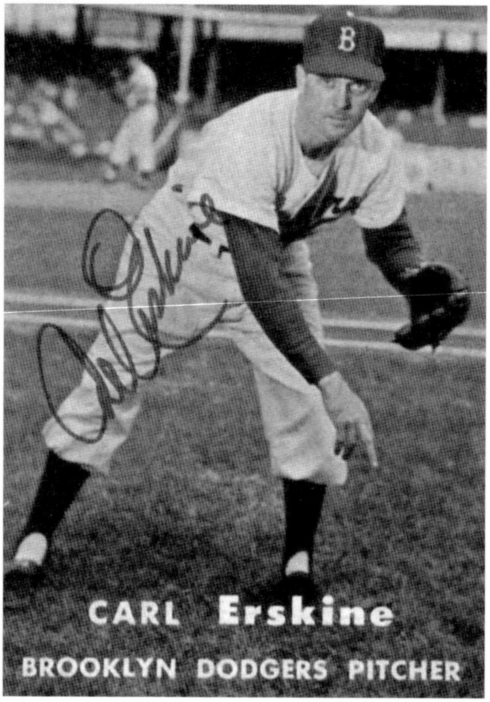

"At Gran Stadium, I'd put my wallet in this little compartment," recalls Carl Erskine. "The Cuban guys would put guns and knives into the trunk. There was a lot of betting going on. Pedro Pages played centerfield, and I noticed he really hustled some nights, and other nights, he couldn't seem to get to the ball. I figured it out, but didn't say anything. Are you kiddin'? He packed a knife!" One night, a fan kept heckling Pages, who eventually disappeared into the clubhouse, pulled his pistol from the trunk, and ran into the stands after the fan, waving the gun in the air.

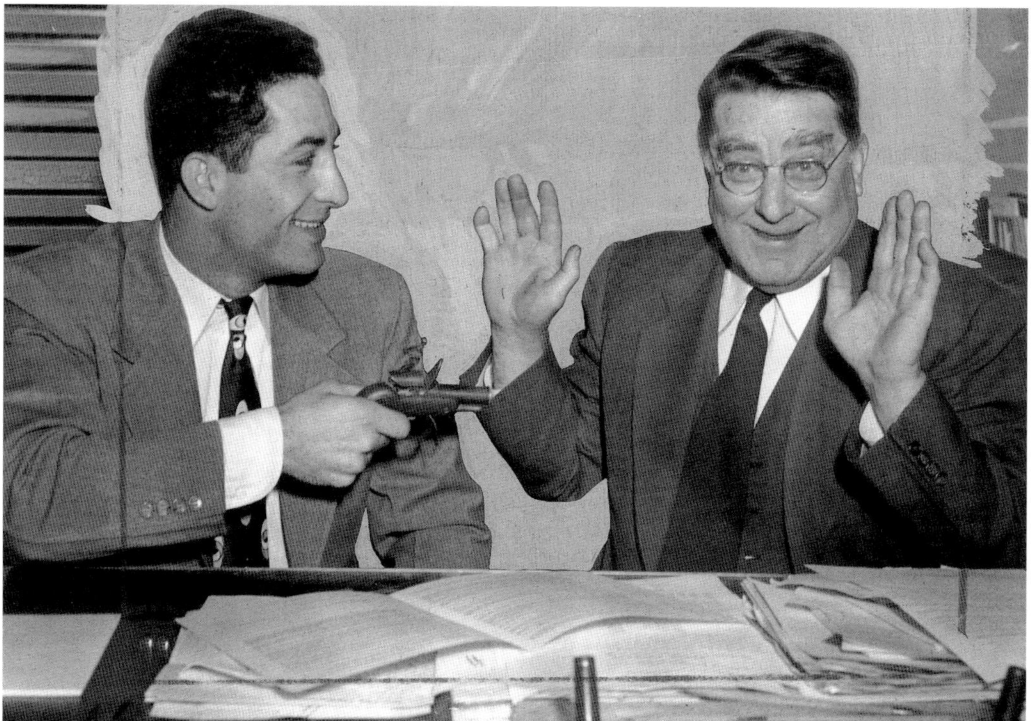

Since everybody else in Cuba seemed to be packing heat, Dodger Carl Furillo apparently decided to give it a whirl in his contract negotiations with Branch Rickey.

At the beginning of his career, Willie Mays played in Cuba. Willie suited up for the Almendares team but was not there long enough to encounter any incidents with firearms.

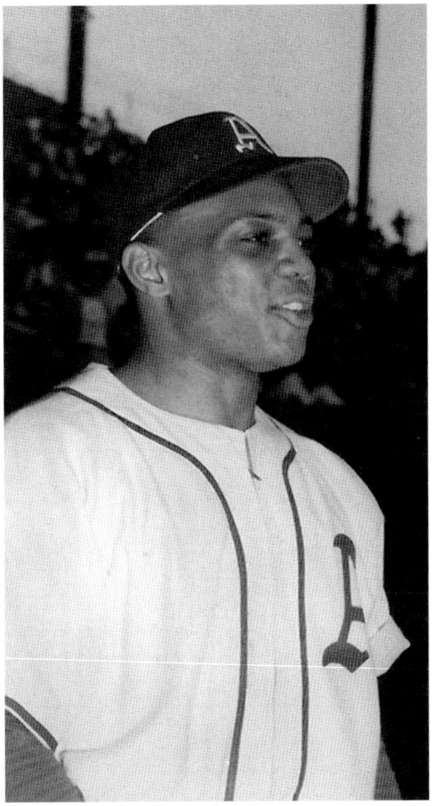

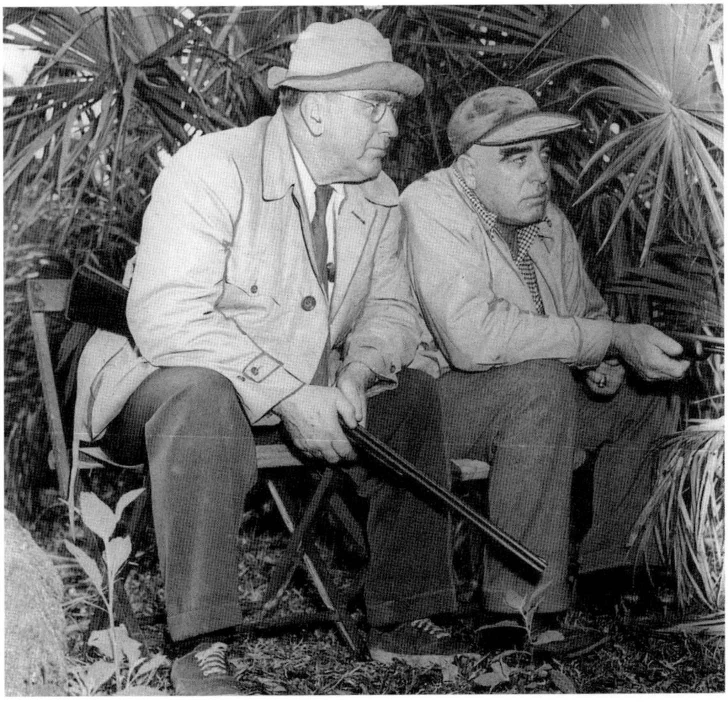

Rickey and Eastern Airlines pal Bud Holman cooked up a plan to take over an old naval air station in Vero Beach, which had been mothballed after World War II. The Dodgers tried the facility out while training in Santo Domingo in 1948 and held their first official camp there in 1949.

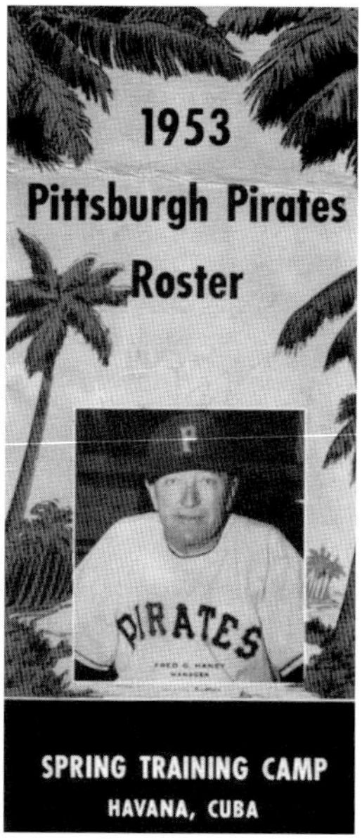

Rickey left the Dodgers in 1950 and moved over to Pittsburgh to try to rehab the sinking Pirates. It was a tall order. In *Baseball is a Funny Game*, Joe Garagiola explained how things went in 1952: "We got off to a slow start. We lost 10 of our first 14 and then had a slump. We won 42—not in a row, but we won them." Rickey's Cuban ties came into play, and to shake things up in 1953, the Bucs held their spring training in Havana.

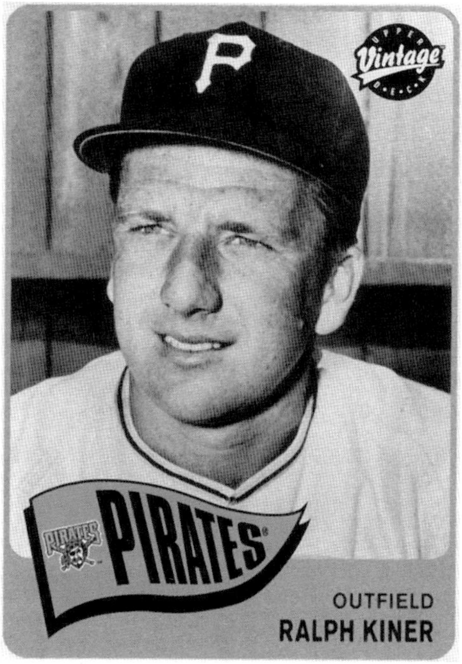

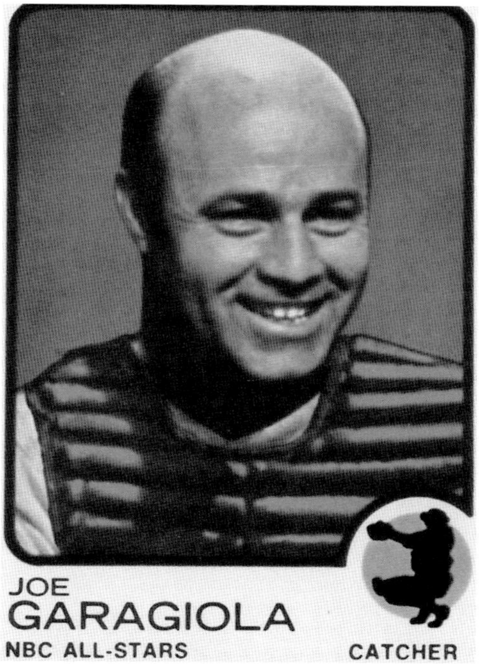

Ralph Kiner (above, left) was the team's only star then, and a contract dispute with Rickey kept him out of camp. "Rickey told him we can lose without you!" recalls Otis "Scat" Davis. Kiner flew to Havana late, then hit a mere seven dingers in the opening 41 games of the season and was traded to the Cubs (with Garagiola) in a nine-player deal. Above right, "Garagiola was a pretty good receiver," batterymate Cal Hogue says. "He had a great sense of humor. He used to burn the guys' shoes. He'd call the ump from the desk and say, 'Pull the shades—your girlfriend's watching!' "

The Philadelphia Athletics visited and split two with their cross-state rivals. Catcher Joe Astroth made the trip, and returned years later. "Soldiers in a jeep met the plane with machine guns to escort us to the park in sugarcane fields. We rode one of the first buses ever made! We held the windows up with screwdrivers. Castro's men were fighting Batista's in the mountains, and we were only 80 miles away."

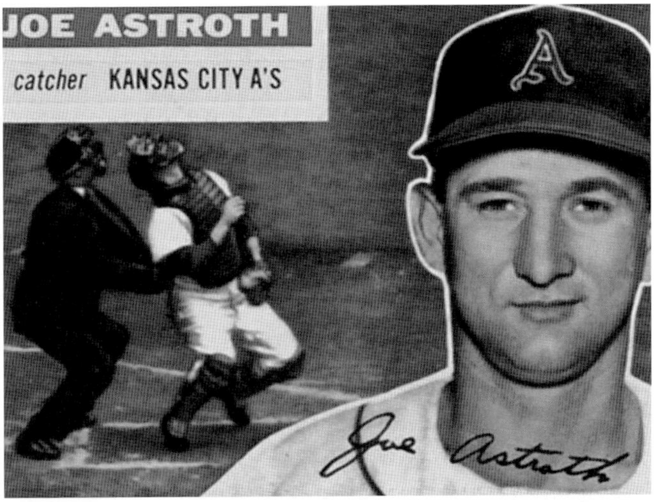

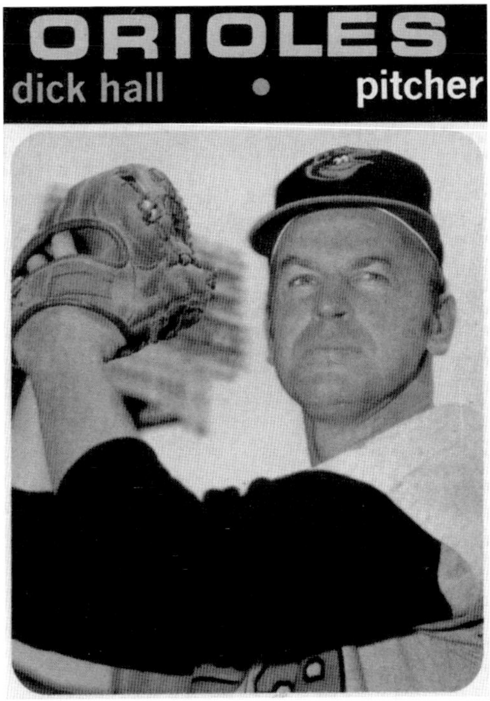

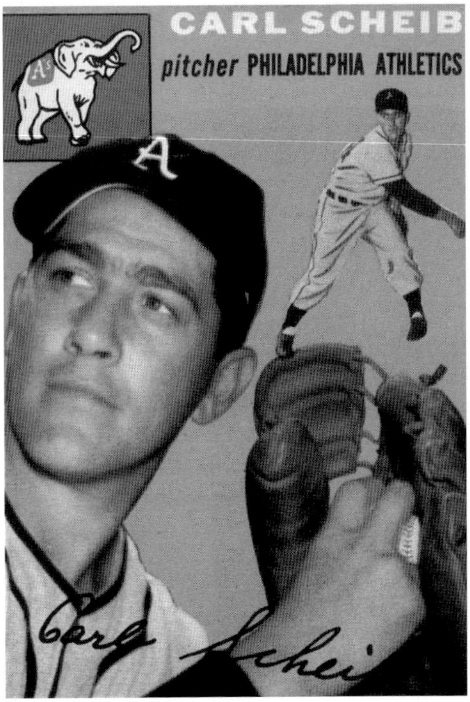

Dick Hall (above, left) was a Pirate outfielder before converting to the mound. Two decades later, he finished his career in the 1971 World Series. "Rickey had this theory: we're gonna finish last anyway, so let's play prospects—they'll get better faster," Hall recalls. After workouts, "I was datin' a girl I met there, Otmana. I'd ride the bus to her house—a big adventure. I'd take her to dances, and some games." Carl Scheib (above, right) got the win for the Athletics. "There was kind of an uproar down there," Scheib recalls. "We wondered what was going on. The fans were pretty lively. They were throwin' snakes at us, and firecrackers. One time, somebody shot a bottle rocket at me." When asked how one throws a snake, Carl explains, "You just wave it around by the tail over your head and let it go."

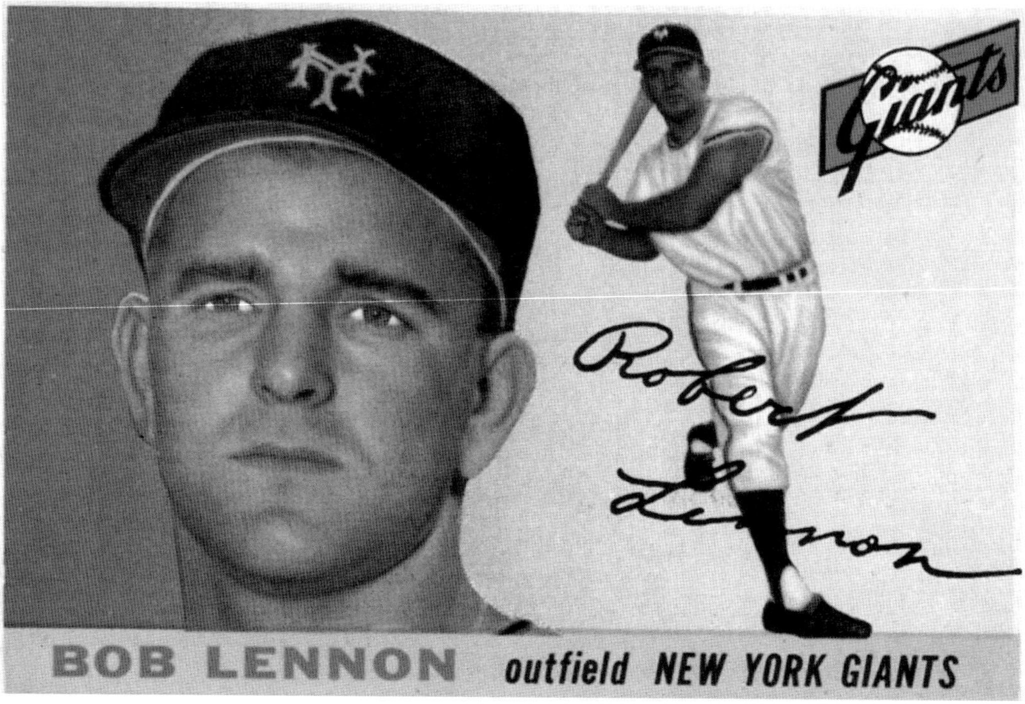

Bob Lennon hit 64 homers for Nashville in 1954. In the Caribbean, he hurt his ankle. Bob recalls, "This voodoo doctor came to take me to the outback! He was a little guy; looked 80 years old. He told his interpreter I had to believe. He told me to stomp my foot. It hurt like crazy. They should've cast it. That voodoo doctor put the kiss of death on me!"

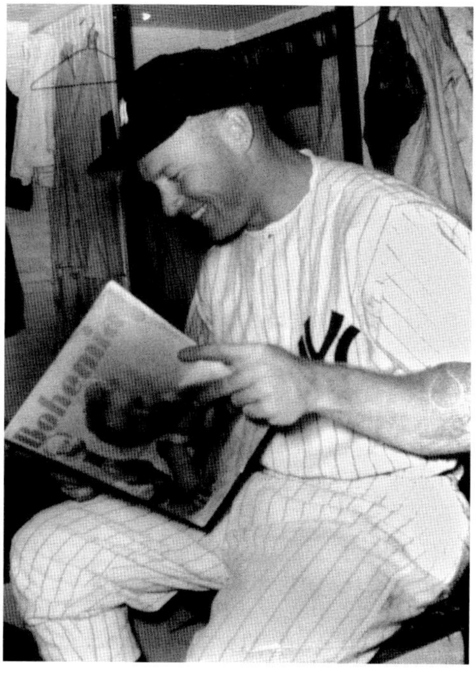

In the spring of 1957, the New York Yankees returned to the Caribbean for a five-team series against the Dodgers, Milwaukee Braves, Havana Sugar Kings, and Tokyo Giants. Coincidentally, the Yanks and Braves would close the season as well, squaring off in the World Series. Mickey Mantle made the trip. The "Mick" thumbed through the Cuban national magazine, *Bohemia*, before running off with Billy Martin to sample the local establishments that advertised in its pages.

After being threatened by Castro during the pregame activities, Lefty Locklin says, "We saw him a couple times at the Havana Hilton. The soldiers took the whole 18th floor. They just put their stuff on the floor, I don't think they used the beds at all. Castro ate with the cooks!" He may have humbly eaten with the cooks, but Castro had no problem seizing the hotel (and the casino it housed, along with its vault) from Conrad Hilton, nationalizing everything in the name of Communism.

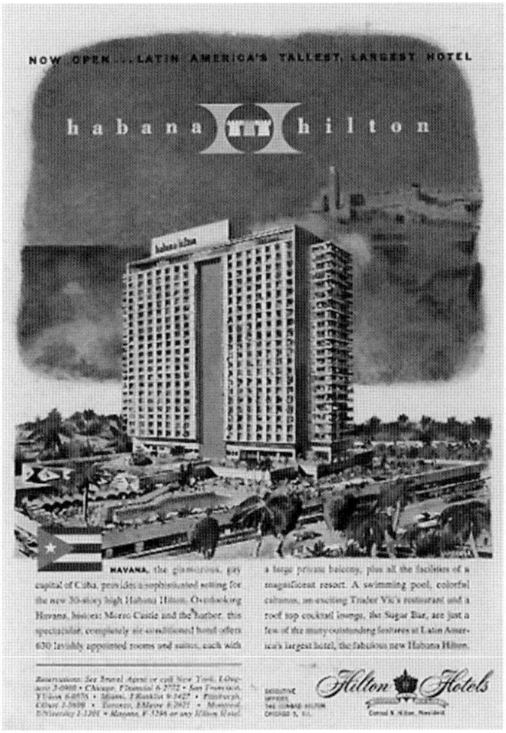

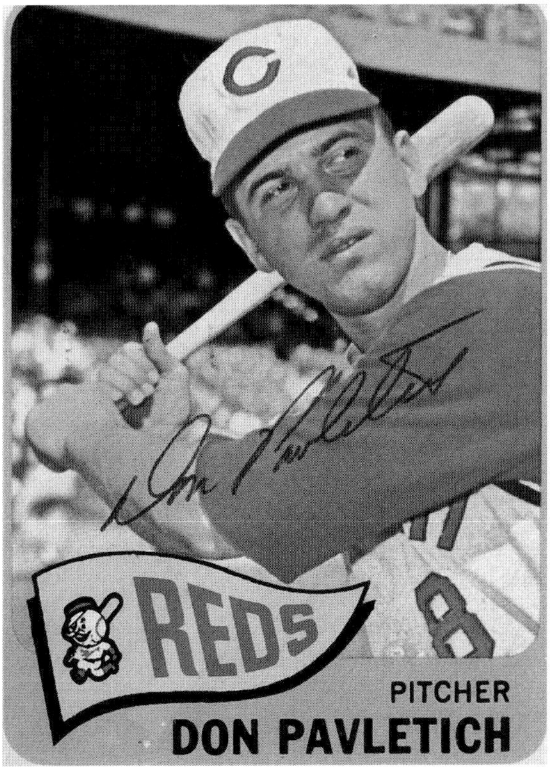

Somebody was always seizing something. Don Pavletich played Winter League ball, Caribbean style. "Every game, they'd have at least two cops with Uzis in the dugout. This terrorist group had threatened to kidnap American ballplayers. The only qualification to be a policeman was one year of training, so these were really young guys, and they got all excited when the game got going, and they'd be waving these things around. You never got used to it."

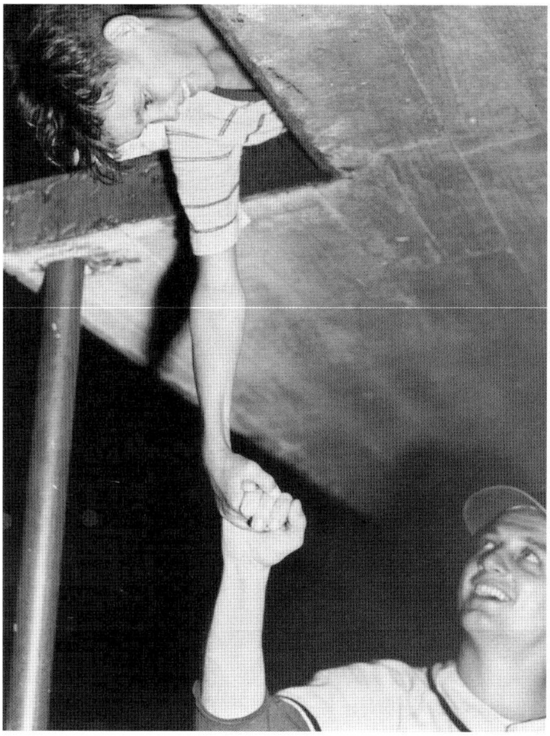

At left, a Cuban fan greets Tommy Lasorda; however, natives were not always friendly. "Between revolutions in Cuba," Tommy says. "I've met dictators, been arrested, started riots, run from riots, pitched with soldiers in the dugout and umpires carrying six-shooters. Now, that's baseball!" One game, men paraded in the stands with a coffin bearing a sign saying Lasorda was dead. "What bothered me most is one pallbearer was my barber, and I'd given him the tickets."

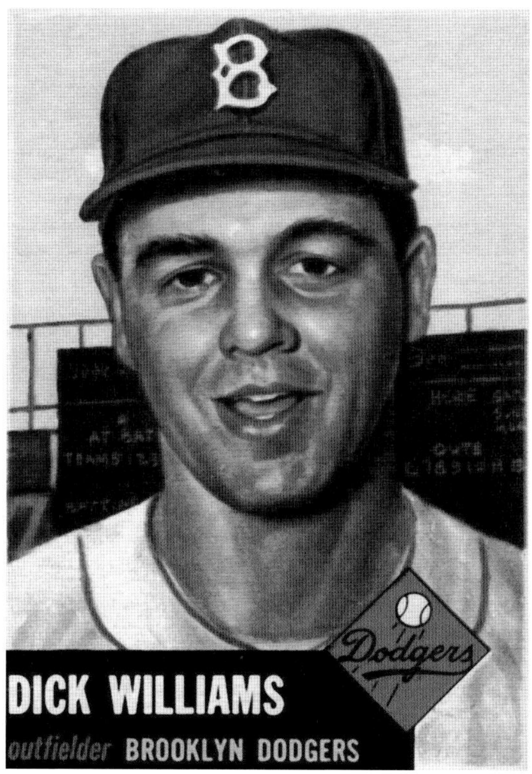

Long before he was a Hall of Fame manager, Brooklyn Dodgers outfielder Dick Williams played in Cuba. Once, he and Lasorda were invited to a radio show. "The interviewer took us into the studio and told us where to sit," Lasorda recalls, "Then he took a large gun out of his pocket, and laid it on the table. I stared at the gun. I couldn't believe the questions were going to be that difficult. Finally, Dick Williams asked, 'What's that for?' 'Well,' the interviewer said, smiling, 'you never know.' "

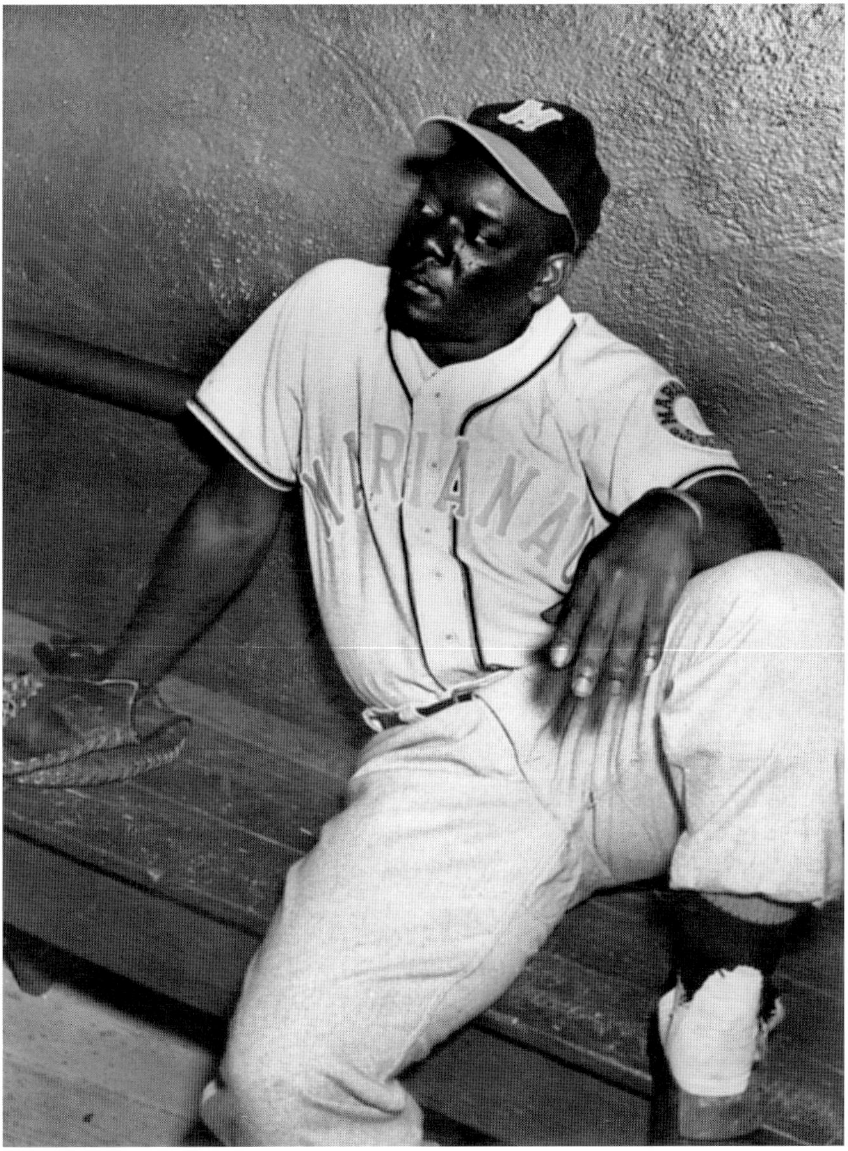

Pitching in Cuba, Tommy hit the wrong batter one night—Chiquitín Cabrera. "It was my fastball," Tommy recalled. "It wasn't really going to hurt him" But Cabrera charged the mound, and Tommy bodyslammed the batter. The crowd roared. According to Lasorda, "This had to be one of the best baseball games they'd ever seen." Cops hauled both to a judge, who asked if Lasorda wanted to press charges. "No, all I want is to pitch against him again." The next day, Tommy was on the beach when four men wearing dark clothes escorted him to a limousine. "We stopped in front of a large iron gate, guarded by soldiers with machine guns. My driver ordered me out." Lasorda was brought to Batista. "I had met presidents of the Elks Lodge, but this was the first dictator I ever met. 'Mr. Lasorda,' he began, 'I invited you here to apologize.' Batista invited me to have lunch with him. Since I had no plans, I accepted. So we spent the afternoon sitting on the veranda, watching armed guards patrolling the lawn, talking baseball."

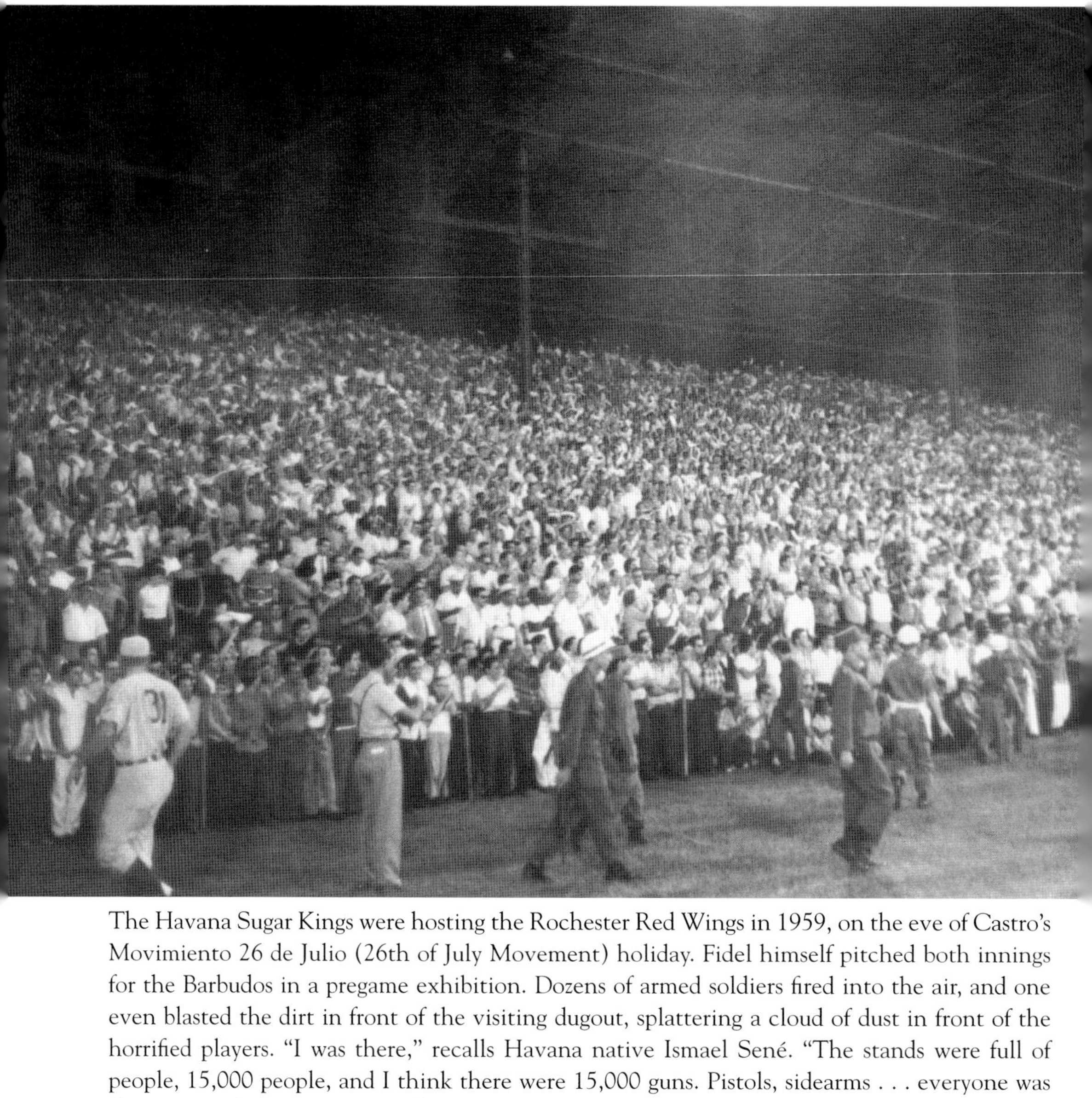

The Havana Sugar Kings were hosting the Rochester Red Wings in 1959, on the eve of Castro's Movimiento 26 de Julio (26th of July Movement) holiday. Fidel himself pitched both innings for the Barbudos in a pregame exhibition. Dozens of armed soldiers fired into the air, and one even blasted the dirt in front of the visiting dugout, splattering a cloud of dust in front of the horrified players. "I was there," recalls Havana native Ismael Sené. "The stands were full of people, 15,000 people, and I think there were 15,000 guns. Pistols, sidearms . . . everyone was shooting in the air. It's a miracle no one was seriously wounded. The players were so nervous, they couldn't catch the ball."

In the 10th inning, Frank Verdi was manning the third base coaching box. Suddenly, Verdi wobbled over as he grabbed his head; a stray .45 bullet had grazed through his cap and just broken the skin above his ear. There was not much blood, but he had indeed been shot while on the field during a game. This was the first time that had ever happened in professional baseball, even in Cuba.

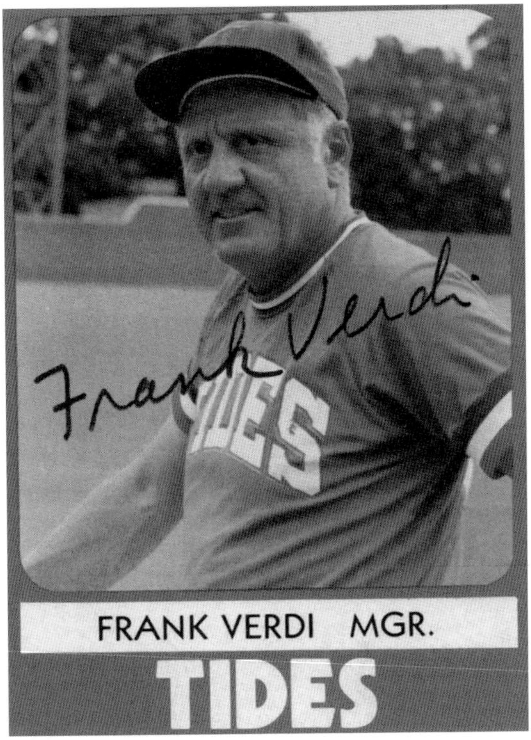

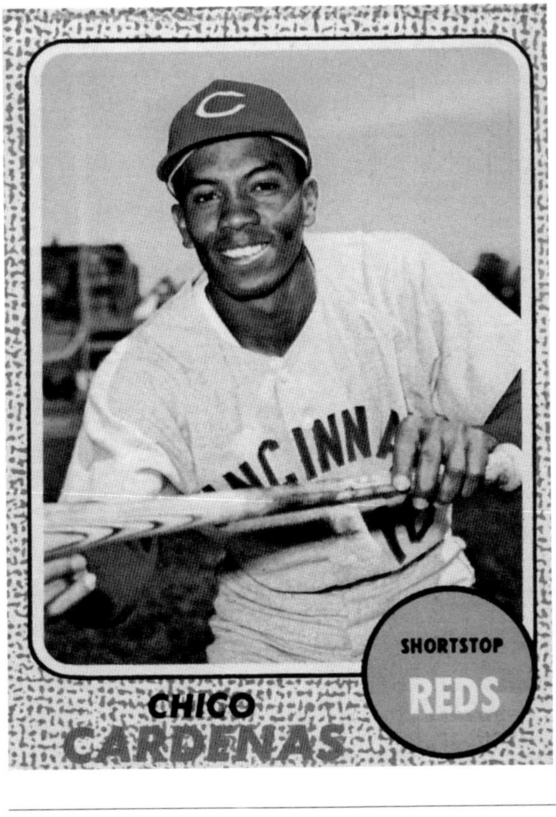

Minutes later, as everyone had gathered around Verdi, it happened again. Chico Cardenas was grazed in the shoulder while standing in the infield, though also not seriously hurt. Everyone quickly scurried for cover, with Verdi "cursing everything from Castro to sugarcane to blackjack dealers," according to a newspaper account.

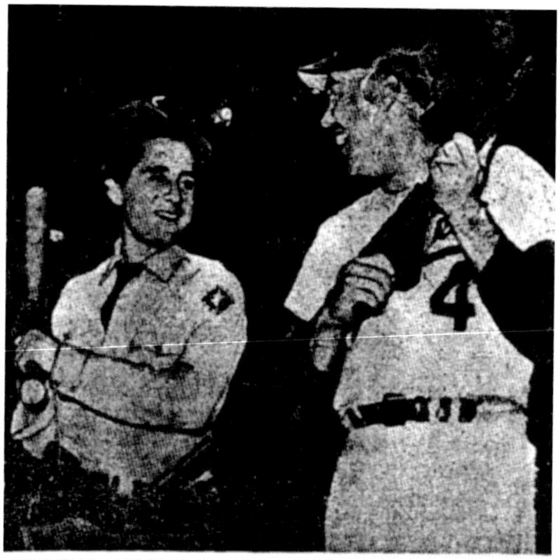

CHANGE IN ARTILLERY—Duke Snider, the slugging L.A. Dodger outfielder, shifts from baseball bat to machine gun with the aid of Pvt. Antonio Castro of Cuban revolutionary forces who is now member of Havana police department.

That spring, the Dodgers and Reds were supposed to play an exhibition series in Florida, but it just would not stop raining. The teams quickly arranged to meet in Havana instead, where Duke Snider turned the tables by trading his bat to a Cuban soldier for a machine gun.

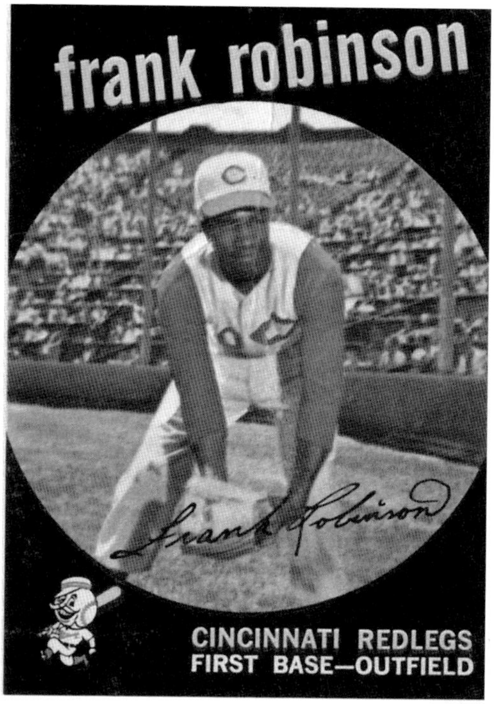

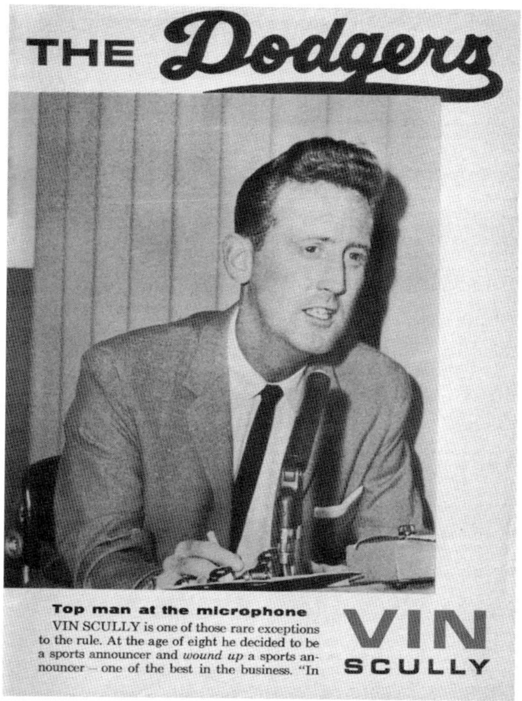

Future Hall of Famer Frank Robinson (above, left), who had seen his share of weapons growing up as a tough street kid in inner-city Los Angeles, took a practical view as a young Cincy outfielder. He was not bothered by all the guns in the stands, he says, as long as "they weren't pointin' 'em at me!" "At the hotel," Vin Scully (above, right) muses, "You'd go down to the bar for a drink, and these guys came in, soldiers in full uniform with their girlfriends, and they'd put their Thompson submachine guns right on the bar, and start drinking . . . and drinking . . . and drinking. I was there with some of the writers, and we got out of there in a hurry!"

Claude Osteen became a star pitcher for the Dodgers but was a Cincinnati hopeful in 1959. "They told us what to expect," he says. The pilot "warned everybody we were gonna see 12, 13-year-old kids carrying guns. I guess if you have a revolution and need to take over a city, you don't ask their age!" Teammate Joe Nuxhall found another weapon rather troubling. "And machetes," Nuxhall adds, "everywhere."

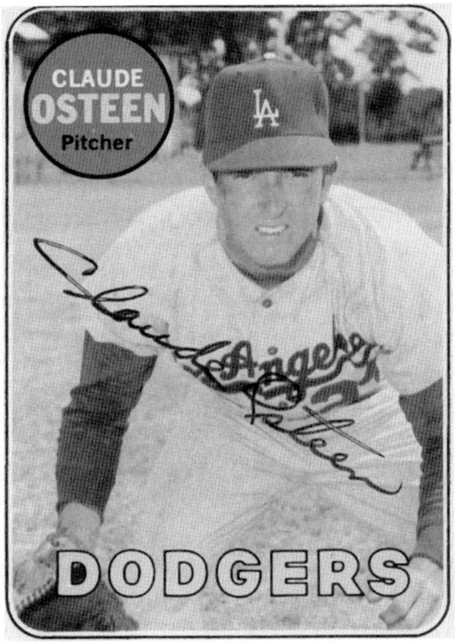

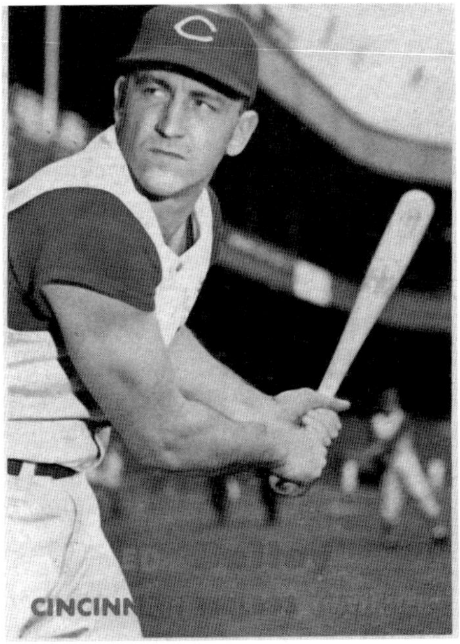

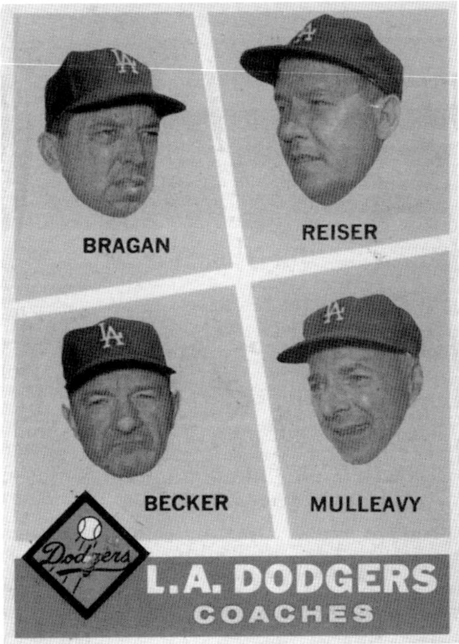

"I caught a pop foul near the screen," says Cincy catcher Ed Bailey (above, left), "and when I looked up, this kid with a machine gun in one hand, which he could barely hold, was holding out his other hand and pointing to the ball. I gave it to him and got another one from the umpire. You think I was gonna say no?" "Greg Mulleavy [above, right] was in the dugout during batting practice," says Dodger Ralph Mauriello. "A *barbuda* points to the balls and says, '*Pelota*.' Greg ignored the guy, but he kept at it. So just to get rid of him, Greg gives him one, and the guy goes trottin' off. But it started this train, and after the 10th or 11th guy comes down, Pee Wee says to Greg, 'We're not gonna have any balls left.' Greg says to Pee Wee, 'See those guns? If any of those guys asks for my jock strap, they're gonna get it!' "

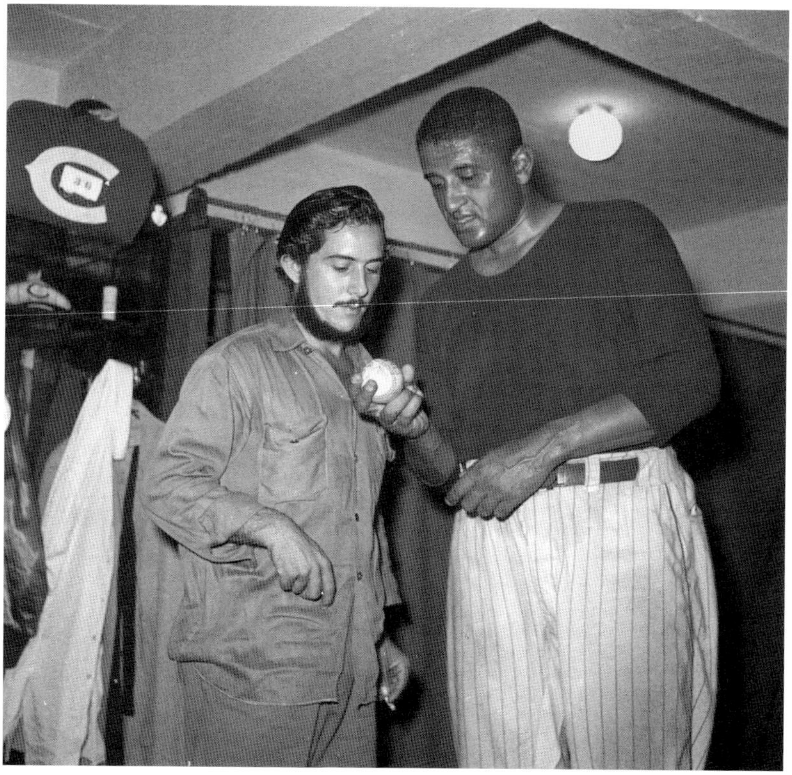

Don Newcombe kept Jackie Robinson company in Cuba during the 1947 experiment, then starred as a Brooklyn pitching ace for years. After the move to Los Angeles, the team traded him to Cincinnati for four players. In the spring of 1959, he faced his old mates during the Cuban series. While in the clubhouse, Newk happily showed his new soldier friend the proper grip for a change-up.

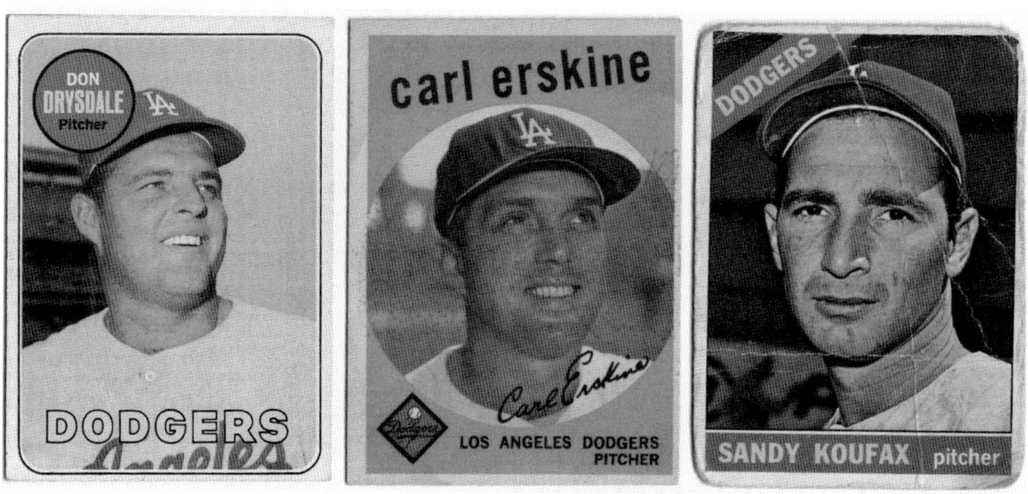

The Dodgers won the first game 3-2, as Don Drysdale fanned eight. The Dodgers also won game two, 4-3, completing the mini-sweep. Catcher Norm Sherry was the batting star, hitting two singles and a home run. Sandy Koufax and Carl Erskine (the winner) pitched well for Los Angeles.

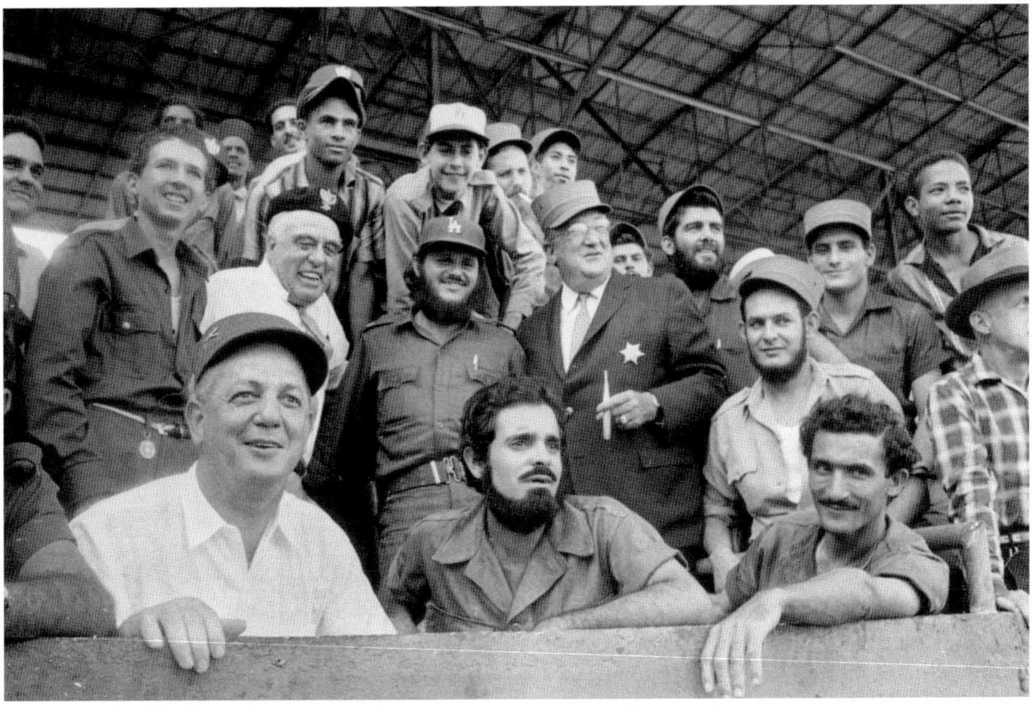

Some friendly locals armed to the teeth welcomed Reds general manager Gabe Paul, Dodger pal Bud Holman, and Dodger boss Walter O'Malley to the ballyard in Havana.

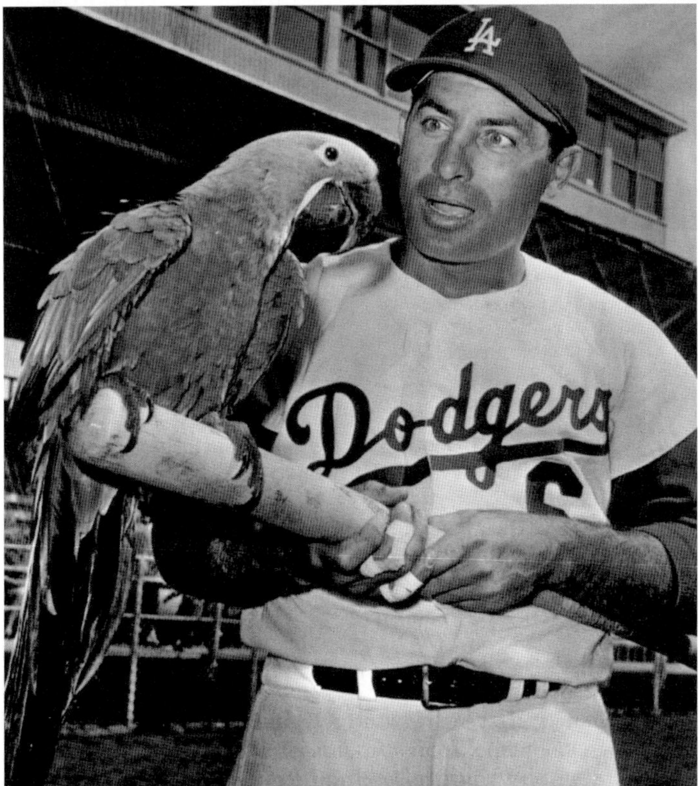

Not many Dodgers lasted from the late-1940s camps to the exhilarating 1959 games against Cincinnati, but All-Star Carl Furillo sure did. His major-league career spanned three decades and seven World Series, all with his beloved Bums.

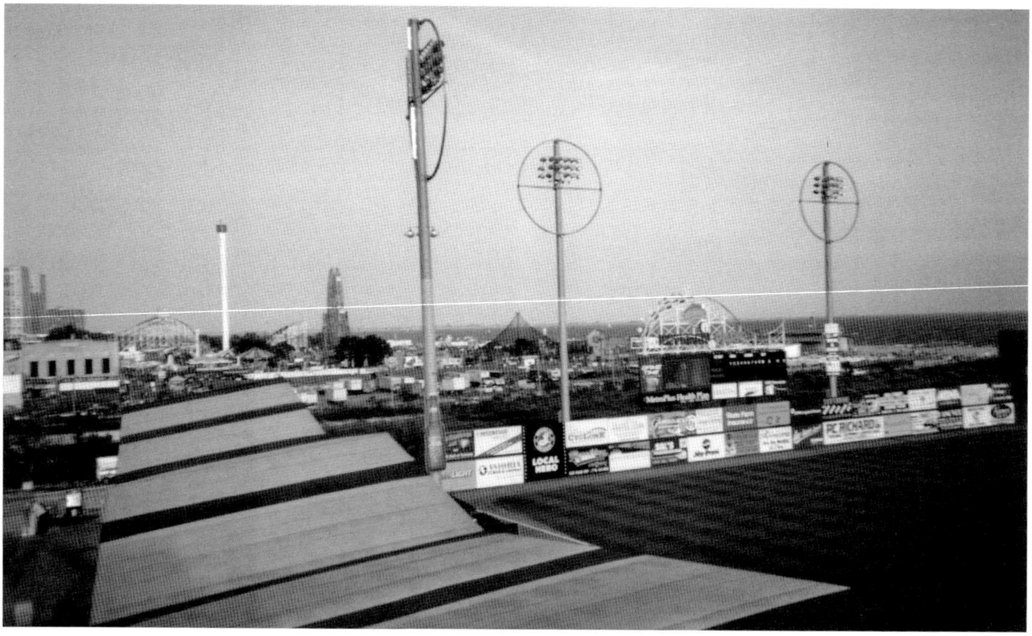

After the Dodgers left Brooklyn, the lonely Long Island borough did not field a professional baseball club again until the Brooklyn Cyclones arrived in 2001. The new "Brooks" are a Class A farm team of the nearby New York Mets. While watching the Cyclones at MCU Park, one can literally see the world-famous Cyclone at Coney Island, as well as the Atlantic Ocean.

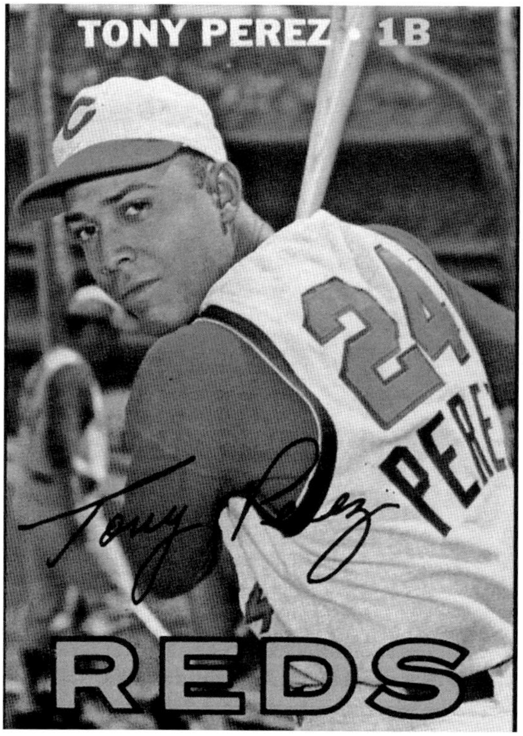

Several ballplayers were already here when United States-Cuban relations crumbled, and they thrived in the majors into the 1970s. Tony Oliva, Campy Campaneris, Mike Cuellar, Tony Perez, Minnie Minoso, and Cookie Rojas made All-Star rosters and kept the dream alive. But the pool dwindled, until a trickle reemerged in the 1980s when Jose Canseco, Rafael Palmiero, the Hernandez brothers, and Jose Contreras re-exerted Cuban muscle in the big leagues. In all, more than 150 Cubans have played in the majors.

In 1999, the Baltimore Orioles played a two-game series against the Cuban national team. Game one in Havana marked the first appearance of a U.S. major-league team on Cuban soil in 40 years. It was held at the refurbished Estadio Latinamericano, the same ballpark that was the brand new Gran Estadio for the Brooklyn Dodgers of 1947. The gates opened to 55,000 handpicked *fanaticos*. Castro mingled with the players, and he tossed the first pitch. In 11 innings, the Orioles won 3-2. In Baltimore, the Cubans came back, 12-6, though Castro did not make the trip. Passions ran high during the U.S. game as Cuban umpire Cesar Valdez body-slammed a demonstrator who ran onto the field.

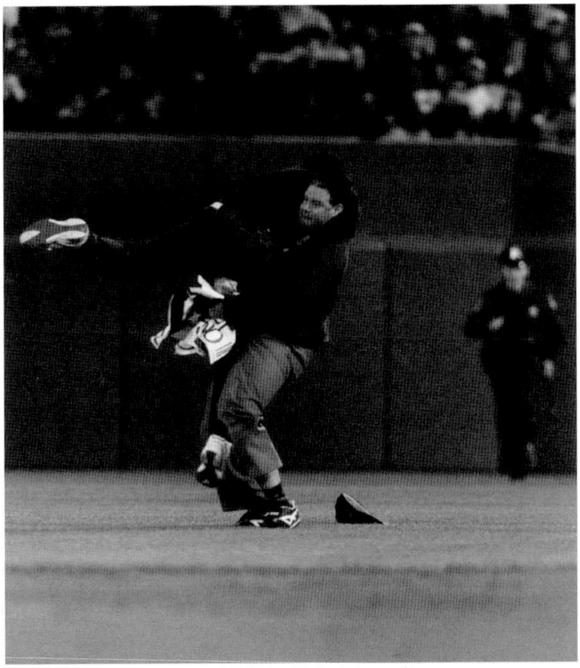

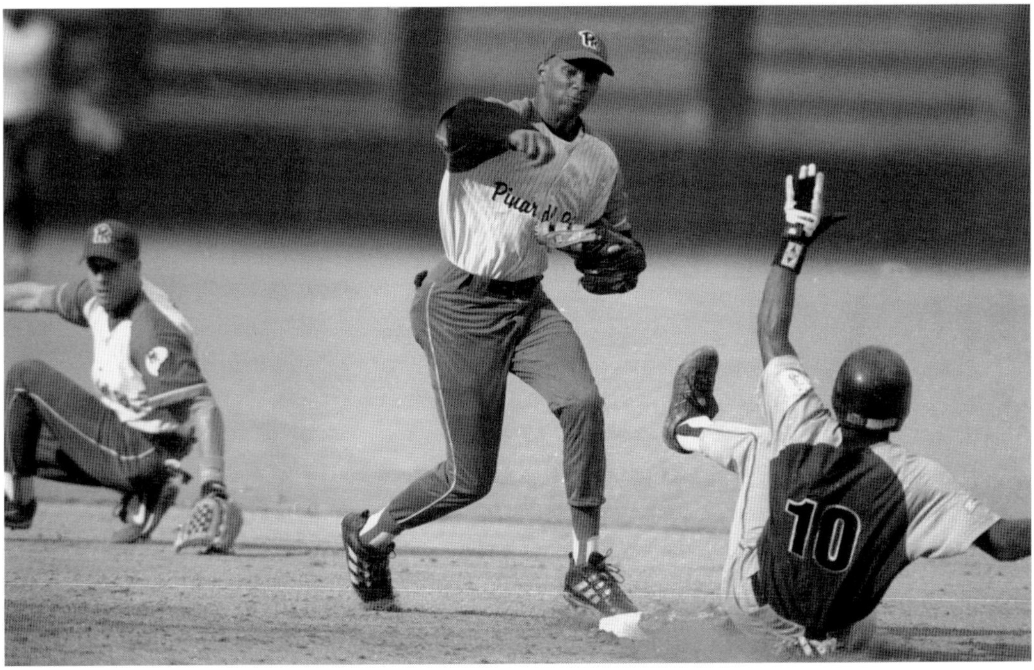

Meanwhile, back in Cuba, professional *pelota* goes on. Above, Pinar del Rio shuts down the Havana City rally. The league fields 16 teams. The national team has more than two dozen world titles and several Olympic Golds (the team took Silver in 2000, behind Tommy Lasorda's Team USA). Teams are named after regional characteristics, making for some interesting monikers such as the Crocodiles, Orange Growers, and Shrimpermen. But alas, no more Dodgers.

Find Your Place in History.

www.arcadiapublishing.com

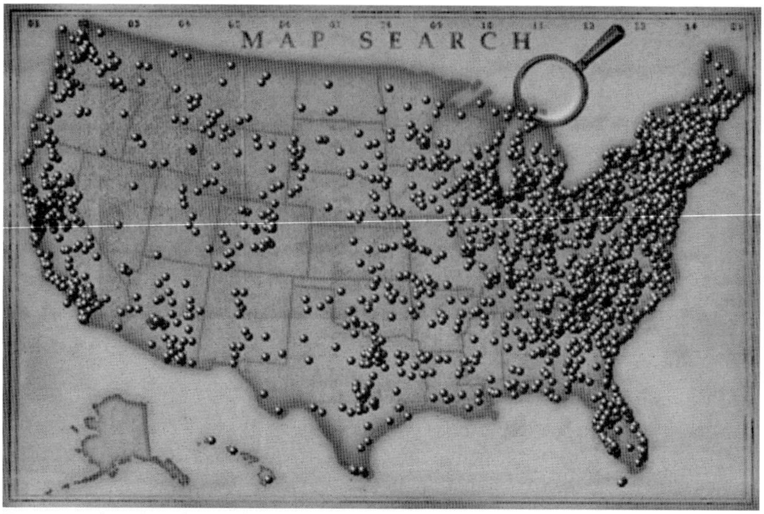

Discover books about the town where you grew up, the cities where your friends and families live, the town where your parents met, or even that retirement spot you've been dreaming about. Our Web site provides history lovers with exclusive deals, advanced notification about new titles, e-mail alerts of author events, and much more.

MADE IN THE USA

Arcadia Publishing, the leading local history publisher in the United States, is committed to making history accessible and meaningful through publishing books that celebrate and preserve the heritage of America's people and places. Consistent with our mission to preserve history on a local level, this book was printed in South Carolina on American-made paper and manufactured entirely in the United States.

This book carries the accredited Forest Stewardship Council (FSC) label and is printed on 100 percent FSC-certified paper. Products carrying the FSC label are independently certified to assure consumers that they come from forests that are managed to meet the social, economic, and ecological needs of present and future generations.